Why are so .... in the mainstream while so many others are not?

What have these women learned that others have not?

What roles have mentors, networks, and women's groups played in their success?

How do successful women handle the problems they share with other women?

What kinds of games are they playing?

How do they deal with money, power, decision making, coping with career and family?

What kinds of men do they marry?

In this perceptive and enlightening book, Ruth Halcomb profiles dozens of women who have made it and offers solid advice on how to overcome the problems women face in trying to balance their careers with their lives.

"EXCELLENT . . . A REFRESHINGLY NEW VIEWPOINT AND ATTITUDE WITH VALUABLE INPUT FOR GOAL SETTING AND SUCCESS PLANNING."

Betsy Berkhemer
President, Berkhemer & Kline
Publisher, *Women's Information Network*

WOMEN MAKING IT

*Patterns and Profiles
of Success*

RUTH HALCOMB

BALLANTINE BOOKS • NEW YORK

Excerpts from the following sources are reprinted by permission:

WOMEN IN THE PROFESSIONS edited by Laurily Keir Epstein (Lexington, Mass.: Lexington Books, D.C. Heath and Company, Copyright 1975, D.C. Heath and Company).

"Invidious Intimacy" by Judith Stiehm, SOCIAL POLICY published by Social Policy Corporation, New York, New York 10036. Copyright 1976 by Social Policy Corporation.

WOMEN TODAY: *Ten Profiles* by Greta Walker, copyright © 1975 by Greta Walker. All rights reserved. Published by Hawthorn Books, Inc.

"Katherine Graham: The Power That Didn't Corrupt," published by *Ms.*, October 1974. Copyright Ms. Magazine Corp.

Library of Congress Catalog Card Number: 79-51129

ISBN 0-345-29348-7

This edition published by arrangement with Atheneum

Manufactured in the United States of America

First Ballantine Books Edition: February 1981

In memory of my parents,
Charles Anthony Moore
and Mildred Smith Moore.

MANY people helped in many ways to make this book possible. I'd especially like to thank the women who took the time and patience to answer my questions. In addition to those individuals who are named in the book, I owe much to the following men and women for the thoughts, support and actual work they contributed: Vauna Abernathy, Debbie Butler, Beverley Chapelle, Maxine Conway, Paul Cooper, Steven Farley, Francis Greenburger, Elizabeth Jaffe, Judy Jewett, Judith Kern, Leona Maertin, Lynn O'Conner and Hedy White.

CONTENTS

I

Women and Success

Not so very long ago a woman's striving for success in a career doomed her to "failure as a woman." Men had careers; women just were. The real woman was the wife-mother-homemaker. A certain mystique accompanied her procreative capacities, but her real purposes were hazily defined, her varying roles were supportive and her actual tasks were sometimes unimportant, sometimes backbreaking and often both.

The successful career woman was a contradiction in terms: an obscene, epicene caricature. The woman who sought success in a career was damned if she did and damned if she didn't. A few women were nevertheless willing to sacrifice the satisfactions of marriage and motherhood for the satisfactions of a career, relinquishing a degree of respect and dignity in the world in order to pursue their destinies as participants in that world. Success, however, remained elusive.

It's not quite that way anymore. Having a career vs. being a woman is no longer an either/or choice. Times are changing, permitting women to emerge from the home or to abandon traditional female roles with far less social disapproval and considerably less internal conflict. We keep hearing that we have options. We're told that we can become professional, fulfill our talents, scale the corporate ladder, wield political power and more, all without endangering our femininity. And yet, confronting the options can be bewildering.

Women are now asking, in effect, *"If we can have our*

1

*cake and eat it, too, then why is it so difficult for us to get
a piece of the pie that men have been eating all along?"*

Why indeed? Is it, as Phyllis Chesler and Emily Jane
Goodman conclude in *Women, Money & Power,* because
the pie is bitter after all, because our values differ from
those of the people running this country—*i.e.,* men?[1]

Women's values are different, although it's hard to say
why they are. I don't think scientists have demonstrated
that basic biological or genetic differences between the two
sexes have much impact on how we think and feel; however, someday more convincing connections may be found.
Most of the differences between men's and women's attitudes now appear to stem from their different social conditioning and experience. These attitudes may change as
society's expectations of men and of women change. Meanwhile, though, most women care more about certain things
than most men do.

The personal side of our lives is very important. I heard
this again and again, expressed in many different ways, in
the course of the interviews I had with women who had
achieved professional success. Near the end of a long interview Virginia Carter, who is vice-president for creative
affairs at Norman Lear's TAT Communications and Tandem Productions, addressed herself to the subject of success in American life. She said, "There's something distorted, I think, in focusing on just one side of life and
letting relationships fall apart. What a difference to go
home every night to a loving environment! What a terribly
important thing this is! I don't think people are designed
to live alone. Most of us need to be close to somebody.
Yet there's such conflict. To be anywhere near the top in
American life, you have to put a very great deal into the
work you do. But," and she lowered her voice, "if you
don't take the time to develop that special idiosyncratic
thing that makes a personal relationship with somebody
else work, then you've missed something. When you get to
be sixty, if you look back on a life that didn't have that,
you've missed something very important. Yes, there are
great pressures to miss the whole enchilada."

The values we women take with us into our professional
lives are different, too. "Thank God they are," said a
woman who was one of several management consultants
I interviewed. "Keeping your integrity in the corporate

world involves some very difficult tightrope-walking. We have to be careful not to fall into the same traps many men have fallen into. The money trap. The power trap. The fame trap. Fame or visibility is especially seductive to women. We have to learn to use these things—money, power, prestige—in order to further the causes and concerns that matter to us most. Men, I think, are beginning to find that out. Men who have traveled steadfastly toward money and power and prestige, developing the tunnel vision necessary to achieve these things, are now beginning to see the dark at the end of the tunnel. They want out."

She went on, "Much as I want to see women succeed in those areas previously dominated by men, I would hate to see women trapped in lives that are as dull and sterile as most men's. I would hate to see women aping men to the extent that they no longer care about the things that have traditionally mattered to us, things like helping people or making the world better. . . .

"It's ironic," she concluded "that men are turning away from money and power and fame right now just as women are discovering them. Let's hope in the whole jumble of rapid changes going on, women don't lose their values."

Right now, money and power are new toys for women, not ones that are really ours, but ones we've glimpsed. We like the way they feel and yet we regard them with ambiguity. Although they hold an electrifying force over us, and we're increasingly attracted to them, we're apt to be repelled by them at the same time. *Women want something more.*

Alas, women have often been willing to settle for something less. Far less. Why?

WE'RE IN THE GAME, LIKE IT OR NOT

Women haven't been programmed for success in the mainstream of society where a rough-and-tumble game is going on.

But many women find themselves playing center court, whether they'd planned for it or not and whether they like it or not, and more women are being tossed there all the time. It's a little too late to be pointing out how comfortable it is to be in the cheering stands in a supportive role rather than out there in the middle of things. From now on, most females will spend only a part of their lives along the sidelines.

The stakes aren't the same for us as they are for men; even when we do win, the rewards are less, and the emotional and psychic costs of our being in the game are high. Often, too, the rules are set by people who don't want to see us win. Although some women play only to survive or to avoid being trampled by the rougher, stronger players, many are now beginning to play to win.

Our ability to make it in the mainstream is blocked both by inner conflicts and by outer obstacles. We need to understand ourselves better in terms of the game that's being played. In addition to looking at the differences between how men succeed and how women don't, we need to know *how women do it*.

What are the ingredients of women's success in what is really a man's world? How do women of achievement handle the problems they share with other women? What have these women learned that women who are still trying don't know? How did they get started? How has their thinking changed? What kind of game are they playing? How does it feel to be a successful woman today?

I started asking women questions about their careers and their lives until eventually I had forty rather extensive interviews in addition to a number of shorter interviews plus materials collected from books, magazines and other secondary sources. The forty subjects include women in vastly different career fields, women whose ages, backgrounds, interests and priorities vary considerably.

HOW WOMEN LOOK AT SUCCESS

My *raison d'être* in the several careers I've had has been usefulness, to respond to a need and to try to help fill that need.

      Felice Schwartz President, Catalyst

Success is just being at this point in time and saying, "Here I am, this is nice." I think life is pretty terrific. Part of it is being in this industry which brings me in touch with so much that's new and young and contemporary, and which keeps me constantly updating myself in every area. I consider my greatest success of all is having four very neat kids and the husband that I have. I can stand back and say, "Gee, they're pretty nice." It all makes life a kind of celebration.

> *Adrienne Hall*
> Executive Vice-President,
> Hall-Levine Advertising, Inc.

Success is hard to define. I guess I knew I'd reached it when my interests and attentions were so focused that I didn't know what time it was. In teaching and in other things I've done, I've watched the clock. Success is being so keyed in that time doesn't matter, getting older doesn't matter. And success is also using my abilities—in my case, abilities I hadn't known I had. I've made money, but success isn't money; success is involvement.

> *Mercie Butler*
> Account executive,
> Merrill Lynch, Pierce, Fenner and Smith, Inc.

Much as I love television, success to me isn't just my work. It's being with my children, being the best parent I can be, and loving my kids. It's loving Johnny with everything I've got. Success is all those things.

> *Marcia Carsey*
> Senior Vice-President,
> Comedy and Variety Programs, ABC Entertainment

For me, success has to be self-actualization, being the best "me" I can possibly be while continuing to grow and learn. It includes being respected and sought after in my field, being a supportive boss and friend, and being satisfied with myself just as I am from moment to moment even as that self changes.

> *Sheila S.*
> Executive, nonprofit organization

We'll be hearing more from these and other women later on. Regardless of how greatly their individual talents, vocations and career milieus varied, the women I spoke with shared some notions about success. They referred to helping others, contributing to society, also to utilizing their abilities, and to personal growth and self-actualization. Often too they mentioned happiness in their personal or family lives. Very few mentioned attaining status or exercising influence or commanding high pay, and almost none attached primary importance to these.

I was surprised. I had expected to find some women who had struck Faustian bargains or who had somehow sold out. I had anticipated that the new successful women, entering areas previously reserved for men, would sound more like men, describing success as money, power and/or recognition.

What surprised me even more was that the definitions given by these successful women were not really much different from those I'd been hearing from women I've known all my life who have achieved far less in their careers. If there's so little difference in basic beliefs and values, where does the real difference lie? Why aren't more women making it?

HOW WOMEN LOOK AT CAREERS

In spite of all the talk about women breaking through traditional barriers, many women in this country don't have careers at all. Instead, they "just work." They get up every morning, put in the requisite forty hours a week and collect a paycheck. Enjoyment on the job is a kind of bonus won by a few. Most women simply work for money, perhaps as a means to luxuries, but far more often as a necessity for their own or their family's survival.

What is sad about this is that many women who are still "just working" are just as well educated, intelligent and talented as the men who supervise them, men who are at a far higher level or on the way there and who are earning considerably more.

Women "just working" fit well with the old order of things. A job was a way to mark time before getting married or a means to help out the family during difficult times. It was something temporary; it wasn't for life. Social and economic circumstances have changed the old order, however. The accelerated rate of inflation as well as the accelerated rate of divorce have contributed to keeping many women in the marketplace far longer than they intended to stay. And women starting employment in recent years have few illusions about only having to work for a little while.

Increasingly, women want "career-type" jobs. And understandably, since working is likely to consume most of our waking hours and is apt to last a lifetime. This is far different from "just working," and when we contemplate careers, we do so very seriously.

Margaret Hennig and Anne Jardim, in *The Managerial Woman,* analyzed why so many women are stalled in middle-management jobs instead of ascending to higher corporate levels. Comparing the ways men and women in corporations define the simple word "career," they found: "Women see a career as personal growth, as self-fulfillment, as satisfaction, as making a contribution to others, as doing what one wants to do. While men indubitably want these things, too, when they visualize a career they see it as a series of jobs, a progression of jobs, as a path leading upward, with concrete recognition and reward implied."

They also point out that women lack a sense of "a game being played, of a temporary adoption of a style for reasons of self-interest." Men, on the other hand, they found, are programmed for game-playing behavior and all that it implies: learning specific rules, adopting strategies with specific goals in mind, obeying signals from peers; also, teamwork, competition, risk-taking, winning, recognition, rewards. In boys this conditioning begins at a very early age.[2]

For women, our life's work is real, serious, fraught with personal, ethical, social and perhaps spiritual considerations. Success for us is far less a measure of ourselves by outside standards or recognition by the public or our peers than it is an assessment of ourselves by an inner yardstick of personal, individual measurements.

When we allow ourselves to be the final judge, success can become difficult to achieve. At the same time, the inner yardstick, with generalized, indeterminate markings, can be a buffer against failure. As one woman said, looking back, "I wanted so much that I really didn't expect to get it all." Relying upon our consciences to evaluate our achievement, women may find themselves floating in a limbo somewhere between failure and success, not wholly discontent, but not satisfied either.

Traditionally, women have been day-to-day creatures, caught up in today's diapers, this week's letters, this month's bills. Our sense of the here-and-now sustains us when sickness or disaster strikes, when children grow up and leave, when husbands succumb to another woman or to a coronary. As another woman said, "I never felt that I was a failure when some phase of my life was going right, and usually something was going right." Through life's disappointments, reversals and traumas women seem to have a kind of psychic continuity that enables us to survive. But by hanging in, keeping our noses firmly to the grindstone, not thinking big and not thinking ahead, women are left behind, still stuffing envelopes, still making the coffee and still poor.

What was a strength in our old roles becomes a weakness in our newer ones. And we're not apt to be disturbed about our lot in life as long as we are in fact surviving. "I'd become a robot," said a former secretary who made a late decision to study law, "but I didn't see myself that way at the time. After all, I had nice clothes, vacations, interests outside of work. I thought I had nothing to complain about. Eventually I realized that I had extinguished part of my mind and part of myself unknowingly and unwittingly, and that I would surely go mad if I didn't do something about it."

CAN THIS WOMAN BE SAVED?

What people really need from life, what brings genuine satisfaction, according to psychiatrist Dr. Thomas Szasz, is not wealth nor power nor esteem but, rather, "games worth playing." Otherwise they fall prey to disenchantment, boredom and psychic paralysis or other symptoms that can lead to mental illness or even to madness.[3]

What happens to the woman who is isolated day after day in the suburbs or whose job consists of tracking details and never making decisions? She may put up and keep going, as many have and still do. But, realizing that she lives in a game-oriented society where the main game is working and getting ahead, she is likely to become bored or bitter or frustrated. She could even go mad.

The real question, then, is: Can she learn what she needs to know and make what adjustments must be made in order to play a game worth playing or do a job worth doing? Can she change?

We're led to believe that many important aspects of both men's and women's behavior is set or fixed early in childhood. This is almost as grim and defeatist an attitude as the belief that we are totally at the mercy of our genes. Either assumption can be used to suppress people by letting them think that they cannot do any better or any differently than they are already doing. Heredity and environment interact in various complex ways, and, more important, individuals themselves have a remarkable capacity for overcoming adverse circumstances of either kind.

Dr. Cynthia Fuchs Epstein, professor of sociology at Queens College and a research associate at Columbia, writes, "I think focusing too much on early socialization has negative consequences. Once we believe all the damage is done early, we can then write off an entire generation as incapable of being changed. It permits the gatekeepers in the academy, business, and the professions to pass the buck to the primary school teachers who made girls take cooking while the boys took science. 'Not our fault,' they assert, 'that women aren't trained to become administrators and heads of departments. They were socialized to be passive, docile, and retiring.' "[4]

Dr. Epstein has been taking a new look at the work of the authorities responsible for these widely accepted theories of early socialization—Erikson, Piaget and others. Her "initial clues" about these assumptions, she writes, "came when, after the women's movement had been sufficiently developed to make career opportunities available to many women, I could see distinct changes in the personalities of women. Those who had severe self-doubts regarding their own competence found that, when they were given additional responsibility, they could handle it well, although they were frightened to begin with. Women who were afraid of taking on new jobs normally reserved for men found they could not only learn things they thought they couldn't (like the economics of magazine production), but they found they liked the new activity. They also liked the power and they liked the success. Nothing, it seems, succeeds like success."[5]

Yes! By the time I spoke with Dr. Epstein and read her ideas, I had interviewed perhaps two dozen women. And while a few of them had chosen their career paths early, many more had started out later. Nearly all had had to conquer some inner fears, come to grips with deep conflicts, assume a different role and change. Certain aspects of their early conditioning proved worth keeping; other aspects were cast off. We are not unchanging creatures doomed forever to the *status quo* by what happened at age four, not if we don't want to be. I met women who'd reprogrammed themselves at twenty-four and at thirty-seven and at fifty-one.

Change isn't easy for individuals of either sex, of course. Some women who are at or near the top now had to hit bottom emotionally before they could pull themselves up.

HOW WOMEN SUCCEED

The women I interviewed didn't succeed by playing a man's game or by abandoning their own values. What gave them the impetus to strive for success was that they found games worth playing within the mainstream that they could play *on their own terms*. We could even say that they're creating new games.

When this happens, the markings on that inner yardstick become not only clear but imperative. "I'll never be able to settle for less than self-actualization from now on," said Sheila, who left her retailing job for an executive position in a large and well-known social agency.

I've known Sheila since college, and got to know her better during the five months or so that we shared a somewhat cramped New York apartment. Twenty years ago she struck me as one of those rare college women who knew what she wanted and went after it. She did her homework efficiently, went to bed at a reasonable hour, pulled mostly A's and even managed to keep her clothing pressed and her hair combed. She was among the most attractive and well-groomed women at our small, progressive college, which is known for many things, but not for its well-groomed women. When the rest of us were analyzing our-

selves and each other, she would either become bored and
leave or she would rip into our theories with a logic that
was hard to fault. She never suffered from second-year
slump, and she seemed crisis-proof, able to get from point
A to point B with a minimum of hesitation and side-
tracking.

Although she majored in art, her choice of a retailing
career seemed well founded. As she said, looking back,
"In part-time jobs I eliminated clerical work, banking and
commercial art. One job in a small gift shop turned me
on. I could do everything there—display new merchandise,
sell, meet people, do the books, learning the business from
the people around me who were willing to teach me. The
latter was more important than money."

She advanced rapidly. A few years after college she
married. There were no children, and in time she found
she had taken on the image of a career woman. "I stayed
in retailing because the challenges, the fast pace and the
variety had me hooked," she said. "I wasn't sure I wanted
my boss's job, but I would say so in order to be looked
upon as a 'comer.' "

We didn't see each other for fifteen years, but every
year came the silk-screened Christmas card with news of
her husband's career progress and the vacations to far-
flung places they took together. Finally I wrote her to say
I was coming to New York to promote a book. "Come
stay with us!" she replied, and I did.

Maybe when women who are good friends meet after
long, long absences, it's apt to be like this, I don't know.
There was a long moment of staring approvingly at each
other's gray hair, I remember, but there was also my feeling that she had changed so very little in other, more important ways. She'd just become more herself, I thought.
The refrigerator was stocked with an array of salads, and
everything that a guest might need was in sight. The living
room had plenty of books and all the right touches: bold
paintings, hand-made ceramic bowls, exquisite textiles. It
was a far cry from the place we'd once shared. Also, her
husband was a thoughtful, charming person. All was well,
it seemed, and although I wasn't unhappy with my own
very different existence in California, I found myself envying her life.

A couple of years later Sheila's crisis struck. The Christmas card came late that year and didn't say much. Later she told me there'd been a serious illness in her family, her own health had faltered for a while and the career to which she'd devoted all those years suddenly seemed meaningless. "It just wasn't challenging anymore. In fact, it was so boring I couldn't stand it," she said. The one stable force in her life was her husband.

She quit her job without knowing what she would do next but with a fierce desire to find *something* to do. "There were times when I didn't want to get out of bed or leave the apartment," she said. "However, I didn't dare give in. So I bombarded myself with as many new interests and experiences as I could, and I found the process energizing. I went through *est,* which left my head in a different place and which speeded up the process of recovery. I saw I had choices. Pulling out of my former career the pieces which gave me the most satisfaction —working with people, supervising, coordinating—I built on these, learned new skills, joined new organizations, got my head into my new field, and ended up getting the perfect job five months later, in a large social agency where what I have to offer accomplishes something I feel is ultimately worthwhile."

For each woman the choice is different, and the process leading up to that choice varies, too. What is most vital and most difficult, however, is deciding *what one wants.* Increasing, women are able to crystallize their abilities, needs and values into realizable career goals early enough to get a head start. But recently, too, many women have done their first concrete career-planning in their thirties and forties and later. Something happens: old ambitions, latent talents and lifelong values all come together. Once these women knew what they wanted, they mobilized themselves and took immediate action. That's not to say that the rest was easy, but the rest was something they could handle.

There's urgency and conviction in the way women describe their eventual career decisions. One said, "There are no compromises. Either you want something or you don't. What you choose either gets you closer to your goal or it doesn't. Halfway measures are the worst self-sabotage there is."

When I heard her say this over the phone, I suggested

that women sometimes must compromise in order to make a living. She said, "No. You work it out. Maybe you work all night or use up your savings, whatever. You stop saying 'yes, but' and 'I'm trying.' You just *do* it."

Talking tough, I thought, giving glib answers—not the sort of thing I want to offer to women trying to *understand*. Meanwhile I was asking other women about success and hearing "I knew I had to do it," "I knew what I had to do to make it real," "There were no alternatives left. I'd fallen flat on my face whenever I compromised, acting against my feelings in promoting a shoddy product or representing something I couldn't believe in."

In somewhat softer tones, these women were saying the same thing. There were no compromises for them either. They'd already considered the options, and once they knew which game was worth playing, they knew with certainty. Nothing temporary or halfhearted about it: they *knew*—and this time they were playing to win.

IT'S OUR WORLD, TOO

When women talk about winning, we don't often think of it as beating out the competition or causing someone else to lose. We win bread for our families, recognition for our achievements, victories for other women, battles for humanity. Our success has to measure up against that inner yardstick.

Our making it in the mainstream is not really just a question of having our cake and eating it too. There isn't much cake being offered to women these days. The job of wife-mother-homemaker, satisfying as it may be, is at best only temporary, and it offers no guarantee of lifetime security. Phased out of the home by technology, population explosion, spousal demise or spousal boredom, many women must find new places for themselves, carving their way through alien terrain where the going is rough and the natives are hostile.

Can we succeed in the system while trying to change the system? Can we get ahead in a world not of our own devising without sacrificing some part of ourselves or selling out other women along the way? As Chessler and Goodman put it: "The dilemma is how women can 'make it in a man's world,' but reject, as a condition for that success, becoming part of the machinery that keeps this a man's world."

We can and we must. The purpose of this book is to explore the ways it can be done.

II

Money, Dirty Money

MONEY is just about the most highly charged single element in our society, carrying with it a complex array of contradictory connotations and confusing symbolism. It is almost as loaded with mystique as sex, and it is surely no less problematic. Like sex, it's something people love to talk about, whether they have it or not and regardless of what role it plays in their lives. People use shared assumptions about money as a way of relating to others and tell lies about it as a way of relating to others. People even lie about it to themselves. Apart from being a medium of exchange, money is a medium for acting out neuroses.

Those without money can look at it as a cure-all for life's problems. The poor may see their lack of money as the curse responsible for all their ills while, paradoxically, consoling themselves with the image of the rich suffering on psychiatrists' couches.

Not all the rich are suffering, however, and certainly not as a direct consequence of having money. When money brings pain, it's because people expect it to do something it couldn't possibly do. Money doesn't bring inner peace, self-esteem, friendship, love, safety or happiness. As one woman, a real-estate broker in a medium-sized city, said, "There are certain things we should do for ourselves, and when we want money to do those things for us, well, it just doesn't work. Money isn't everything. Money is only money. Some good things can be bought with money, but others can't. It sounds so simple, doesn't it?"

Women and money. A lot has been said and yet women are still having problems. We have trouble thinking about money, trusting ourselves with it, figuring, planning ahead and—most important to our working lives—we have a hard time asking for raises or negotiating fees for our services.

Within the broad boundaries of women's values, there's room for vast differences in how we look at money. Also, not all money hang-ups are unique to women by any means. But some beliefs about money are clearly self-defeating; some attitudes not only prevent us from becoming rich but also impede progress in our life's work and keep us from becoming the human beings we'd like to be. Lacking a Masters and Johnson of money, we must analyze our own money problems and probe our own dysfunctions.

One message about money—that it isn't everything, that it can't take the place of many other good things in our lives—gets through to women rather well, far better than it gets through to men. For middle-class men, money is a very real means to having friends, love partners, a spouse and rosy-cheeked children, and for them it easily becomes an end in itself. Women traditionally haven't needed money—at least, not our own money—to have the things that matter most to us.

"Women's satisfactions have always been different," says writer Nancy Shiffrin. "We've traditionally sought inner satisfaction in our relationships, our homes and our families rather than in our work, so we've been spared the dreadful onus of having to be materially successful ourselves. Although money has been necessary for our survival—and more women, I think, have had to take a responsibility for their material needs than anybody realized—money hasn't been necessary for our identity the way it has for men."

In some ways women are saner about money than men have been. But is our sanity keeping us poor? And can we reconcile our inner values with the game-playing techniques and strategic thinking we need in order to survive?

CLEAN MONEY AND DIRTY MONEY

Through centuries of feudalistic and other hierarchical societies, the "best money" was old money, gained by the happy accident of inheritance. Those spending it never had to contemplate the toil or sweat or injustices that went into making it.

Today there remain vestiges of the notion that women —to be pure, respectable, virginal—should be safely removed from the nitty-gritty of making money. As Chesler and Goodman perceptively note, "Real Ladies come already paid for. And a Real Lady is the best kind of woman there is. Or so women have been made to feel."

The most envied women are still those "already paid for" in one way or another: by trust funds, wealthy fathers or highly paid husbands. Real Ladies could and still can afford to be crusaders, helpers of the poor, guardians of culture, patrons and even practitioners of the arts. Men feeling uneasy over how they gained their wealth have always been able to take comfort in their wives' and daughters' compensating efforts.

Women without money did and still do devote themselves to social and artistic causes, but at great sacrifice, so that poverty itself becomes a cause. "Poverty is not a virtue, but a lot of women go through a stage of believing that it is," said Toni Carabillo, co-founder and co-owner of Graphic Communications, a small but thriving graphics concern, and editor and publisher of the National Organization for Women newsletter, "and I think even the women's movement inadvertently endorsed this for a while— the more you sacrificed, the holier you were supposed to be. Actually, the more you sacrifice, the more uncomfortable you are. Adamantly not wanting to make money is as wrong as wanting to make money just to be making money. To me, success has a lot to do with the quality of life. You don't have to be rich, but you sure can't be poor."

The extent of women's sacrifice isn't always apparent these days, even to the women themselves. Well-educated women from middle- to upper-middle-class families may think of themselves as comfortably well off when their incomes barely exceed the poverty level. Usually they're counting on a man or a miracle. They're not facing their situation realistically nor are they counting on themselves.

"They're the pseudo-rich," said Inez T., "they think they don't have to work for money." Inez, who now holds a vice-presidency in heavy industry in the Midwest, was once

a comparative-literature major who went to work in publishing, a field where women employees have always been
expected to be independently wealthy or to have few material needs. When I met her twenty years ago, her Green-
wich Village apartment was filled with books, but so
underfurnished that her guests either sat on the bed or on
the white metal cover of the bathtub, which was in the
kitchen, conveniently placed next to the sink. "This is luxury compared to how I lived in Paris," she assured me
then.

When I asked her to look back on those days, she said,
"I thought there was something classy about being able to
regard pay as incidental. Nothing was more boring to me
than hearing personnel discuss the retirement plan. . . .
People kidded me about having a rich fiancé, and I fully
expected to have one."

Like many women who were in college in the 1950s, she
expected marriage to solve her money problems, but she
married a man who was also "pseudo-rich," having exquisite tastes and very little money. They were divorced
after two years, having had no children. Nearing thirty
but still earning very little as an assistant editor in a
publishing house, she began to reconsider her goals. "I saw
that I simply couldn't afford the luxury of a publishing
career and have the other luxuries I wanted, too," she
said. "I hadn't tossed out the idea of marrying again, but
decided that I wanted a worthwhile existence in the meantime."

Packing up her few belongings, she left New York and
enrolled in an M.B.A. program at the state university
near her parents' home. She worked as a secretary to support her schooling.

Today, at thirty-eight, she has her own house in the
suburbs of a large Midwestern city. Books are everywhere,
but neatly arranged on built-in shelves. Classical music
follows her from room to room at the flick of a speaker
switch. She points proudly to pottery collected on business
trips to Europe and South America, where she has also
had an opportunity to use the foreign languages she
learned in college. "Business is challenging and fun, and it
gives me the life I want," she said.

In many ways women integrate their knowledge, interests, values, with their material needs. For some women

a sense of personal financial responsibility coincides with an acceptance of their single status.

Nancy Shiffrin spent her twenties in a variety of creative pursuits including dancing and poetry. "My thirty-third birthday was a day of awakening," she said. "I realized that no man was going to save me, really save me, that nobody was going to support me while I wrote poetry on the second floor of my house. I knew I'd have to get on with my life and take responsibility for myself and my material needs." Soon afterward she became a serious writer of articles and non-fiction books, including some dealing with the subject which interests her most: the human potential movement.

Often this realization that one is responsible for one's own material well-being comes as a rude awakening after a divorce. A mother of three who was in her forties before beginning her real-estate career said, "We were all raised to wait for Prince Charming. For me, as for so many others, Prince Charming has been here and gone!"

Novelist Carolyn See launched her writing-and-teaching career after her husband left. "With three mouths to feed, you'd better believe money is important," she said.

But it still isn't easy for women to stop looking at money-making as a matter for the great unwashed or the ungodly, the greedy or the unfeminine—in other words, for persons other than themselves. A college woman of twenty, the daughter of a woman achiever, said to me, "Money doesn't matter a lot to me. As long as I have something to eat and a place to sleep, I'll be okay." As recently as 1972 a study of college women (and nuns) by Paul F. Wernimont and Susan Fitzpatrick, reported in the *Journal of Applied Psychology*, revealed that a majority thought of money as "evil" and pooh-poohed the idea of making money. Although attitudes are changing, some women still fear that making money will soil their hands, tarnish their souls, or worse.

Telling people that money isn't good for them and that striving for it is sinful has been a way of keeping suppressed classes poor and in their place for centuries. It's amazing how effectively this message, like the sexual taboos in our culture, has gotten through to people—especially to the middle classes, who have continued to believe in the corruptive power of money even as they've become richer.

The old myths and taboos about money have, never-theless, all but vanished from the mainstream, the game-playing arena where money is "the bottom line," the *raison d'être* for most institutions. The woman who brings a heavy load of guilt over money to the game is going to find herself severely handicapped. And a belief that money is evil incarnate will prevent her from playing at all.

WHAT DOES THE STOCK MARKET HAVE TO DO WITH THE PRICE OF BEANS?

Why do women persist in thinking small, worrying over the price of string beans for dinner instead of, say, keeping up with the price of soybeans on the commodities ex-change? "Women are great managers of the *Knippel*—which is the symbol of the nest egg and the cookie jar—but are afraid of economic realities and terrified of high finance," said therapist Dr. Tessa Albert-Warshaw. Women play a penny-ante game with money, and though they sometimes play it well, saving a dollar here and a dollar there, they're often losers in the larger money game.

Success in other phases of our lives, including our careers, doesn't guarantee success with money. As Erica Jong said at a Washington benefit for the Women's Cam-paign Fund, "We successful women feel we are doing something unwomanly by making money. When we try to invest it wisely instead of going out and losing it all, we tend to feel conflicted."

True enough, women are victims in a society that makes us want more of everything while often not letting us earn the wherewithal to take care of our basic needs. When I wrote my book *Money & the Working Ms.*,[1] I thought that women's money problems would be greatly alleviated if only we stopped buying clothes, cosmetics and other frills to combat depression or assuage guilt or compensate for low self-esteem.

Stay out of the dress shops, I warned. Scrimp, scrounge, but save a few pennies for a few shares of stock or what-ever small investments you can afford. It won't be much, but it's better than nothing. This advice may have helped some women, and I got letters from around the country saying that it had. But how many women are still scrimping, scrounging and floundering, I wonder, still listening to the rattle of pennies in the *Knippel,* working hard, struggling and not expecting much? Looking back, I think my advice was more a symptom of the real problem than it was a cure for it, and I now apologize for adding fuel to the forces that keep women from thinking big and looking ahead and fighting back. Self-denial is not by itself a virtue any more than poverty is. Instead of spending less, most women need to earn more.

Women can derive real satisfaction from achieving economic goals that they've set for themselves. Having economic goals doesn't mean we must become mindless worshipers of the "bitch goddess," as males metaphorically call money. But, living in our present society, we need money goals along with career planning in order to have the kind of life we want. Money goals, like career goals, must derive from our own values and reflect our real needs.

Some very valid money goals are personal ones—money to buy a house or a weekend cottage, to retire someday, to travel, to educate one's children, even to afford time for pursuing non-paying adventures.

Money goals can also be political. Women are beginning to realize that to participate in the important decisions being made in society, one must be where real money, big money, is being allocated and spent. Very few women are in such positions. One who is, Katherine Graham, chairman and chief executive of the Washington Post Company, once said, "I get a lot of flak at the *Post* when I talk about profitability. They get up pretty tight at the mention of M-O-N-E-Y; they think I'm some heartless bitch. I have to do an endless song and dance about how excellence and profitability go hand in hand—which isn't an act. I really think they do."[2]

Women who still think of money as evil need to remember that, although it took money to create a Watergate, it also took money to expose it, as the *Post* decided to do. Difficult as it may be for most women to identify with the chief of the $250-million Post empire, at some deeper levels they may have more in common with Ms. Graham than they realize. Women need to believe in whatever they're doing the way Ms. Graham believes in the *Washington Post.* More women need to be in positions like hers, and if they get there it won't be by ignoring profitability. The women I spoke with believed too, though they expressed it in different ways, that excellence and profitability can go hand in hand.

Even when big money ceases to appear evil, however, it's still awesome. Many women are still more comfortable with the *Knippel* or the cookie jar.

Women think of money the same way they think of time: they see both portioned out in small segments. They worry over the Saturday grocery shopping, the bills coming due next week, the rent for next month, all the while resisting serious consideration of their income five years hence or the financial assets they'll have for retirement.

Surely one reason we have difficulty looking ahead is that we're apt to feel threatened when we try to picture ourselves in the future. Instead of imagining our achievements and rewards, we may instead see age and loneliness. I remember one would-be achiever saying, "Who needs to think about being seventy when there are more pressing problems at hand?"

Her problems, however, were essentially cookie-jar problems—a bill from the plumber, the cost of minor car repairs. They were important, but they certainly didn't warrant her staying away from a career seminar or a job-planning course. Or her staying on at a low-paying, dead-end job to get this year's Christmas bonus.

Somehow, once one starts looking at the future realistically, the smaller, more immediate problems, no matter how pressing they once were, are swept away. The energy that women once expended in worrying over auto repairs or comparing produce prices goes into planning for the future, not only making their own and their family's lives more comfortable, but ensuring their own independence in later years. Anyone planning to live past age sixty-five needs either an ample and very secure pension fund or, minimally, a six-figure sum of money. And it's not possible to invest for the future in stocks, bonds or real estate with cookie-jar money. To think ahead one must think big.

Although the tyranny of age is lessening as women find sources of fulfillment outside their home and family and beyond their child-bearing, child-rearing years, the financial realities of growing older still elude them. *Ms.* magazine surveyed 20,000 women of all ages, 43 percent of

whom had advanced degrees or graduate training. A total
of 61 percent were entirely confident about their financial
futures, and only 12 percent doubted that they would have
enough money to live comfortably for the rest of their
lives. And this was despite the fact that only 5 percent of
the 20,000 were earning $25,000 a year or more at the
time of the survey.[3]

But time plus an ominous vision of age and poverty can
also be motivating forces for women. California Superior
Court Judge Joan Dempsey Klein witnessed the ravages
of the Depression from a home that was torn by alcohol-
ism. Her first goal was to become a physical-education
teacher, and she worked her way through San Diego State
College as a swimming instructor, a dishwasher and a
schoolbus driver, among other things. During World War
II she was an aircraft riveter on B-24s. After obtaining a
master's degree in education she worked as a playground
supervisor to support herself in law school.

When I asked her about the relentless energy she displayed, she said, "I was determined to get myself out of a
place where I'd be poor. I didn't want a lot of money. I
wanted to be self-supporting and independent. We were
very poor and I saw my mother trapped by lack of funds
and with no skills to earn a living for herself and three
kids. Her life was totally without options. Something kept
me going. I have tremendous drive and determination,
also tremendous physical energy. If there's a force behind
me, it's the fear of poverty. I've always known that I
didn't want to be what they call 'an old lady,' whose usefulness is spent, over, and who, most likely, is poor and
dependent upon others."

She has a strong commitment to helping other women
structure their lives so that they too will have options.
"Women were never taught to achieve goals," she said.
"We need marketable skills and we need to be able to
take risks. Women need to understand from age three
that they need to have financial goals!" When I spoke with
her in her chambers, her voice filled with the same in-
tensity it has when she addresses groups of women, relay-
ing to them this same message.

Another woman I know had worked alongside her husband in his insurance office for years. The two of them
were nearing sixty and looking forward to a modest but

comfortable retirement together when the husband died suddenly. He left his wife some money, but her own retirement began to look very bleak compared to the way it might have been had her husband lived. Slowly and with difficulty she adjusted to being alone, keeping her job in the insurance office for a year and a half. Then, just after her sixtieth birthday, she had a new burst of energy. "All around me housing prices were going up and I saw an opportunity in real estate. People laughed at me when I talked of quitting my job and studying real estate. I knew I had to do it," she said. She dipped into her husband's insurance funds to support her schooling, then to make some small but sound investments. By now she has helped her three grown daughters make investments in real property and she has the kind of life she'd always dreamed of having, which includes European travel, cruises and vacations in Hawaii. But not all women getting off to a late start can run as hard as she has.

Men not only make career plans early but also generally decide just how much money they're going to make in five years, ten years and twenty years. Often, too, they picture where they'll be at fifty or at sixty-five, the sort of office they'll occupy, the house they'll live in, the people who will surround them. Although plans may have to be changed, their financial goals are real and workable ones which are effective in getting them mobilized. Men—and not only businessmen but researchers and professors and writers—know when they're on schedule. Being able to visualize oneself in the future, and having precise plans for that future, makes a rather enormous difference.

Until recently, precise planning has been almost impossible for women. One might or might not marry, one's husband's future came first, one might be unexpectedly pregnant, and unexpectedly, too, husbands might be transferred. In anticipation of a life beset by uncertainties, one learned to cope rather than to plan. Said one achiever who was in college in the 1950s, "Dreaming was okay, but planning, no. Actually, I had plans, but I kept them secret from my peers and from my parents. Nobody would have understood."

Spurred on by career workshops, counselors and new self-awareness, many women are now setting five-year plans for themselves; more and more women of all ages are looking ahead, establishing their own timetables and mapping out their futures with an eye to economic realities.

When they appeared on a panel together, Nora Ephron asked Erica Jong, "After you get through the dire psychological effects of having money, is it okay?" Ms. Jong replied, "It's wonderful!"

Nearly all of the women I spoke with were happy with the money they were making, enjoying money far more than they had anticipated, in fact. Their testimonies ranged from practical to philosophical.

"Money is freedom," said Mercie Butler, who is married to a professor and who had worked most of the time while raising their three children, but who did not start her career as an account executive with Merrill Lynch until she was almost forty. Her income now eases the burden of college tuition and makes other things possible, too, including travel. She described the beach house to which the family escapes on weekends, then went on to tell me, "Not long ago we got there only to find that it had been flooded by the rain. The floors were soaked and so was everything else for several inches up. A while back this would have been tragic. As it was, my husband and I looked at each other and started to laugh. I'm more relaxed now than I used to be. That's the kind of freedom I'm talking about."

"Money is energy, money is fun," said Carolyn See, who had once been content with a Bohemian existence. "I used to be a very grumpy person. In college, there I was in a black turtleneck sweater carrying my copy of *The Idiot,* my eyes focused downward. . . . Life doesn't have to be all about poverty and suffering if you don't want it to be. If you're going to work, why not make money? If you're going to write, of course you want people to read your books. You have to give the universe a little nudge, that's all. And when things start looking up for you, of course you begin to feel better."

Planning, looking ahead, getting what you want—again and again I heard women saying that it paid off, it was worth what it took. They'd weighed the trade-offs and made things work—*their* way.

Yet there's another side of the coin. One of the high costs of a goal-oriented life is forever missing the present, the here-and-now. Lisa Clewer, who founded her own company, The Works, which performs a wide variety of motivational services in advertising, promotion and training, said, "If only we had the gift of knowing when we peak . . . if only someone could tell us, 'You are in your finest hour!' Because, when everything is a stepping stone to something else, when we're so preoccupied with *where we're going* that we can't savor *where we are,* we may only realize later, 'That was it, and now it's over!'" Later she added quietly, "To get ahead, you have to see ahead. While I'm finishing something, I'm also working on a contract for three months ahead and a proposal for something I'll do in six months. I've always lived in the future. I need to start living more in the here-and-now."

The best-laid plans may not acknowledge the price we must pay for success and for money. There's a line in the film *Citizen Kane* that goes, "It's no trick to make a lot of money if all you want is to make a lot of money." The conflict that women feel over money isn't always the result of old sex-role conditioning. Sometimes the conflict arises from sheer unwillingness to pay the price for money.

FEAR OF FIGURING

Women's fear of numbers has kept us out of better-paying jobs in business, finance and technology and has made us feel helpless with the money we do earn. What is really happening when an intelligent, knowledgeable woman cringes at the mere arithmetic of taking out a loan, investing in stocks or filing a tax return? Nobody knows for sure.

We've all heard by now that females generally test lower than males in mathematical skills. While some maintain that this is an actual case of gender difference, it may turn out to be yet another result of sex-role conditioning. Little girls aren't taught to love numbers; parents and teachers don't expect them to do well with math.

Los Angeles attorney Edna R. S. Alvarez, who specializes in tax work and who lectures to groups of women about the ways economics affects their lives, confessed that she had thought her pre-adolescent daughter was less proficient in math than in other skills. Tests proved otherwise, however. "I was surprised and pleased, of course.

But this shows how effectively we've all been socialized to have lesser expectations of females," she said.

Many women were protected from exposure to math during their school years and later, too, but women are now discovering their own native mathematically abilities that remained undeveloped until they decided to do something about it. An article in *Fortune* about the ten top women in thirteen hundred major corporations included Carol Goldberg, who is president of Stop & Shop Manufacturing Company. In addition to being the daughter of the chairman of the board as well as the wife of the president of the holding company, Stop & Shop Companies, she has had an impressive career of her own that began with other businesses. Yet at the age of forty-seven, according to the article, she was taking a "math anxiety course."[4]

Merrill Lynch account executive Mercie Butler explained how she overcame her own math block. Today, as part of her job, she invests for pension funds and other large accounts as well as for individual clients. Statistical theories on what makes the market tick, such as the "random walk" theory, hold little mystique for her. Amazingly, though, she had insulated herself from numbers and number concepts for years, having had no formal training in math after high school. "I was good at all the things girls are supposed to be good at," she said, "but I thought I wasn't good at math, so I carefully avoided courses in it." Her college major was art. She later taught, painted, worked as a high-fashion model and had three children besides.

A career in business simply didn't occur to her until she was in her late thirties, still in demand as a model but becoming bored with fashion and wondering about her future now that the children were almost grown. Then the world of investments—stocks, bonds, funds, options and real estate—began to fascinate her. She started reading the business pages of the newspapers. Using some of the earnings she had saved from her modeling jobs, she made a small investment in real estate.

"It did well. The property increased in value overnight almost, as I'd thought it would. That gave me confidence," she said. She then began investigating a career in finance. Brokerage houses, in 1970, were just beginning to interview women for non-clerical jobs, although there still

prevailed a strong suspicion that any woman who wanted
to work in investments had something wrong with her.

Refusing to be deterred either by the rampant sexism
she found or by her own lack of experience, she began
studying. After taking the qualifying exam at one brokerage firm in order to pinpoint her strengths and weaknesses,
she knew just what she had to do: learn business math.
She kept studying, and with the help of instruction books
complete with lessons, quizzes and answers which her professor husband brought home for her, she passed the exam
at Merrill Lynch with flying colors. "If I can do it, other
women can," she said. "The important thing is to get the
education, learn."

She now contributes to the education of other women
by lecturing to women's groups about investments. A few
years ago she convinced a major Los Angeles department
store that a combination of investment lecture plus fashion
show would draw a crowd. It did, only the women were
more interested in investments than in fashions. Now she
gives most of her lectures minus the fashion show.

A knack for numbers can be developed early or late
when there's good reason for it. A block about handling
figures can hamper one's ability to deal with dollars, and
when that block stands in the way of career goals or personal financial plans, it had best be demolished. And it
can be.

That's not to say, though, that all women must conquer
the math obstacle simply because, like Everest, it's there.
When it doesn't stand directly in the path of one's goals,
a circuitous route around it may be effective, too. Not all
women's success rests on a foundation of figuring ability,
and some women, such as Carol Goldberg, have succeeded
very well, even in terms of money, without much mathematical wizardry. A small electronic calculator, plus knowledge of simple arithmetic, can go a long way. Some successful people simply don't care for figures and don't need
to. When the figures they have to deal with are large or
demand complex calculations, they depend on experts they
know they can trust.

Lisa Clewer and I were discussing an article she'd assigned me for a magazine she edits and publishes. The
conversation turned to money, as such conversations must.
I was somewhat surprised to learn that she didn't write

her own checks, didn't even carry a checkbook, and I began pumping her for information about her business manager. Everything from loan applications and tax returns to her clothing budget is controlled by a C.P.A. and another accountant in the same office who gives particular attention to her needs.

"It's so much easier," she said. "They keep records for taxes that would take too much of my time. Let's face it, I just wouldn't do it. There are things I'm good at and things I'm not. I don't have time to get bogged down in a lot of details."

Already I knew Lisa as an "idea person" who could entrust details and follow-through to others. "Whatever I'm doing, I have to see the over-all picture, the bird's-eye view, and I don't dare get entangled with things that really don't need my attention." Besides a business manager, the other professionals who handle her financial matters include an attorney, an insurance broker, an investment broker and, occasionally, a real-estate broker. All these individuals were carefully chosen and all, she feels, are cognizant of her needs and goals.

"At what point in your career did you decide you needed a business manager?" I ventured to ask.

"I've always had one," she answered matter-of-factly. "Even as I was just starting out in business," she explained, "I surrounded myself with people who assumed I was going to make a lot of money. Believe me, it has helped."

"Didn't you start small?" I wanted to know.

She shook her head. "No. It's just not like me."

"I believe you," I said finally. "But how can you avoid thinking small in the beginning? How can you afford expert help when you're starting out?"

"You don't hire everybody all at once," she began. "And when you're starting out, it doesn't cost all that much. You might have an attorney picked out and on standby. You already have a banker. Don't just get to know the tellers at your bank, get to know the person in charge *before* you need credit. And a business manager will frequently take someone on for a percentage. You're going to need somebody to do your taxes at the end of the year anyway, and if you haven't kept good records, that could cost you a lot in accounting fees. I know people who spend more having their taxes done than I do all year on a business manager because they pay for having their books unscrambled. . . . This kind of help isn't luxury when you're the kind of person who isn't good at these things. Most people don't get the help they need until they find out that trying to do without it is actually costing them money."

There's an important lesson here for women who may still berate themselves for not being adept with those aspects of money matters that are strictly arithmetical: Don't be swamped by details. Get help. Just make sure that the money matters affecting your career and your future are handled expertly—and on time.

Fear of numbers can sometimes translate into apprehension about individuals who deal in numbers, some of whom do their best to cloud matters in obscure language and awesome complications. But it's possible to cut through this when you choose your experts carefully. Some of the women I spoke with mentioned that they had found the professionals through networks they belonged to. Other network members either were professionals themselves or they could recommend individuals they'd worked with. Edna Alvarez urges all women, married or not, working or not, to find bankers, investment brokers, possibly an attorney, and others with whom they can communicate. She tells women not to be intimidated by these professionals: "Interview three or more before hiring one. Ask them questions. Know what their self-interest is, what they're selling. And don't work with anyone you can't feel comfortable with."

Hiring experts to deal with financial matters doesn't mean abdicating responsibility as women have done in the past. There are basic things one needs to know, and expert help makes learning easier.

As Lisa said, "You should be able to read a financial statement and even be able to prepare one of your own. And there's a lot you can learn from studying financial records which someone else has prepared. You have to know where your money is going, what's costing what, where you should cut down and where you should spend more." Understanding what the figures on a page mean is more important than making rapid-fire calculations.

While Lisa is planning a sales campaign that may yield

millions for the company that has hired her, the accountants she hired are tallying the charges on her statement from Visa and Carte Blanche. Another lesson here, and a more difficult one, is this: Don't be afraid to think big even at the start of a venture. Thinking small may not be your style any more than it is Lisa's. Don't listen to people who, for one reason or another, try to hold you back. We're not little girls being wowed by multi-digit multiplication anymore. We don't have to be.

IF YOU DON'T WANT A RAISE, SOMETHING IS WRONG

Women themselves have been passive objects whose bodies have been (and still are) bought, sold, rented and traded. Considering this history and the connotations of price along with the money mystique and the numbers phobia, is it any wonder we have a hard time putting a price on ourselves in today's job market?

Wilma B., a businesswoman looking back on her first job in the 1940s, said, "I was a secretary to some very bright and well-bred men, and I felt grateful to them for letting me work in their office. Later, when they bestowed the title of administrative assistant on me, I was grateful to have additional responsibility and to do tasks that were more interesting. It didn't occur to me to ask for more money. My gratitude saved those people a considerable amount."

Wilma wasn't unique. I have encountered writers who had been grateful to be published, teachers who had been grateful to be teaching, and so on. Some younger women have difficulty understanding this. "I do not consider working a privilege," said one. But when I asked her if she thought she was being paid what she was worth, she shrugged, admitting that she still had trouble measuring her skills and services in dollars and cents.

Earnings, after all, are not an absolute assessment of one's real worth as a person. A salary (or a fee for services rendered) simply reflects what one is worth to the people who are paying. It's an endorsement of competence and an index to where one stands among one's colleagues or rivals. Beyond that, it's also a sum arrived at by bargaining or negotiation.

"If you don't want a raise, something is wrong!" Wilma literally thundered these words, bringing a bejeweled hand down on her mahogany desk so hard a paperweight jumped. "The system never—or almost never—pays women enough. Anyone who considers herself overpaid where she is now should be out looking for something more challenging. When you've learned all there is to learn in one spot—move on. And a woman who loves her job so much that pay doesn't matter is smothering. Or else being smothered. That's unhealthy. If she honestly doesn't need the money, then she should give it away. But she should still ask for that raise. You know something? The woman who doesn't want more and doesn't ask for it is a traitor to other women who do want it and need it!"

After this outburst, she relaxed in her leather wing chair and gazed serenely at the paneled walls. "Money is part of the game, that's all. The woman who glosses over this fact is going to be treated as an office volunteer or office mascot and she isn't going to be taken seriously by her male colleagues. Why would anybody want to work and not be rewarded for it?"

She continued, "Of course, we work for reasons other than money. The person who is too hungry for money and wants to gobble it all up right away may win in the first round but not in the second. You have to see the whole picture, the whole game, remembering that there's a next round. Your first triumph will pay less than it really should because the people who are paying want you to have something more to work for."

Wilma acknowledges that she got most of her raises *after* doing something that made her employers take notice of her abilities. "But once you've proven your competence, there's nothing wrong with asking for money *before* you do something big. If you know you're the person for the job, they'll be afraid not to give it to you."

Some women have to put their jobs on the line in order to move ahead. Before her position as executive vice-president of Catalyst, Jeannine Green worked for an old, established business-and-economics-research institute. She wanted to be a director of the organization, but was informed that she was "too young" to manage a staff of twenty.

"Needless to say, I was shocked," she said. "I had managed a staff in my past jobs. Finally I saw what the problem was. In the past, I'd been paid very little for administrative work and I'd never been given a respectable title! Naturally I argued that although there was nothing I could do about my youth, I felt I was qualified for the job, giving some concrete reasons why.

"Management was taking its time. Since I really wanted the job, deserved it, had earned it and was ready for it, I decided to help force a decision for my career.

"I sent management a letter saying that I planned to leave for a month's vacation—I had already arranged to go on an African safari—and I asked for an answer before I went. If a decision wasn't reached by then, I explained, I'd assume that someone else had been selected for the position and, in that case, this could be considered my letter of resignation. I was relatively well known in my profession by that time, so I felt that I could surely get a similar job elsewhere and I was prepared to do so. The president of the organization called me in, offered me the job and wished me a good safari. What a relief!" With this promotion, she became the organization's first woman director.

She wasn't the only woman I talked to who had, in effect, issued an ultimatum. But anyone wishing to carry it off must be willing to follow through. She must be sure of her abilities, must be sure that her boss knows what she can do and must also know that a demand exists for her services elsewhere. Given these things, her bargaining position is excellent.

Independent professionals, freelancers in creative fields and others who derive income from various sources must negotiate fees far more often. A lot depends on bargaining position and on confidence, too. Lisa Clewer looked at it this way:

"I've walked away from a contract when somebody didn't want to pay my price, which was a fair price, at times when I literally didn't know how I was going to make payroll without the job. It was risky, but I'd say to myself: 'When you do a job for less than it's worth, you're cheating the other clients who pay you a fair price.'"

She went on, "I work with freelancers a lot, artists and writers. They have no idea of the disservice they're doing when they lower the price because they need the money. Should the price of widgets go down just because the widgetmakers' rent is due that week? Of course not. What's fair one week is fair the next."

"No exceptions?" I asked her.

She thought for a minute. "Deliberately bidding low? The only time I've been able to justify that has been when I'm tackling something new and different. I'm going to be learning from the experience, so I figure I won't charge the client for educating me. Maybe I'll even lose money, considering all the costs, including my time.

"With one client who was very important to me, I gave a very low bid, then turned in a terrific job. The next two jobs they offered me, I turned down. Pretty soon they were asking, 'Why aren't you taking our jobs?' I said it was because I'd bid so low on the other work I'd done for them.

"The moment of truth had arrived—would they remember that I was cheap or that I was good? It's a big gamble. Sometimes they'll remember that you were cheap. This is the time you do your real selling—point out the little extras the client may not be able to get elsewhere. Fortunately for me, the client I wanted so badly remembered that I was good and so was willing to pay my price. I wasn't sorry that I'd given this client a discount in exchange for the training and experience I got."

What about increasing one's price as one becomes more competent? Old clients, after all, may not see that one is getting better all the time. Lisa said, "Every time I've moved ahead, I've dropped work that I didn't want to do anymore. That's part of the fun of it all: getting a new contract, then taking a look at all the things I've been doing and saying to myself, 'Do I really need this work?' Some of it I don't need if it's no longer enhancing my competence and expertise, not at any price. But even when there is no new contract pending, but when you're sure you're worth more than before, you have to act with confidence and ask for a fair price. Never, never work for less than what's fair."

How does one know what is a fair price or a fair salary? Ideally, this should be based on one's own experience and proven abilities compared to those of others performing the same services. Sometimes considerable research is required. Today women who are colleagues and even competitors are comparing notes to find out what's fair, and they're finding, too, that their male colleagues often don't mind talking about money. But it's difficult, especially when you're starting out, to take a detached, objective view of what your work is worth. One woman who confessed, "I used to believe 'I am what I do,'" and who had considerable difficulty bargaining because of her identification with what she produced, had this advice: "Join trade and professional associations. Hook into networks of women in your field. Having good relationships with people who do the same kind of thing you do yields all kinds of useful information, and, even more important, it lets you know where you stand among your peers. It bolstered my confidence enormously."

Wanting more money has nothing to do with greed or avarice or any other of the seven deadly sins. On a subjective level, it may have to do with need, but needing money is never a valid reason to ask for more, just as it isn't a valid reason to accept less. Need only affects one's bargaining position in an adverse way. Wanting pay that's enough and that's fair because it matches your expertise shows willingness to become a serious player in the larger game. Other players—especially males—expect this kind of move. Money is a very important part of the larger game for those who play to win. It's not the whole game, though, whether the arena is a university or a business, a gallery or a bank. The highest stakes of all have to do with power.

III

Power—Uses and Abuses

"WOMEN don't know a thing about power. It used to be we weren't even supposed to use the word," said Frances "Sissy" Farenthold, the first woman ever nominated for the vice-presidency of the United States and, since 1976, president of Wells College.

Power is another dirty word. It's supposed to be addictive, corruptive, disruptive, destructive, but also a turn-on. "The ultimate aphrodisiac," Henry Kissinger called it. Power is what makes some people feel alive, and, despite its many negative associations, the notion of power is gaining respectability. The same women who said they had little interest in money often admitted that they were students of power, intrigued and fascinated by it. Those who had some power nevertheless admitted to being impressed by greater power.

WHAT IS POWER?

When women are turned on by power it's usually power concentrated in male attributes. Power is sexy. Power is *macho*.

Power is strength. Males function as our protectors, but underlying this is the notion that females cannot and should not fend for themselves. Our protectors are also the "gatekeepers," as Dr. Cynthia Fuchs Epstein calls them. They decide where we should gain entry into the

36

mainstream of society. Their power enables them to define our self-images, our options and our horizons for us.

Male authority is woven into the very fabric of our society. As Eleanor Holmes Norton stated in a *Newsday* interview when she chaired the Human Rights Commission of New York City, "Society is organized so that it depends on discrimination against women."[1]

Male power is perhaps most insidious on the psychological level, where women sometimes become willing victims because our thinking reflects the deeply ingrained attitudes of our society. As Dr. Epstein writes, "There is an entrenched theoretical framework which underpins the assumptions that women don't want success or don't have the capacity to achieve it. That is, the set of ideas itself serves as a mechanism that keeps women in their place and out of the competition for the good things in life and keeps them from achieving power. Furthermore, the structure of our society works hand in glove with the structure of our thinking, resulting in the most minimal access of women."[2]

Numerous forces—physical, economic, social and psychological—all working together, have discouraged our rebellion, rewarded our conformity and kept us where we were.

When women want to talk about power, men talk about biology and they're likely to tell us we're already powerful. One important issue in women's striving for equality is, as Erica Jong said, that women are "the only exploited group in history who have been idealized into powerlessness." At some stages in a society's development, the production of babies is a viable contribution to the economics and the cohesiveness of that society. In our present society, men and women agree that babies are nice and that the whole process of making them has awesome aspects. However, there's now a problem of overproduction not likely to reverse itself.

Women's other idealized contributions—as helpmates, companions, guardians of culture, keepers of the faith—no longer guarantee us a livelihood in a society where the position of wife is likely to be only temporary. True enough, women with leisure can rise to places of real power through various volunteer activities. Also, marrying the boss of a corporation is still the surest route for a woman to advance to the peak of a corporate pyramid, and marriage followed by widowhood is still the surest route to a Senate seat or a governorship. For the vast majority of women, however, the position of wife yields little if any power and the position of widow or divorcee yields even less.

In the mainstream, by choice or by chance, women can no longer depend upon others to direct their lives and must instead forge their own destinies. The prospects are dizzying for those who were programmed for passivity and who grew to adulthood with no concept of power.

Women are nevertheless readying themselves for responsibility. And responsibility isn't work alone. It's taking charge of our own lives. It's decision-making and innovating, making things happen and making things change.

"The whole concept of power is just beginning to dawn on women," said California Superior Court Judge Joan Dempsey Klein. "We don't aspire to take over a country. Maybe we aspire to *save* a country. I don't think women want power merely for its own sake, but we need to explore what we do want."

Women often think of power at its destructive worst, as force. The ultimate power game is war, and even in peaceful times power may manifest itself in coercive action. Theodora Wells, communications and management consultant, author and group leader with extensive business experience, had this to say: "Most power is coercive. Power in our society is deeply imbedded in the competitive model. It's I-win-you-lose, manipulative and exploitive. The whole issue, I think, boils down to *who controls whom?* But power can be collaborative; control can be shared more widely. Humanity needs to learn to use power wisely so all parties and nations can gain some of what they want. We may be blown to bits, though, before we learn."

In her book *On Violence!* Hannah Arendt explored the idea of the collective power which can be established in groups through communication of ideas. She wrote, "Power is never the property of an individual; it belongs to a group and remains in existence only so long as the group keeps together. When we say of somebody that he is 'in power' we actually refer to his being empowered by a certain number of people to act in their name."[3]

Shared power or collective, collaborative power is far different from personal power. We need to learn more about both kinds.

WOMEN'S USES OF POWER

I asked a number of individuals, men as well as women, who is the most powerful woman in Washington. Invariably the response was: Katherine Graham of the Washington Post Company. As chief officer and chairman of the board, she is also the only woman at the helm of a large corporation and one of the most powerful executives in the United States.

Casting her as a role model presents difficulties. She didn't come up through the ranks, but was the daughter of one powerful man and the wife of another. Envying her, other women may tend to overlook the hurdles, both private and public, which she has surmounted. The pattern of her life, with its transitions and reversals, actually parallels that of many other women. And her achievements demonstrate well that a woman, once in power, needn't be corrupted by the vertiginous possibilities nor compromised in her convictions.

She was the fourth of five children. Her father was a newspaper tycoon and an investment banker, while her mother's accomplishments included translating Thomas Mann. It was her father who insisted that she leave Vassar after two years to attend the University of Chicago, where the official curriculum was classics and the intellectual climate was liberalism of the most *engagé* sort—or what we'd call radical today. She studied political science, both in classes and in late-night student haunts. She participated in union struggles, too, and after college she worked as a reporter and a columnist.

The first phase of her career in journalism ended with her marriage to Philip Graham, who had been president of the *Harvard Law Review* and who became publisher of the *Post*. Brilliant and charming, he was well liked by everyone from reporters to presidents. For two decades she lived in his shadow and raised their four children.

Turbulence shook this idyllic existence, however, when Phil Graham began to suffer from manic-depressive illness. Another woman entered the picture, too, and was said to be his fiancée. In the face of scandal and sickness, the job of wife must have been exceedingly difficult. Then in 1961 he shot himself.

No ordinary widow at the age of forty-six, Ms. Graham nevertheless confronted some of the problems shared by women who have been far less lucky. And she perceived an opportunity, though she surprised many people when she decided to take the reins of the *Post*. People who worked with her in the early days remember that she was shy, that she worried how her hair looked, and also that she was never afraid to ask questions. She gathered confidence and won respect.

The rest is history, but let's hope that history remembers her part in the exposure of Watergate as an early and important example of a woman not afraid to take a big risk even in the face of extreme vindictiveness from a troubled administration. This is the kind of power that can save a country, even change a country.

But the power that can make a difference still rests almost exclusively in male hands. Males are still in command of the three great bastions of power in this country: the corporations, the government and the military. As of 1978, Katherine Graham was the only chief executive of a company on either the first or second *Fortune 500* list, and in *Fortune*'s investigation of 1,300 companies' proxy statements, which disclosed the names of 6,400 officers and directors earning more than $40,000 a year, only ten, or 0.16 percent, were women.[4] Women's recent strides in government are similar to those in business. Increasing numbers have edged from the bottom to the middle, with almost none reaching top positions. Nor has there been progress in the military, at least at levels where important decisions are being made. The kind of power that makes a difference is the kind women do not have.

How likely is it, though, if more women gain real power, that there will be any real change? It's possible to point to Katherine Graham and to a few others: Martha Griffiths, former Congresswoman from Michigan, who pushed the Equal Rights Amendment out of committee and onto the House floor, or Yvonne Burke, former California Congresswoman, who introduced the Displaced Homemakers Act.

Among the women I spoke with personally, Yvonne Burke was one whose whole career has been motivated by a dedication to social change. The same was true of Jewel Lafontant, Chicago attorney, representative to the U.N. in 1972 and a member of the board of several corporations. Others are also trying in different ways to make things better: Felice Schwartz, president and co-founder of Catalyst, is helping women choose, start and advance their careers and is also working with organizations in changing their hiring practices . . . Adrienne Hall, executive vice-president and co-founder of Hall-Levine Advertising, Inc., is upgrading the image of women in ads . . . Virginia Carter, vice-president for creative affairs at TAT Communications and Tandem Productions, is seeing that various causes are accurately portrayed on some of the country's favorite television shows. The list could go on. A majority of the women I interviewed, whether they were in politics or industry or universities, were deeply committed to helping people and to making human lives better in some way.

Women want things to be different. One study indicates that women of several age groups are less conservative than their male peers, more open to social changes and more tolerant of dissenting and non-conforming attitudes.[5] Women want change; that is, here and now we do. After a few more years and a few more inroads, will we be the same?

It's an academic question, of course, but I think it's worth asking. Could a woman have created a Watergate? Very possibly, yes. But could a woman have led a mass of people to their deaths in the Guyanese jungle? I don't think so, but I truly don't know.

THE POWER GAME

The game has become a trendy metaphor for all events and actions where power is at stake. A game in itself isn't good or bad. Like power itself, a game can have its various uses and abuses.

Games are played wherever there are organizations or

groups of people, wherever power may be seized, shared or redistributed as the result of established rules, individual strategies or clever plays. Much has been written about games in the corporate world, where, as business became larger, the rugged individualist gave way to the organization man, who has in turn been toppled by the astute game-player. The war game is the oldest and is still the prototype for many other games, and politics is perhaps the most exciting game of all. Game jargon is heard less often in the artistic community and the academic world, but the measure of power that exists in these areas is shuffled and reshuffled by power plays, star grabs and surreptitious strategies just as it is in the corporate world. Working independently at a small craft or business keeps one's playing arena smaller though not necessarily less complicated.

To understand power—personal or political—one needs to understand games. In *Games Mother Never Taught You*, author Betty Lehan Harragan has some excellent advice for women entering the corporate world which can be valuable to women invading other institutions as well. As she points out, a knowledge of football or other sports may be helpful, but nothing can replace on-the-spot participation in one of the mainstream game arenas.[6] The desire to win is a mind-set women don't always have but which we are learning.

Winning may be individually defined, but, as one woman said, "You can't win anything in a vacuum. You win because other people agree that your goals are worthwhile." Winning amounts to far more than fame, than riches, than power.

Winning means innovating and motivating, all the while maneuvering ahead of the competition, no matter what the goal is. Describing the process of getting a bill passed, former California Congresswoman Yvonne Burke said, "Legislating is an art and a technique. You can learn how to develop your bill, how to modify it so that you can win over the competition, how to lobby it. You learn how to get different groups participating and supporting your ideas. Like anything else, you just learn, and if you don't, your bill doesn't get passed and never becomes a law."

You just learn. . . . The mind-set becomes firm. The

whole series of plays is the same whether the goal is an election victory, a successful sales campaign, a creative project or a scientific invention. Come up with something new and different, get others to believe in it and keep rivals at bay.

For those who enjoy playing hard, such sport can be self-extending and breathlessly exhilarating. For some of the more seasoned players, it becomes easy, like Zen tennis, a supreme exercise in mind, will and intuition that yields satisfaction from minute to minute.

Some seasoned players, no matter how committed to their goals, nevertheless develop a personal detachment that keeps the game from being a life-death struggle. Yvonne Burke was in the middle of her campaign for attorney general in California when I talked to her, but she showed the same controlled, serene style she's become known for in Congress. "An election is something you can't take personally," she said. "The fact that you may lose somewhere doesn't mean people are rejecting you. Winning is really a matter of how you developed the techniques of presenting yourself or presenting the campaign. My feeling —and I could be wrong—but my feeling is that if I don't do this, I'll do something else."

When they do lose, good game-players start looking for another game, maybe even have one lined up ahead of time. Some game-players, though, including some very skilled ones, are motivated by a fear of losing and have a harder time dealing with losses and cutting their losses.

I had explained this much to a woman friend when her face lit up in a smile of recognition at the idea of politics as a game. "But what about business?" she wanted to know. "What do you have when you've finished? If it's not the money, what exactly do you win?"

I had to think about that. Finally I told her that game-players never finish, that there's always another move or a new play or a whole new game. Sometimes the very process of playing takes precedence over actual goals. Barring a crisis of consciousness, game-players are continually looking ahead for the next challenge; they're not the sort of individuals who will ever be content to cultivate roses in a retirement garden. The result of successive wins, however, can be real power: the ability to influence things and to change them. By winning, one gets to a place where one can achieve increasingly important goals.

One's own goals in any power game aren't necessarily understood by the other players, and yet they must more or less correspond with the goals specified by a given arena of play. In a business, success equals sales and profits, and one is fully expected to try to garner a portion of profits for oneself. Elsewhere, prizes, popularity or visibility may matter even more than actual dollars. Visibility counts in that it allows for a certain amount of influence, but visibility alone shouldn't be confused with power. The names behind real corporate power are scarcely known to the general public. Media stars usually have less real power than the producers and backers who control their stardom and much more. Great power is often felt without being seen or heard, but skilled game-players are in tune with where the power is.

Since the power game is based on the oldest game of all—war—many power structures still parallel the way ancient armies were organized to meet their foes. Most of our present-day institutions, regardless of their purpose, are militaristic hierarchies. Everyone has a specific, well-defined position in the system, and everyone but the top boss reports to one superior. Although upward mobility is possible, the rules usually specify taking one step at a time along prescribed lines within the established chain of command. There are various levels of entry, however, which enables a certain elite to start nearer the top. Some individuals are earmarked to become officers, while a vast number of others are meant to remain workers or foot-soldiers. But not all officers have an equal chance of reaching top command posts.

A group of experts, advisors and specialists who started at mid-level are needed where they are and are very rarely promoted on up; these are staff officers. Women who've made some career progress find that the roadblock standing in the way of further advancement is not only sexism but the inherent structure of the system itself. Line or field officers are promoted; staff officers are not.

Good game-players understand the structure well, deferring to superiors and knowing which privileges go with each rank. Such players will be aware that the seeming incompetent with a large office is really an old friend or a relative of somebody further up, and that the recipient of nepotism is valuable in keeping open channels of communication to the top.

Those who win sometimes do so by breaking rules, skipping steps and taking long leaps ahead, and they are admired by other winners for doing so. But forging ahead blindly without understanding the rules or the system invites failure, as some women have learned the hard way. Naïveté can confuse things enough to clear a line of attack, but naïveté without skill is rarely rewarded.

The more aggressive players choose their arenas of play carefully, avoiding places where the structure is too rigid, seeking instead spots where there are loopholes that make winning easier. Somewhat less aggressive players may be content to be on winning teams. Virtuoso players are those who lead their teams to victory.

Neophyte players must also choose their bosses well, selecting someone who is destined to rise within the system but who is also sympathetic to, not threatened by, a female who wants to get ahead. One reason for this is that team players are more likely to respect a female leader who is already endorsed by a male of higher authority.

Males respect authority. They do so to an extent that can be nauseating to women. As one woman confessed anonymously, "I used to get ill watching my male peers brown-nosing their superiors. How seriously they took themselves, I thought, and yet how little self-respect they must have! Little did I know that my own individualistic stance would leave me out in the cold, but that their back-slapping would be rewarded with raises and promotions. They knew how to play the game even down to the symbols they chose—not the Continental and the tailor-made suits the big bosses had, but medium-priced cars and good-quality ready-made clothes that were, after all, appropriate to their status."

Absolute loyalty to one's boss is expected, too, unless he or she is embezzling company funds. While it's better if that loyalty springs from genuine feeling, smart game strategy isn't often colored by real human sentiments. Right or wrong, one obeys one's captain, never stepping beyond or outside his or her authority.

I once had a job editing a house organ under the

supervision of a personnel director who had a firm grasp of power principles. I felt that the house organ should be outside his jurisdiction as part of a larger communications department. The sales force was expanding and needed literature to help sell products. I sensed what I thought was opportunity at my own doorstep. Without telling my personnel-director boss, I took on an assignment to produce a promotional brochure for the head of the sales force. The work was nearly completed when my boss found out. I defended my decision to take on this task in terms of costs saved to the company, pointing out that I hadn't neglected any other duties to get it done.

"You work for *me!* And don't forget it!" he roared through gritted teeth. I could almost see flames surging from his eyes.

I was angry and humiliated, didn't want to give in to this tyrant and didn't want to give up my long-range scheme either. Quickly phoning the head of sales, I explained what had happened. "Can't we take this to Mr. D——?" I asked. Mr. D—— was the president of the company, and, formidable though he could be, he might see my point or befriend me now, I reasoned, especially if I had the sales chief for an ally.

"Better not," came the head salesman's reply. He advised me to listen to my own boss and not go over his head. He didn't like my boss, I knew, but he was smart enough not to tangle with him over a matter such as this. Although I was sorely disappointed, I learned one of the most important lessons a beginner can learn: Don't go over the boss's head or sidestep his or her authority. Good intentions probably won't be rewarded; playing by the rules will.

Learn the rules and don't think about breaking them until you're sure of them. One woman after another echoed this advice, and several thought that not knowing the rules was the main reason women aren't getting ahead faster. "The fact that you're in a man's job—as they see it—is already a violation of the rules," said one woman. "They're watching you. They'll notice if you're doing a good job, maybe sooner than if you were a man. But they're also ready to trounce you for the slightest goof. Know the protocol, and don't forget to salute!"

The very presence of a woman in the game changes

the game, challenging male players to try new strategies to preserve the power they're used to. Their most effective strategies are subtle, insidious. When a woman moves up to a better job, that job becomes downgraded in the total scheme. When she is turned down for a job, the excuse is legitimate-sounding enough, yet designed to undermine her confidence; she'll be told that she doesn't have the experience or the education or the personal qualifications.

After Jeannine Green finally got that supervisory post for which she was originally told she was "too young," she found herself at the center of a phenomenon all too common in male-dominated organizations. "One major obstacle to my being able to get the information I needed to work effectively was that I was the only director not on the executive committee," she said. "It took me three years to become a member. Then the committee disbanded six months after I joined it!" The same committee soon surfaced again, but was restricted to vice-presidents. Directors were excluded. "Needless to say, direct routes to the top became nearly non-existent," she recalled.

Another ploy of the male player whose game-playing ability is handicapped by his own lack of confidence is this: he allows a female assistant to take major responsibility for a project that involves considerable risk. When the project fails, he intimates to all that it was solely hers. Should it succeed, of course, he's ready to take the kudos.

A woman will rarely receive praise from male game-players who are confused by her role as a team member. When a group of female engineers received low performance ratings from their male supervisors, investigation revealed that the supervisors were too shy to pat them on the back the way they did the young men. What's more, they were also too reserved to offer the criticism the women needed to do their jobs well.[7]

A woman who doesn't understand the canons of the game and the motives of the male players will be less a threat and more a source of amusement between plays. She may herself become an object of minor plays, even a trophy to be carried off. One woman who thought that having an affair with her boss would enhance her position had this to say years afterward: "I guess I thought the closer I could get to power, the better, but sex is definitely not the way to power. I really had some power over him all the while he was making his conquest. By giving in, I gave my own power away. He stopped telling me things and teaching me. Fair or not, I'd had an advantage. I simply handed it over." In instances like this, the man scores points, the woman loses.

"What's wrong with men is they don't forget that they're men and we're women," said one businesswoman. Even well-meaning males who speak out eloquently for equality and women's rights may not be able to ignore that part of their programming which makes them see women as mothers, wives, girlfriends, daughters, maids and whores. Secretaries often assume the combined wife-maid role. The assistant who unfailingly takes care of multitudinous details is allowing herself to fall into the mother slot. When there's sex, the woman may see herself as office wife or office girlfriend while being seen as office whore. The eager-to-learn tomboy daughter who inspires a father-figure boss to pass on knowledge and advice is best off, but, even so, she may not necessarily convince him of her competence.

Businesswomen and others who are smart game-players told me that the most effective relationships on the job were like those that exist between members of a team: that is, good working relationships rather than more personal ones. Juliette Moran, executive vice-president of GAF Corporation, stressed that even so-called mentor relationships are an outgrowth of team playing and that mentors sponsor several qualified people, not just one. Mentoring, several women stressed, isn't purely benevolence; training talented people is simply good for business.

Conventional wisdom and even some research maintain that men are more task-oriented, more compelled to get the job done, while women are more socially oriented or more interested in people and their relationships with them. Game-players are, almost by definition, task-oriented, geared to getting things done.

Sharp game-players are, if Michael Maccoby, author of *The Gamesman*, is correct, individuals who not only tolerate change but welcome it.[8] However, the purposes, rules and structures of the games were determined long ago, and expressing a desire to change the system is tanta-

mount to conspiring to mutiny or trying to direct a whole
fleet away from the battle it's fighting.

Both players who are sharp and those who aren't talk
a lot about being fair, and some organizations do stress
fair negotiation techniques, assertiveness training and
other strategies that evoke a feeling of "I win, you win,
everybody wins." But these can be like Tom Sawyer—
getting others to paint the fence by talking about how good
it is to paint a fence. Some of what passes for open communication is really subtle motivational expertise.

Right now hierarchical structures ruled from the top
with an iron hand are less effective than they used to be.
Workers at the bottom are usually organized, and, increasingly, so are workers in the middle. Often too the
structure is shaped like a diamond rather than a pyramid:
it bulges in the middle with workers who command data-
processing equipment or other sophisticated automatic
machinery. The old militaristic set-up, "designed by a
genius for execution by idiots," as someone once said, is
becoming ineffective as well as anarchronistic. But although research abounds, little has been done to reorganize
large organizations along more democratic lines, to allow
power to be shared. Theo Wells remarked, "There've been
models of participative management, but they haven't
caught on." Why? I wanted to know. Can't women be the
bridge to better systems? "I'm not optimistic," she said.
"Individuals who have authority don't like to give it up."
Humanizing efforts are valued by top-level game-players
only in so far as they actually enhance productivity. Alternative systems must prove themselves profitable. Money
bows to power, but power listens to money.

Toni Carabillo said, "I think women are more sensitive
to the evils of hierarchies than men traditionally have
been, and yet a certain amount of structure seems to be
necessary to get things done." Another woman explained
that a network to which she belongs designates offices
simply by functions rather than traditional titles.

After talking with and reading comments from women
at various levels in different fields, it's my hunch—and
my hope—that women won't become the same kind of
game-players men are now, couching manipulation in
motivation, tightening their blinders, narrowing their horizons, fearing that someone may be catching up to them

and unable to look beyond the boundaries of the playing fields. Not all male players want to play that way, not anymore, and some power centers are already starting to shift.

TAPPING OUR POWER SOURCES

Just as some individuals seem to be programmed, almost from birth, for power, certain others seem to have been programmed for powerlessness. Although debates over free will vs. determinism can go on endlessly, it seems to be true that individuals who perceive themselves as being buffeted about by the cruel hand of fate live hard lives, while those who see themselves as masters of their destiny manage to make things happen.

Many more women are now seeing themselves as being in control of their fate. Not all the women achievers I spoke with were optimistic about the collective power of women. Invariably, though, they discovered that they had something within them that enabled them to direct their own lives. Powerlessness may not be the feminine condition after all.

Some of these women had an early awareness of that "something" within themselves. For others, awareness of their own resources came late—and painfully. Some had experienced the real powerlessness that results from not knowing what one's options are or not even knowing that there are options. Then there were outward indicators that something was wrong—tears, self-pity, headaches and backaches. When the doctor couldn't fix these things, what next?

Many of them got mad, and getting mad can be a step up and away from utter helplessness. "Listen to your feelings . . . you have a right to be angry . . . stand up and fight." We've heard all this before, though not as many times as we've heard: "It's not nice to get mad."

Getting mad gets women mobilized. Theo Wells explained it best of all. "We all have X-rated feelings," she said. "When you recognize that your feelings are okay, you discover that anger doesn't have to mean destructiveness. It can mean growth." The Chinese word for anger, *shang ch'i,* she pointed out, means to produce *ch'i* or energy.

"We need to get into the guts of anger," she said. Using ideas from Raymond W. Novaco's book *Anger Control,*[9] she conducts workshops for women and for community groups of both sexes in channeling anger and putting it to positive use.

Negative anger, according to Novaco's classification, is anger that doesn't accomplish much. Shooting first and asking questions later is merely disruptive, and it can backfire. Defensive anger—the attack one makes when threatened, or the process of justifying one's actions—focuses on something other than the problem. Instigative anger, including aggressive actions and hostile internal dialogue, has no effect on the problem. Anger indicates that there *is* a problem, something that needs to be done or changed.

The point is: Don't use anger *against* something, use it *for* something. Get things done, make some changes. Wells advocates that a person experiencing anger against something should first stop and think, "What results do I want?" or "What are my options?" In this way, one moves from non-productive, scrambled emotions toward positive problem-solving. Early pressure from anger is a signal to step back, "buy time," look at one's options and make a choice. Then anger can be expressed in an assertive way: "I don't like that . . ." and "I want. . . ." And anger that needs physical expression can yield vigor to meet constructive challenges.

Get mad, get mobilized. Judge Joan Dempsey Klein characterizes herself as a person with a lot of energy. Looking back at the forces that got her out of poverty, into college, into law school and finally to the bench, she said, "I had a lot of anger. I felt rage against the world in general. For some time I didn't identify discrimination against women. But somebody seemed to be out to do you in. . . . It wasn't tangible for a while. Once I was aware of discrimination toward women, I was also aware of its devastating effects. As a lawyer, I could bring my training and experience to the problem and work to eradicate it." The anger is gone, but the energy is still there, channeled, directed, contributing to the collective force of women.

52   WOMEN MAKING IT

Besides generating power for collective change, women's anger fuels creativity. During the final phases of a disintegrating marriage, Carolyn See recalled, "I was mad all the time and it gave me incredible energy for writing. I wrote far more than I ever had before." Now, a decade later, she encourages her creative-writing students to take their negative responses to criticism and "Plow them back under. Put the energy into the writing," as she said. She went on to stress that "You have to get past anger eventually, transcend it, get to another level. There's a conspiracy to keep people down in the dumps, failure-oriented, poor. You have to get beyond all that. Once you begin to experience getting your way, you know you're not helpless and you begin to cheer up. You begin to know what you want. Only now you're drawing on a different kind of energy to help you get it." Yes, self-affirmation yields energy, too. As self-esteem goes up, levels of energy increase.

Women are no strangers to anger. Anger, I found, had mobilized them to write, paint, go back to school, start businesses, lobby, meet with legislators, make speeches, resign jobs. And it occurred to me that a lot of energy is wasted cleaning kitchen cupboards or rearranging desk drawers when a women hears that her significant other is seeing somebody else or that another applicant has been hired for that job. Stored-up anger is a veritable reservoir of energy. As Theo Wells said, "We have to get into the guts of anger." Understand it, feel it, pick the target, direct it, but direct it responsibly.

The choice of target is vitally important. Theo Wells urges responsible social action as well as personal affirmation. But not everyone agrees with the basic assumption that power is to be shared, not simply attained for its own sake. There's a lot of talk these days centering on "How do I get what I want?"

"How do I get what I want?" This is the question of the "me decade," and it's also the point where seekers of inner fulfillment and assertiveness-trained gamespeople meet. They share the same jargon and some of the same concerns. Both have inner yardsticks, and both are talking about "me"—that is, about themselves.

Hearing women talk about getting what they want, how good it feels, how it builds their self-image and widens their horizons, I felt exhilarated for a while. This is surely what more women need, I thought, a more profound awareness of themselves and a growing sense of their own power. One day, however, I encountered a woman who let me know that she was very well paid for giving special seminars and for making speeches, all in a self-help vein. I asked her, finally, if she didn't ever speak or give workshops to women's groups without charging. So many of the other achievers did this, even when they had nothing to gain but the satisfaction of helping other women.

No, she didn't, she assured me, and, what's more, she said that she had refused chances to appear on television, to talk about abortion or other issues which nevertheless interested her personally. "What's in it for me?" she asked.

I went home shattered. Also, I began to feel concerned about the extreme degree of self-absorption some of my achievers displayed. Some time later I spoke with Judge Klein about this in her chambers. Did she see any danger in this inner-directedness, this preoccupation with the self that I was picking up from so many successful women? Did she perceive a trend away from responsibility to the group and to society and to women's issues?

She was thoughtful for a long time before answering. "In order to see yourself in a group, you first have to know who you are. Women have been arrested in their development and have to deal with that. With maturity there's the necessity to get beyond the self. What's happening now is surely just a stage on the way to greater maturity. I think it's transitional. I hope so."

I hope so, too, and I think so. But I still sometimes wonder.

IV

Rites of Passage

WHAT does it take for a woman to have a successful career? I pondered this question for some time, as have many women who felt left behind in the late 1960s and early 1970s. "What does it take?"

I wondered briefly if certain fixed or unchangeable circumstances helped determine success. I read a lot about women who were first-born or only children. In Hennig's original study of twenty-five successful women executives, every one was either the eldest in a family of all girls or an only child. According to some studies, too, women from the Midwest and the East seem to have an edge over others in business, and men who are corporate executives are most likely to be Midwestern Episcopalians.[1]

Interviewing forty women in a variety of fields, including business, however, I found no similarities of this sort. More than a few had older brothers or sisters. They'd been raised in all parts of the United States and in other countries as well. I didn't ask about religion, but I'm sure this varied too.

Actually, I didn't spend a lot of time looking at the things women cannot change in their lives, because I wanted to learn about the things they did change, how and why and when. Their individual circumstances became important, however, as a background for the ways they coped, adjusted and defined themselves.

At first, too, I thought they all must have been aware of a certain drive or ambition at least since adolescence.

I asked one woman after another about her girlhood hopes
and plans, but their responses showed little consistency. A
few knew at an early age what careers they wanted to
follow. Some had displayed a great deal of unchanneled
drive early, but had focused on a specific career target
only later. There were those, too, who grew up believing
they had no place in the mainstream but who made a
serendipitous discovery of their capabilities after they were
well into their adult years. A few others had had careers
all their lives but had at some point switched interests or
vocations.

Women's career patterns vary enormously, I found. The
necessary drive may develop early or late, but somehow
it is there when the individual woman needs it . . . as a
teenager with a deep sense of her own values . . . as
a divorced mother forced to make a new life and a living too . . . as a homemaker needing new challenges and
involvement . . . as a working woman needing a new
and more fulfilling career. Women's success seems to be
a matter of challenge and response.

Women undergo the rites of passage into the mainstream at different ages and stages, but, at whatever time
their energies are ready to be tapped, the vision of what
is to be done becomes clear and dreams crystallize into
realizable plans. Something happens; something clicks
and brings it all together. This is the one consistency. It
may occur suddenly or slowly and with varying degrees
of drama.

EARLY TARGETS—HITS AND MISSES

Some individuals know from the cradle, almost, what
they want to do with their lives. Most of them, however,
aren't women. And yet a few women do have an early
sense of their own value and capabilities which provides
accurate and steady guidance toward a career target. The
inner gyroscope doesn't waver.

"I really decided to become a lawyer when I was in
my early teens," Yvonne Burke said when I asked about
her career decision. "I remember going to a birthday
party for a friend whose uncle was an attorney in a
famous civil-rights case. I was aware of this case because

it affected blacks and whites living alongside each other in East Los Angeles, where we lived. My mother was a real-estate broker, so I knew the effect this could have on our lives. I talked to my friend's uncle, the attorney, and I was very impressed. I decided I wanted to be a lawyer. Interestingly enough, so did his nephew and his son and others. His son is now on the bench. He had a great effect on all of us."

Her values were already forming, and her career ambitions grew out of her concern for and awareness of civil rights. Women's career goals, I found, usually spring from their most profound interests, but, typically, the vocational choice isn't galvanized so soon.

Yvonne had another advantage: role models. "I didn't know about the obstacles facing women and blacks at the time. My mother was a professional. She was a teacher, then a real-estate broker. It never occurred to me that I wouldn't be professional too. Once we were having dinner in a restaurant and my mother pointed out to me a young black woman who had just graduated from law school. I was very young then, but that made an impression. This woman was Martha Louis, Joe Louis's wife. She had a successful law practice near where we lived while I was growing up. Eventually I was fortunate enough to meet her and to visit her at her house. In college when they'd tell me that a black woman couldn't be a lawyer, I'd think to myself, 'They don't know.' And they *didn't* know about people like Martha Louis," she explained.

As a student at UCLA, she was a sorority queen, also a good singer and a good dancer as well as a serious student. Majoring in political science, she went on to study law at the University of Southern California, where she received several honorary campus awards. Classmates remember her as personable, likable, smooth. Yet the thought of a political career didn't even occur to her until after she'd been practicing law for about ten years. "I never was interested in running for political office until I ran," she told me.

Her political career evolved, like her legal work, from her values and her commitment to doing something for black people. After the Watts riots, she was appointed to the McCone Commission, an investigatory body which analyzed why the riots had occurred. "We asked ourselves what was wrong with politics and with representation. Why did the people hold this attitude toward elected officials? We decided some of us should get involved," she said. She credits Sam Williams, another attorney on the McCone Commission and a longtime friend, with having encouraged her to run for office the first time. In 1966 he became the manager of her successful campaign for a seat in the California State Assembly.

Then, in 1972, just before she was elected to the House of Representatives, her serene and capable demeanor as vice-chairman of the Democratic National Convention put her in the national spotlight. She became the first member of Congress to ask for and get maternity leave. The bills she sponsored—like the Displaced Homemakers Act —reflected her lifelong involvement with civil rights and a deep concern for women's rights.

Her life parallels the classical pattern of "the achiever who defers nurturing," but not intentionally. Her first marriage ended in divorce, and she married for the second time in 1972. William Burke had been her opponent's campaign chief in the congressional primary; he left this job to be at her side during the campaign. Their first child was born when she was forty-one. "There are some things you can't keep putting off," she explained. "So many women are waiting for the right time to have a child. I kept waiting and waiting, and that time never came. For some of us the perfect time never comes. I wanted to have a child and I decided to have one."

When I asked her if she had ever seen career vs. family as an either/or choice, she replied, "My mother had both a career and a home. I didn't think that much about it. I guess I assumed that I could be a lawyer and have my own office in my own house, because at that time many lawyers worked out of their homes."

Jewel Lafontant is another black woman who knew from an early age that she wanted to study law. Her father and her grandfather, both civil-rights attorneys, were role models in a sense, and her mother had interests outside the home too—she was an artist who taught painting and sold her work. "I knew when I was about ten that I wanted to be a lawyer," Ms. Lafontant told me in answer to my question about her career choice. "One of my classmates from grade school tells me that I went around saying, 'I'm going to be a lawyer and I'm going to be the best there is!' "

For her too a career in law meant a career in public service. In 1948 she became, as she said, "the first bona-fide black" to be admitted to the Chicago bar. "Because of my father and grandfather, we heard a lot about the racial issue at home. So, when I was twelve I taught myself to type and went to work in my father's law office. I remember my father defended the Hansberrys, Lorraine Hansberry's family, in their right to live in a home they'd bought in a white neighborhood. From an early age I was convinced that through law you can bring about change."

She held three appointments in the Nixon administration, was Representative to the U.N. in 1972, and, the following year, Deputy Solicitor General of the United States. A corporate lawyer for thirty-two years and senior partner in the Chicago law firm of Lafontant, Wilkins & Fisher, she serves on the boards of five corporations.

Role models guide and strengthen early commitments. But the values and interests that set the inner gyroscope in motion may begin to take shape long before role models appear, and then the influence of a parent can be decisive.

Dr. Barbara Fish, a researcher in child psychiatry who "always wanted to be a doctor," attributes her motivation to the influence of her father, a mechanical engineer who delighted in answering her questions about nature and how things worked. Attending a private, progressive school on scholarships from kindergarten on, she proved to be proficient in a variety of subjects but still wasn't deterred from her ambition to study medicine. It wasn't until after she had trained in general medicine and pediatrics that she went into psychiatry. "I'd originally chosen medicine as a way to help people," she said, and she eventually realized that, for her, psychiatric research was the most effective way to do this.

"I was always going to be a writer," said Esther Shapiro, who grew up in a "very European family," where she spoke French and Spanish rather than English until she entered school at the age of six. Even before she was a teenager she told her father that she wanted to write, so he brought home a typewriter for her. "It was an

incredible thing to do at the time," she said. "I think he
had to pay for it at the rate of fifty cents a week! He
was still supporting members of the family in Europe. He
appreciated good writing and encouraged me to do better
all the time." By the age of fourteen she was selling verses
to greeting-card companies, but her sense of humor
eventually became too sophisticated for this outlet. She
kept on writing and selling her work throughout her years
in college (on a math scholarship) and during a brief
stint as a teacher. She married an accomplished film and
television writer who became her mentor and sometimes
collaborator. For the next eighteen years she worked at
home writing television plays, continuing full-time even
after her daughters were born. Besides creating episodes for
a number of popular shows, she wrote television films such
as *Minstrel Man* and *Sarah T: Portrait of a Teenage Alcoholic,* both of which were nominated for awards. Also,
she wrote and produced the television movie *Intimate
Strangers,* which is about a battered wife.

Then her career changed; but rather than moving in a
completely different direction, it broadened in scope. She
joined ABC Entertainment as an executive producer for
motion pictures and novels for television. In less than a
year she became vice-president for novels and limited series, a job that entails, among other things, working with
writers. *Roots* was one of her pet projects, and when I
spoke with her she was just embarking on *Passages.* "I'm
a creative junkie," she said. "I love creative people. Part
of this job is trying to get the best out of all the people
who are working, getting them to do their best and getting
their ideas instead of superimposing my own." All along
her goal has been to show material unlike anything seen
on television before.

Two attorneys who have also made a contribution in
politics, a psychiatrist who has done original research and
a writer turned network executive—they have quite a
lot in common. They had goals which got them off to an
early start, but in each case the career advanced beyond
early ambitions, yielding more than they had anticipated.
None was guided by a hard and fixed concept of what
eventual success would be. They chose their professions,
and subsequent developments evolved from those choices
and from their early values.

And all had some distinct psychological advantages—role models or parents whose encouragement and support were fortuitously present in the face of racial or economic disadvantages.

Other women I interviewed had also overcome some serious obstacles while they were quite young, responding to challenges in their environment. Options that are open to more-advantaged women didn't seem to occur to them, but neither did some of the more typical fears and conflicts. It was as though they had not stopped to dwell upon a life without work.

The lack of alternatives can minimize distractions. I understood this better after speaking with Juliette Moran, who began as a chemist and went on to become one of the highest-ranking women in industry today. Somewhat naïvely, I asked her why she had majored in chemistry. "Wasn't there a temptation to follow a more traditional course for women—say, to study liberal arts and work in publishing?" I inquired.

"This implies a kind of choice that didn't apply to someone who was poor, growing up in the thirties," she said. "I was intrigued by chemistry," she went on. "Think of a child raised by a widowed mother who had just gotten off the boat from France and who had learned little more than embroidery and reciting in a French boarding school. I went to high school in New York, where you have to take science, and I didn't even know what chemistry was. After about a month or so I went home and announced to my mother, 'I'm going to be a chemist!' "

For decades, actually, women who could consider themselves lucky to go to college—women from poor backgrounds or minorities or both—have studied career bulletins and visited vocational counselors before they chose their major, or have even arrived at college with a definite vocational goal. I was a moneyless student myself and I remember well the burden of having to make a wise career choice. Wise meant not too risky; typing or teaching could always bail you out. An M.R.S. degree too soon, even during the marriage-minded 1950s, could spell disappointment to those back home who were counting on you. So, in addition to the marriage-vs.-career conflict which most women felt, there was the dilemma of choosing between a career that was exciting, daring, and one that was more of a sure thing.

Unlike Yvonne Burke and others who were certain of their professional goals early, there were those who sprinted fast from the starting line only to find out later that they were headed in the wrong direction. Or were, at least, off course.

California Superior Court Judge Joan Dempsey Klein admitted that she was driven to find her way out of poverty at a very early age. With no early role models, she initially made a safe career choice, one that would help consume the extraordinary energy she knew she had: she studied to be a physical-education teacher and even took a master's degree in education. "Teaching was a way of earning one's keep, and a nice, acceptable vocation for females," as she said.

But a sensible choice can be so very wrong. "I soon realized teaching wasn't my thing," she went on to say. "I recognized all too well that aspects of my personality could cause me difficulty in working for somebody else. I needed to be intellectually independent. People kept telling me I'd be a good lawyer." One of these people was an attorney and also an Olympic swimmer whom she met while working for a year in Europe as a professional swimmer-dancer. Back in California, she enrolled in law school, where she was supported by scholarships and part-time work. Admitted to the bar in the mid-fifties, she went to work for the state attorney general's office, where the cases she tried included criminal appeals. "At every turn I would see two sides to a conflict. Other people's emotions became my emotions, and other people's problems became my problems. I began worrying about the lives of others." First appointed judge of the Municipal Court in Los Angeles, she won election to the Superior Court twelve years later. She now gives readily what time she can to causes affecting women and to helping them with their career problems. "The fact," she said, "that I was so alone in law school and before is one of the reasons I feel I must make myself available to talk to other women."

Novelist Iris Bancroft also went through a practical phase, though not initially. A missionary's daughter born in China, she spent her teenage years in Illinois writing poetry and dreaming of becoming a professional singer. After finishing high school, she was notified that she'd won a conservatory scholarship. She resgistered there only to learn that the offspring of missionaries were eligible only for a 10 percent rebate, not the full scholarship which she needed. Disappointed but not defeated, she entered Chicago Teachers' College. At about eighteen she fell in love with a young man of a different religion. "Here was someone who responded to my youthful poetry," she remembered, "but, knowing that we would have severe problems because of our religious beliefs, we broke up. In a fit of despair I destroyed all my poetry. It took a very long time to recover, not from the loss of love but from the loss of my poetry. I decided then to become a very practical woman. I would be a teacher." She earned a master's degree in education, and she married "a very practical man." That marriage lasted sixteen years. Her second husband was supportive of her less practical and more creative interests. During her forties she began writing and selling articles, and she was over fifty when she wrote her first novel. Part of her motivation to write, as she explained, was "the desire to express why I had left my first husband and my two sons to pursue my own identity." Part, too, was that she and her husband faced early retirement and possible financial hardship. "The practical side of me again," she said. "But I also needed something I could always do, something I couldn't be retired from. In writing novels I'm finally doing what I really want to do."

Too often women have the wind knocked out of their sails early on and never manage to get under way at all. For some the problem will be solved as women increasingly see the need for hard-headed career-planning at an early stage. But choices that are too practical and that ignore certain inner needs can be cause for eventual regret and a sense of time wasted. They may even be worse than no choice at all.

GRADUAL FOCUSING

Many women reach adulthood with a broad spectrum of interests but without a vocational specialty. Or their specialty is one which lacks practical application. Middle-class young women especially have been allowed to dream but not encouraged to plan. Yet the dreams, vague ambitions or even flights of fancy that women have during girlhood sometimes hold portents or fleeting glimpses of what they will become.

Several who have become successful writers wrote poetry at an early age, others dreamed of becoming actresses. If there is a great American female fantasy more romantic than the dream of Prince Charming coming to rescue us and make everything right forever, it is the dream of becoming a stage or screen star. As fantasies go, it isn't all bad; at least it contains some elements of independence and self-reliance.

Two of the women I interviewed who today occupy vice-presidencies in "glamour" industries once had dreams that included both acting and writing.

Marcia Carsey, senior vice-president for comedy and variety programs at ABC Entertainment, whose story is told in detail in Chapter XI, originally wanted to become an actress.

Adrienne Hall also loved acting and writing as she was growing up. "I put together a four-page newspaper when I was in the second grade," she recalled. "I went around interviewing people. . . . There was a whole range of things I thought I'd like to do when I was very young." Acting was her prime passion for a long time and she did actually appear with a professional repertory group. "I also dreamed of becoming a foreign correspondent. Or a lawyer. Or maybe working for the State Department. Yes, I was thinking of the more glamorous professions. Sometimes when I look back I wonder who my role model was. . . ." Describing her childhood, she remembered having been intensely aware that her mother had given up a promising career as a concert pianist. "I'm not sure that I had a role model," she said finally. "I knew, though, that I'd have a career."

In college she was active on the newspaper, on debating teams and in politics. Marrying soon after graduation, she went to work to help her husband finish his graduate studies. As luck would have it, her job was in an advertising research organization. Then, after a brief stint working for a small ad agency, she and another young homemaker, Joan Levine, started an agency of their own. "We had a couple of very small clients, so we set ourselves up in Joan's garage. We certainly weren't planning big things," she laughed. Today, Hall-Levine Advertising, Inc., has about forty-five employees. As executive vice-president, Adrienne Hall is responsible for developing and supervising major accounts. She is also active in political and professional activities and sits on the boards of several corporations.

A number of the women I talked to found their career direction while they were working to help their husbands through graduate school. Edna R. S. Alvarez, though the daughter of an attorney, didn't think of studying law until several years after finishing college, where she had studied liberal arts. Taking a job as a clerk in a library to support her husband in graduate school, she first decided to become a librarian. After finishing library school, she worked in a legal library, which, in turn, stimulated her interest in law. With the help of a scholarship, she went through law school, finishing the same day her first child was born. She now has her own law firm and finds time to devote to many community causes, including those benefiting women.

Many experts now feel that the lack of an early career decision is a serious detriment to women, and this would certainly be true in the field of medicine, where professional training is still largely closed to all but recent college graduates. But many successful careers—for men as well as women—start gradually, with the actual vocational goal coming as the result of varied, often on-the-job experience. Important as it is for women to give some serious consideration to their working lives at an early stage, in college or before, it would be equally wrong if *all* young women were pressured into making early choices as young men have been. Choices derived from real work experience are likely to be sound enough to make up for the loss of a few years' time. One knows better at that point what one wants to do, what one can and cannot do. Combining work with education—not a new idea in education, but one that is growing in favor—surely has advantages too. But, besides needing experience before knowing what they want to do, some people simply need time. Time to know themselves better.

LATE EMERGING

All but one of the women mentioned so far in this chapter had assumed from an early age that they would work. Those who'd had role models or some other form of encouragement early in their lives always thought of their future employment in terms of careers rather than just jobs. Others—those whose mothers had worked—grew up believing that they too would be working women, and work outside the home was something they valued, at least as essential to survival and sometimes as essential to a full and rewarding existence.

I had expected *more* women of achievement to admit that they'd somehow been on their way to having careers or to being working women at an early age. One after another, though, looked at me in amazement when I questioned them about their youthful career plans or goals or dreams. Here are two of the responses I received:

"I'd expected to devote my life to my husband and children. This was what my mother did. I never thought much about it until after my divorce," said one woman professional.

Another woman, now an executive, said, "I never wanted to *be* anything." She mentioned having just reread Irving Stone's biography of Michelangelo, *The Agony and the Ecstasy.* "In the book we are told that Michelangelo yearned, lusted to be a stonecutter. I don't think many women have yearned passionately to *be* anything. It's not in our culture. If you do work, you simply do whatever you got A's in, if that's possible."

Until recently, many women didn't especially want to be anything in a professional sense. Women were taught that being a mother-homemaker was a full-time job, and they were often led to believe that it was a lifetime job as well. They were programmed to wait and hope rather than to want and plan. Or, for some, becoming a wife and then a mother was in itself a goal.

Along with the messages about marriage and motherhood, though, there was almost invariably a cautionary note, much like the fine print we see at the bottom of some packages these days—contradictory but ominous. It was the warning that a wise woman should learn a trade or have a marketable skill, to be held in reserve "in case something went wrong." The things that might go wrong were all bad: spinsterhood, divorce, widowhood and/or poverty. Employment was the way to make the best of a bad situation, but something to be avoided otherwise. A woman's true fulfillment was supposed to come through other people, through loving and serving them but not through herself, her vocation and her outside accomplishments.

And so, many women settled into a life-style centering around home and family, only to have their needs or the impulse for a real career awaken later. Perhaps one of those things which could go wrong actually had, but often, too, the life that a woman had hoped for and dreamed about turned out to be strangely and shockingly incomplete. The career impulse sometimes quite literally erupted, and nobody but the woman actually experiencing this and coping with the necessary adjustments understood.

Theodora Wells, whose father was a chemical engineer and plant manager, studied chemistry, then business administration, both unusual fields for a college woman in the 1940s. "But I also had a strong identification with my mother," she recalled. "During my high-school years I was encouraged to go to college, but the unspoken objective was marriage, home and family—with something to fall back on if it became necessary. Yet I somehow knew there was something else for me. I labeled myself a rebel without knowing what I was rebelling against."

She married a young optometrist shortly after her graduation from the University of California at Berkeley. As Theo later wrote, "I was a lovely bride, complete with Gorham's Greenbrier, rather ordinary crystal and my hand-embroidered, cedar-scented linens. He gave me his name and I became a woman."

After a couple of years spent helping her husband establish his professional practice, the babies came, both boys, born only thirteen months apart. "My husband could never understand why I needed some nurturing—'pampering,' he called it—during my pregnancies. 'After all,' he'd say, 'a Chinese woman just comes in from the rice paddies, drops it and goes right back to work. What are you making such a fuss about?' "

Supposedly she had everything a young woman of her

generation could hope for: a husband with a promising career and two healthy boys. But after the birth of her second son she desperately needed time away from her twenty-hour-a-day routine of babies and bottles. Her husband had his Thursday-afternoon golf and his Saturday-afternoon socializing, ostensibly for business purposes. For her, however, there was neither diaper service nor the occasional babysitter. What was wrong?

"Why wasn't I happy?" she asked herself. "I cried a lot and couldn't smile anymore and I scared myself by gleefully trying to smash two hurricane lamps his mother had given us. I hated those lamps, but only one smashed. Then fear of my violence and guilt at my glee set in. *What was wrong with me?"*

This was 1952. Her doctor said the trouble was "postpartum blues," and sent her to a rest home, where it was called neurasthenia. Not adjusting to the wife-mother role at that time meant that one was ill and in need of treatment.

Shock treatments were prescribed. "Before seeing my assigned psychologist, I refused to sign the necessary papers," she remembered. "Later I confessed to him my rebellious stand against authority. His only response was, 'You did what you thought was right for you, didn't you?' It was. For the first time in my life I had defied an order and stood up for myself," she said. She was twenty-three years old.[2]

With the help of this therapist ("He was a humanist who didn't try to make me adjust to a role," she said) she began to rebuild her life. Her marriage was ending. Working at a full-time job and singlehandedly caring for her two small boys, she resumed her graduate work in business administration. She'd gained considerable strength, but it wasn't all easy sledding.

Before completing her master's degree she married again, only to discover that her new husband was an alcoholic. On the positive side, her association with Alcoholics Anonymous and with Alanon (a group for families of alcoholics) deepened her spiritual consciousness and added to her sense of personal integrity. "This was the beginning of a growing spiritual awareness which for me is essential," she said. "I need to feel connected with a larger energy, whether you call it God or Universal Intelligence or a higher power. At this time I was learning to trust my inner self."

At work, she gained valuable experience as the finance director of a large social agency. Internal politics, however, eventually resulted in her dismissal. A colleague wrote to her, "Don't let it get you down. You were fired for your strengths." Looking back, Theo said, "It was gratifying to hear that. Being fired was agonizing, especially because the reasons were political. I had always taken pride in delivering top-quality work. One thing I learned from being fired was that, to feel effective, I had to work near my capacity. I also needed people who were willing to build trust so we could get things done instead of playing games. I learned, too," she added, "that top-quality work sometimes takes more time than is needed for doing ordinary tasks."

In the mid-1960s she read Betty Friedan's book *The Feminine Mystique,* which confirmed her earlier suspicions and had a lasting effect on her beliefs. "It was as if she had read my mail!" Theo said.

She became involved in the women's movement and, at the same time, began taking on added responsibilities in jobs she held in business. Both men and women managers she worked for were supportive, she feels, in a personal as well as a professional sense. One of the women managers ran interference when the second divorce was imminent—her husband's activities could have jeopardized her job.

She left the corporate world, and in 1969 she formed her own Beverly Hills consulting firm, Wells Associates. Specializing in communication and decision-making processes, she consults and leads workshops with industry, government and professional groups. She also works with women's groups and teaches at UCLA Extension and other campuses. Co-author, with Rosalind K. Loring, of *Breakthrough: Women into Management,* she was finishing her new book, *Keeping Your Cool Under Fire: Communicating Non-Defensively,* when I last spoke with her.

Theo Wells is one of a number of women I talked with who prefer working independently. "When I worked for other organizations, I learned that I can function well under pressure," she said. "But I'd rather put that extra effort into work where my values count instead of where people matter less than profits. I don't yet see widespread concern for basic human rights or for growth of the individual in the business community." She added, "And human values are important to me."

Her story is more episodic, more turbulent than most. But so often it takes years, even decades for women to realize what they can do and what they want to do. Their experiences enable them to see themselves more clearly and to assess more accurately what matters most to them. This surely is what maturity is all about.

A few of the women I spoke with regretted having lost time before finding their career direction. Mercie Butler, the Merrill Lynch account executive, who'd worked in a variety of fields until almost the age of forty, said, "I should have been in business twenty years ago. But how was I to know that?" Another woman was quite bitter about the years she looked back on as "wasted." She said, "You think of how much further ahead you could be and remember all the time you spent polishing kitchen floors. It makes me mad whenever I think about it."

Generally, though, the women who'd spent time as homemakers and mothers or who had meandered into various jobs or several careers had no regrets. Some were simply unwilling to cry over spilled milk. The past was over and done with, why not accept it? More women, however, stressed that these years had been a time of searching and learning and growing. The various things they'd done had all helped them become the persons they are now. It was all worth looking back on.

A GOAL-ORIENTED LIFE?

As time goes on, fewer women should have to undergo the agony and confusion that accompany role-changing and life-planning in adulthood. Presumably, more women will launch their careers early, and at the same time will undertake some careful planning to integrate the various roles in their lives. Trying to fit a career and a family into a precise timetable can be a tall order, of course. And things don't always turn out as planned.

Terry Learned, who started working at seventeen, made some very precise plans for her life. "At the age of twen-

ty I had outlined my goals for a ten-year period, but since
career goals are only part of being alive and some people
mattered to me more than things, I had a ten-year life
goal. At age thirty I wanted to be living in Connecticut
in a white farmhouse, to be married to the best man I
could possibly find, to have a son and a daughter and to
be a retail fashion-store buyer earning ten thousand dollars
a year," she explained. At the time she formulated these
ambitions, World War II was in process and she was living in Evanston, Illinois, where she earned $35 a week as
a secretary for the Army.

By the age of twenty-eight she had achieved all of it,
including two children of her own and two stepchildren
besides. The Connecticut farmhouse had eleven rooms and
a guest house, surrounded by a five-acre lawn, flower and
vegetable gardens and wooded areas. The family fished,
hunted, chopped their own wood and shared good books
together. Her family had top priority, Terry said, and she
hadn't been sure that she could manage a job in addition
to all her other other responsibilities, especially since her
husband, John, sometimes liked to travel on the spur of
the moment and wanted her to come along. But her boss
at G. Fox and Co. in Hartford, where she worked as a
buyer, permitted her to take time away from her job.

"My next ten-year goal," she went on, "was to write a
novel and have it published, and to spend time in Europe,
all the while working and making sure my children grew
up to be citizens of the world." Most of this she achieved,
too. She rose to become divisional merchandising manager
at G. Fox, and she is especially proud of her children.
But not everything went according to these well-laid plans.
The suitcase containing the manuscript of the novel was
dumped into the Grand Canal in Venice by a careless
gondolier. "Since it was handwritten in ink rather than
typed, it was a total washout in all possible meanings of
the word," she said wryly.

Then, after she turned forty, a series of tragedies struck.
Her husband died suddenly and her parents died within
the next year. "This was the major crisis in my life. Besides the grief I felt, there was also an identity problem.
I'd suddenly gone from being the youngest adult in a family to being the oldest, with the job of raising two young

children alone. I was too depressed to make a third ten-year plan," she said.

Quitting the buying job she'd held for eighteen years "to rethink my life," she left Connecticut. She continued her retailing career with Cluett Peabody in New York for two years, then decided she preferred living away from the city. She moved to Williamstown, Massachusetts, where she stayed for six years. Her career branched out in several directions. She bought and operated a small gift shop, also became a marketing consultant, first for small stores and eventually for shopping centers. During this time she also renovated eleven houses and three stores from start to finish, working as both contractor and designer. "This was very rewarding," she noted. "Remodeling a building has the advantages of yielding visible results, which is somewhat more exciting than the figures on a profit-and-loss statement."

By now she had helped with the education of her step-children and had been responsible for educating her own two children. Vacationing on the West Coast during the summer of 1977, she decided to move to Seattle. She established herself as a management and merchandising consultant there. "I'm very pleased with the work, the city and the people," she said. When I last heard from her she was busy with her consulting work and had just completed a one-year assignment as director of marketing for the Seattle Art Museum in conjunction with the King Tut Exhibition, which meant starting from scratch to design, stock and staff two stores.

Even with difficulties, Terry's life and her career have afforded her many satisfactions. Her early vocational goals and achievements helped provide her with added options for coping with unexpected later developments. And unexpected developments do occur in lives that are well planned as well as in those that aren't.

Her career pattern—an early sense of direction and a solid foundation in her field followed by a looser, more open-ended orientation later on—is still somewhat unusual for women. But it's one that may become increasingly prevalent as more women are well established in their careers by mid-life. With or without a crisis to cope with at that time, women—and men too—who've achieved a measure of career success may find they crave freedom and flexibility they haven't had before. And they will have at that time the maturity and the options to strike out in new directions or keep going without the precise, finely pinpointed targets they needed earlier.

V

Cashing In on the Options

THE word "options" gets kicked around a lot. As one of the key words of the seventies, it has a certain magical ring to it. But the meaning becomes fuzzy at times.

The whole notion of options isn't new, of course. A couple of hundred years ago the word "freedom" held the same magic for many, though there were those who felt threatened by it, afraid that freedom of the people would usher in chaos. Whole civilizations have believed wholeheartedly that individual freedom simply would not work, that individuals themselves should be considered only nameless, faceless units who generally could not be trusted to act responsibly and who therefore had to be kept in tow for the good of society. What has mattered in the minds of human beings during most of the time since we first climbed down from the trees and began to talk has not been individual persons, but the group or the clan or the country, which had to be preserved at all costs. Acting for one's own good rather than for the good of the group was considered deviant behavior and usually incurred punishment of one kind or another. And individuals weren't even supposed to think of themselves as separate entities whose wants, needs or desires were worthy of consideration.

Certain individuals, however, those with power, could go about satisfying their own wants, needs and desires pretty much as they chose, all the while keeping those beneath them convinced that to act or think similarly was sinful. And not only political institutions and religions, but language as well has kept the masses thinking of themselves as mere worms whose will must be constrained. Even the very word "people" didn't mean individuals or persons until recently (and still doesn't, according to some dictionaries). It meant *the* people, the common people or the masses; it was a political term.

It is also a concept that has been in the process of changing over several hundred years. Gradually, "people" has ceased to mean the masses, and has come to designate instead a group of individual beings with individual wants, needs—and rights. And in the last couple of decades individuals have been becoming aware of themselves as individuals at an ever accelerating pace.

Through new religions, new therapies, self-help groups, business seminars and groups designed to help women specifically, we're learning to "take control of our lives," affirming "our right to choose" and focusing on our "inner experiences." We're living in what Tom Wolfe calls the "me generation," which shows no signs of subsiding.

There are those who think this self-preoccupation is taking us back to chaos. Right or wrong, though, it is highly effective. People, enormous numbers of people, are changing the way they talk and think and the way they live. Not all oppressed groups have got the message yet, but women are getting it loud and clear, and are putting it to use. Probably the most important progress women have made has been on this inner level: looking at ourselves and our lives as things that matter, beginning to trust ourselves to be responsible for making things better for ourselves and being convinced that we as individuals are in charge of our fates.

Although assimilating the new vocabulary is easy enough, a lot of our talk about choices and options is by now clichéd and nebulous. Sometimes the new, liberated language obscures real issues and problems, too. We can get high on words and fail to look at what's behind them. "Options," if they are to be of value, must be something more than the key word in a slogan. Options are alternatives or possibilities to be analyzed, weighed, measured, evaluated, reevaluated and eventually exercised.

IS CRISIS NECESSARY?

"When you're wandering around in a fog, it means you're not following the old formula, whatever it was. And that's good. It means you're ready for something else. The fact that you're bewildered is good," said writer Nancy Shiffrin.

I wished that someone had told me this earlier. Maybe somebody did, but I wasn't listening. Maybe I had to be in the thick of the fog to understand.

Is a sequence of crisis-chaos-confusion necessary? By the time I began the research that led to this book, I was almost certain that serious career commitments made by women past the age of twenty-one must spring from some sort of crisis. This book was conceived during my own crisis, which was minor compared to many others I heard about from women, but very real to me nevertheless. Prince Charming had departed, shattering hopes and dreams, also taking half the community property with him. I had a teenage son to support. I'd supported him and myself much earlier on very little, and although I'd now made a fairly good living from my writing for more than a decade, I'll confess that just making a living had been my *only* goal for some time. I now needed a better living and some new goals, a new *raison d'être*. I hoped that the woman friend who'd been my editor on several books would help me think of a subject for another paperback geared to women. But at about this time, too, she decided to leave publishing and work for a graduate degree in psychology. I made an appointment to talk with her replacement, who, as it turned out, mistook me for another writer when I walked into his office. What's more, he didn't have any ideas and didn't inspire me to think of any that day or in the days to come.

I went home to the suburban house which I'd been able to keep during the divorce by forfeiting cars, furniture, books, stereo and all else that could be hauled away. The roof leaked, the bathroom floor was mysteriously sinking and before long the plumbing had given way. Somehow I managed to get a loan. Only one article assignment sustained my interest, one having to do with widows and widowhood. It left me very depressed, however, and afterward nothing else seemed worth doing. I couldn't think of topics to write about, and the bills began to mount. Always a firm believer in conservative money management, I wasn't buying luxuries. No, I was using my major credit cards to pay the mortgage and taxes and was horrified at myself for doing so. In retrospect, I guess I was buying time.

Meanwhile my friends were starting careers, finding new ones or finally writing the books they'd always wanted to write. Somehow I found the strength to start calling these other women, asking them how they'd managed to get it all together. I began to hear their stories, which weren't too different from mine except that they were now through the crisis and the confusion. They all had words of empathy and encouragement and, sometimes, advice too. I thought long and hard about what they were telling me, and gradually I realized that here in fact was material for a book, a book about how women succeed— this book.

Gail Sheehy's *Passages* helped, too. The phrase "mid-life crisis" set bells ringing in my head. Now at least I had a harmless label for what was happening, and I knew that I had plenty of company in my misery. I felt even better knowing that males go through it too.

Soon I was telephoning women near and far, friends of friends at first, and then others whose names appeared in newspapers and national magazines. "Did you ever have a crisis?" I would ask them.

No, not all of them had. And some women's crises were only vaguely related to their careers. Women certainly shouldn't wait for a crisis in order to consider their options.

A crisis, however, can trigger change and often accompanies it. Crisis can provide the fuel to launch a new career or to make an about-face in one's career direction. It can bring one's real options into sharper focus. Many mature women embarking on a first career or a new one have just undergone or are right in the middle of major upheavals in their lives. Often enough, one of those things our mothers warn us may go wrong actually has. But sometimes, too, these are events that mothers never dreamed of, and more than a few women launch impressive careers after undergoing heartbreaking personal disasters. In many instances, there is no specific external event that a woman can point to. Something intangible has gone wrong, resulting in ennui or boredom or depression or simply a sense of something missing, and this, too, can very nearly take away the will to live. But out of the gloom or the boredom or the tears, possibilities appear on the horizon. They may shift kaleidoscopically for a time or they may click into place with amazing speed and ease, but, in one way or another, many women hit rock bottom before starting their ascent. They find success because they have to find new reasons for living.

OPERATION BOOTSTRAP IN ACTION

Sometimes the fact that one's options are severely limited makes the possibilities that do exist appear far more clearly.

Janet Wentworth, a slim, attractive blonde in her early thirties, greeted me in her office on one of the upper floors of Los Angeles City Hall in a wheelchair.

Fifteen years earlier she'd been a freshman at UCLA who listed her major as English but who thought she might want to go into nursing. As far as she knew, her only serious problem was being overweight, though she'd recently noticed a certain clumsiness. "I'd been a klutz all my life, so that didn't seem to be anything to worry about," she said. Seeing a doctor about her weight problem, she mentioned the awkwardness. She was referred to an orthopedist, who sent her on to a neurologist. She understood there was a chance she might have cerebral palsy.

"The day I was supposed to see the neurologist was the day President Kennedy was shot, so the appointment was canceled. I had to wait until after Thanksgiving, and then I was told, 'You don't have cerebral palsy.' I said, 'Well, that's good.' The neurologist said, 'But we don't know what's wrong with you.' I was also told that if I had any fainting spells before my next appointment I should come in to the emergency room. That was a kick in the head. I hadn't thought there was *anything* wrong."

She was hospitalized during Christmas vacation for diagnostic purposes. "By the end of December I was told 'possible multiple sclerosis.' By February I was legally blind. By the first of March I was paralyzed."

MS is a neurological disease in which the body begins to destroy the sheathing around the nerve endings, causing messages between the brain and the muscles to be intercepted. It affects victims differently, depending upon which part of the nervous system is attacked, but usually the disease works its way more slowly. "It happened so fast," she said. "I was lucky—not terribly lucky, but I consider it lucky that I did not have to live through the yo-yo of not knowing from one day to the next if I was going to wake up better or worse. Also, I was fortunate that I hadn't yet made a career commitment that I wouldn't be able to fulfill. I hadn't married and didn't have a family that I was responsible for. There were some emotional problems I didn't have, at least.

"But I was young and I wanted to be young and to be involved. Meanwhile the doctor said, 'Don't compete, don't fall in love, don't get married, don't do this, don't do that.' Then the Department of Rehabilitation told me I was not rehabilitable, and twice I was turned down for services. I was nineteen and at a dead end. It was very difficult. I was very depressed," she said.

She clung to the thinnest shred of hope. Her mother knew of someone with MS who had begun to improve after five years. "I thought to myself, 'Five years, that's reasonable.' " So she began waiting for her situation to get better. She remained with her mother, a very strong, independent woman who had her own business. Though managing to continue her studies by taking one course each quarter at UCLA, she did little else. "After five years with no change, I began to think, 'Well, gee, maybe it isn't going to change,' " she said.

Handicapped people aren't perceived as having the same needs as other individuals, she explained. "Outsiders don't realize that before being handicapped we were ordinary people. It's very uncomfortable for them to try to identify with us. So we're portrayed, currently, at least, as 'sanctified.' We're put on a pedestal, separated from others. We're not supposed to mind what has happened to us because we don't know what we're missing, or we're not supposed to resent the fact that other people don't understand because we've reached some 'higher state of consciousness.' No, I can't say that I've reached a higher state of consciousness or awareness. But that spring day I was beginning to value myself and to feel that I had something more to offer. I began to realize that there must be a place for me. I just had to figure out where that place was and what I was going to do to justify my existence here."

The house where she lived with her mother was near UCLA. That same spring day when she decided to do something more with her life, she resolved to be more than a student and a patient. She would become a hospital volunteer, selling newspapers to patients.

"I knew it wouldn't be easy," she said. "People who survive with great obstacles seem to survive because of them. In reality, they survive *in spite* of them."

The resolves and the plans she made that day were difficult, though not impossible. As "borderline legally blind," she can only read a page held close to her eyes. Her legs are paralyzed, she cannot wear shoes, and she has diminished sensation in her hands. Her arms, however, are strong enough to propel a wheelchair. Since she had special parking privileges, she could exchange her space for a ride to and from campus.

"One day I rolled into a room with my newspapers," she said, "and there was a man who asked, 'What's it like being in a wheelchair?' I didn't know why he wanted to know, but even if he was just curious, I was prepared to be straight with him. So I told him that it might not be the worst thing that could happen, but that it wasn't easy. But I asked him why he wanted to know. It turned out that he'd been a railway employee who'd had a back operation and the operation hadn't worked. He was over sixty, and instead of having the kind of retirement he'd dreamed of, it was going to be very different. He said I'd been the first person who'd been honest with him. I was glad I had been able to tell him the truth." She began to see her role as more important than merely selling papers.

Although her self-image improved and her activities broadened, she stressed that there were setbacks. "I might take two steps forward only to take one step back," she told me. "It's still that way. That's part of growth."

Part of her self-initiated recovery program was to take up various arts and crafts. "I have a terrible time with colors, but I love to paint, draw, sew . . ." she said, pointing to a bag of needlework by her desk and to some attractive watercolors on her walls. "I enjoy being creative, but that's one of the things we're not supposed to do." She smiled wryly and went on to tell me that in an art class a teacher had looked at her designs and said, "Why don't you try poetry or politics?"

Also, she began dating. "I had my heart broken for the first time when I was twenty-eight, which I needed. I needed to feel equal to other women in that area. I enjoyed the pain. I loved crying," she laughed and shook her head. "Since then I've dated other men, including some able-bodied ones who are far more mixed up than I am," she added, touching her wheelchair. "It can be a little hard for someone to get past the fact that I'm rubber and chrome as well as flesh and blood."

As her horizons expanded, she made many friends in the handicapped community and soon became an activist for handicapped people. "In any minority group—racial, women's or handicapped—the activists are a very small, very closed group. They're the ones who take the responsibility and who get involved," she said. Her work with the Los Angeles Council for the Handicapped, a grass-roots organization, led to her appointment as a community-services representative and eventually to her becoming a senior project assistant in a federally funded program for the handicapped, Projects with Industry, which is part of Los Angeles Mayor Tom Bradley's Office for the Handicapped. In an attempt to implement and enforce laws benefiting the handicapped, she works with the public, with employers and with handicapped persons, seeing that qualified individuals get fair treatment in hiring. It's a job to which she brings her deepest values and commitments, and getting to where she is today is an experience she can share with others who haven't yet found "their place" or may not yet believe that they have one.

Janet Wentworth's story is exceptional, not typical. And yet, for many women too who now have satisfying and successful careers, the option they were to exercise eventually didn't always appear as an option at first. All that appeared initially was an obstacle or a problem, a personal one, that seemed insurmountable and sometimes very nearly was. The problem might have been large or small, but nevertheless it seemed to leave their own lives in ruins. Then, as they began to look beyond themselves and saw that others shared the problem in one way or another, they found their own role in helping alleviate this same sort of problem for others. Their careers grew directly from their personal crisis, and the experience of that crisis gave them more to bring to their careers: more in the way of experience as well as more will and determination than they had ever summoned forth before.

Helene Landress hadn't worked at a paying job at all during her marriage. "My husband considered me the leading volunteer in Los Angeles. On occasion he would go to some association and 'unvolunteer' me," she said.

But when she was forty-five, her husband died. "I looked at my life and I thought to myself, 'I can't go on this way.' I decided to go out and actively seek a job, but I didn't know how hard it would be."

Before her marriage she'd been an advertising copy-writer. Applying for jobs in related areas, she was told again and again that she was "overqualified." "I became convinced that it was an age problem," she said. "Employers who are willing to hire women generally prefer to hire younger women. We live in a youth-oriented culture where people don't want to think about growing older. Aging is something that happens to other people until quite suddenly, one day, you realize that you *are* one of the ones who are older."

After accepting several short-term jobs which she looks back on now as "meaningless," she went to work for the National Council on the Aging as Western media representative. Describing her job, she said, "I work with the television industry in trying to change the image of aging as currently portrayed on television shows. I talk with producers and writers about the fact that people who are over sixty or sixty-five are not senile. They're not all shuffling along. The women aren't all dowdy and they don't all have blue hair and wear tennis shoes and have daisies in their hats. They're bright, perceptive people and are certainly capable of doing their job, whatever it may be. . . . It's wrong to promote stereotypical images of any group. Rather than applying pressure, however, what I do is more on the level of raising the consciousness of people. Television is the most pervasive and most persuasive communication tool that the world has ever known. If we're going to change people's perception, television is the tool." And she brings to her job the sensitivity of someone who has survived the very problem she hopes to solve for others.

Several women I spoke to came to the "helping" professions after being victims of the very situations they are now working to change. Their personal challenges, once overcome, grew into social responsibilities.

But it would be a mistake to wait for a crisis to occur. For some women it never does, yet they don't necessarily lead unexamined lives. Those who said they had not undergone severe difficulties often confessed that they had nevertheless reached a point where they were bored or burned out or generally dissatisfied. Just as women who've been mothers and homemakers yearn for something more, women whose careers seem to be progressing beautifully also reach a point where they must take a second look at what they've been doing and make some changes.

Women who've enjoyed a measure of career success are apt to have many options. But breaking from the past and from past achievements, often hard-won, can be difficult.

Anita Lands has been, by most standards including her own, a fortunate woman. She was the only child of parents who raised her to believe that men and women could perform the same jobs and assume the same responsibilities. Also, her parents encouraged her involvement in sports and her academic achievements as well.

After working in industrial-relations research in Canada, she went to New York. Starting as a sales-promotion trainee for technical-trade publications, she rose to be sales manager just fourteen months later. After a year and a half she left to take courses toward an M.B.A. at Columbia University and, at the same time, began working in the university administrative offices. She stayed at Columbia nine years, during which time she became associate director of placement, counseling students and alumni on jobs and working with employers as well.

"I'd hit a plateau in my life. I wasn't growing. I'd lost momentum. I was very discouraged, very down," she said. She wasn't short on options. There were many, in fact, but the question was "Which one?"

Like my friend Sheila in Chapter I, Anita went to *est*. (I should point out that I'm not an *est* graduate, but I interviewed several women who were. For both those who've been there and those who haven't, *est* seems difficult to summarize or explain. It doesn't promise career success or personal happiness or anything in particular. Men and women attend a couple of weekend seminars—which are apparently unlike most other seminars—and come back saying they've changed. While this seems like a too-fast, too-easy solution to complex problems, the women I know who claim they have benefited were not individuals who would have been satisfied by fast, easy solutions.)

"*Est* offers ideas that are similar to what people are getting elsewhere," Anita said. "So many of us seem to need to readjust our whole way of thinking. For me it was the combination of *est* and other things, too, that happened at about the same time that really catapulted me from where I was."

I wanted to know more about the ways her thinking had changed.

"*Est* made a difference in the way I look at priorities," she began. "Now I can ask myself, 'What is important?' or 'Does this really matter?' or 'Will it matter twenty-four hours from now?' This lets me focus my time and energy on important things and let little things go by.

"I have an acceptance that I didn't have before, but by that I don't mean a passive acceptance. It's more a matter of being realistic about any situation. Certain things are just going to be the way they are. With important things—situations, people, relationships—I think you have to give them a chance, but at some point I'll ask myself, 'Is this really going to change or isn't it?' If it isn't, I can decide whether I'm going to live with it or to extricate myself and go elsewhere. Most people waste a lot of time trying to change the unchangeable. In *est* that's called 'efforting.'

"We have another phrase—'putting it out there.' You see, people will put one foot in the water, and if they get it wet and don't like the sensation, they may not go near the beach again. But the next time they might like the water, they might experience it differently, who knows? The point is: Try to interact with the environment as much as you can, don't give up the whole idea of going to the beach because something went wrong the first time. Just one thing went wrong, after all; the whole idea wasn't wrong. This makes it easier to take a risk, a calculated risk where you know what the odds are and there's a chance you may win as well as a chance you may lose.

"I can look at life in a more open-ended fashion now. I'm not constantly concerned about how things will turn out, because I know I can cope with however they do turn out," she concluded.

Following *est,* she conducted an intensive job search. "I tell people, 'Getting a job is your job until you have one,' " she said. First going to Catalyst as director of programs for women, she counseled women, managed the campus recruitment program and worked with corporations placing women. "It was an excellent steppingstone to the job I have now," she said. When I spoke with her, she had just assumed her post as director of the East Coast office of the National Association of Bank Women, a professional organization devoted to helping women in banking advance their careers in various ways.

The darkest hours, one faces alone. But women have found help from various sources—feminist organizations, psychotherapy and, in several cases, churches and religious groups, as well as friends and family. And the messages they got were similar. They learned that they had choices; that although some things couldn't be changed, others could; that some risks are worth taking; and that they could cope with unknowns. It was a kind of rebirth into new roles and responsibilities.

FACING THE OPTIONS REALISTICALLY

They knew they could do it! Or they were reasonably certain. Not all women have the same options, of course, and any optimism about options is bound to be clouded by a realistic look at the obstacles that exist in the real world. Discrimination against women is one, but some of the women I talked to faced double doses of discrimination.

Anyone who suffers from bias or prejudice, whatever the reason, has to struggle to avoid "buying" the stereotype that the rest of society has bought. Suppressed people have traditionally accepted the image others have had of them, allowing their options to be limited even further. Generations of women have accepted men's notions that we cannot do certain things, and many believe there is still less we can do beyond a certain age.

Women rarely aim too high. Often they aim too wide, not really focusing on specific targets soon enough. And many, many women aim too low, becoming nurses instead of doctors, secretaries instead of supervisors, teachers instead of many other things. They think they are being practical, after all, stacking the odds in their favor by choosing vocations where their services will be in demand. But in many instances they are being modestly unrealistic about themselves and their abilities. They have "bought" the image others have of them; they have "bought" the stereotype.

"Don't underrate what you can do," I remember one woman saying. "You'll always find plenty of others to do it for you! No matter how good you are at what you do, there will be people who think you're not good enough or that you're not serious or that you'll never make it. Just keep telling yourself that you can do it. Stay away from people who think you can't and stick with those who think you can."

Women so often think they're not good enough—not smart enough, not educated enough, not skilled enough, not working hard enough. Writers rewrite endlessly, not submitting their work to publishers, actresses keep going to classes instead of auditioning, women managers check and recheck subordinates' work. A number of successful women can remember a time when they overworked themselves and concealed their efforts for lack of confidence.

"I finally realized that I can do what I'm doing better than anyone else can," said one woman who began her career in her forties, "but I didn't know that until after I'd been at my job for some time." Experience builds confidence, of course, but many women need their self-esteem bolstered before they can start to gain experience.

These days, fortunately, there are places to go: career conferences, courses in career-planning and counseling facilities especially geared to women are springing up all over the country. Women in larger cities can find career-related events to attend every evening of the week. In smaller cities and towns and in suburbs there are counseling and placement agencies which are sometimes linked to larger organizations. Catalyst, headquartered in New York City, helps women research and plan careers through a network of 201 centers through the country.

Programs for women have become big business these days, however, and women would be wise to do some comparison shopping before deciding which one best fits their own needs. Some programs represent a considerable investment in time and money, particularly if testing is offered.

Testing is a highly controversial element of the job search. Preference tests can be ludicrous. Sociologist Dr. Cynthia Fuchs Epstein took one in junior high school which indicated that her interests pointed to a career as a fashion coordinator. I myself remember being steered toward becoming a speech therapist after such a test.

Some tests, however, can be valuable in sizing up your abilities or achievement level alongside those of others. You can find out if you're qualified for graduate or professional school. You can also discover whether or not you have the native ability or aptitude to learn a specific activity that's entirely new to you. You can see how much you've picked up since you left school and where there's work still to be done.

Taking a test that doesn't matter can also be good preparation for taking one that does. Mercie Butler first took the qualifying exams at brokerage houses where she did not want to work. She found that her reading of the *Wall Street Journal* and the business pages of newspapers had indeed paid off and that what remained to be done was buckling down and studying business math.

"I look at testing as one more tool," said Anita Lands. "Testing can point out certain things. And it can generate ideas, so if it's followed by counseling and a change of ideas, it can be a good starting point. But it's not enough by itself and never will be enough unless used in conjunction with other activities."

Mere numbers can only tell so much. Many careers have no entrance exams and many employers are not in the least interested in test scores. The abilities that count in many careers are intangibles that tests cannot measure.

Women are often amazed to learn how good is in fact good enough. As one woman said, "I had been awed by people who were doing well in the field I had chosen until I found myself among them. I'd imagined them as superbeings, with superbrains. They're bright and they're interesting, but then, so am I," she laughed.

Although many of the women I spoke with still measured their abilities and skills by the inner yardstick of personal standards, their confidence was nurtured by looking outside themselves and becoming involved. Anita Lands said, "There's a point where you realize you have to get it all together and channel it. And when you start to do things, you start to change. All of a sudden there's input from different directions and you find yourself handling it. You identify, focus, channel." She added, "Success is doing more than you thought you could do."

And a lot of women are now doing more than they thought they could.

SEEING OPPORTUNITIES AND SEIZING THEM

Is there a state of mind that enables certain women to know instinctively when it is opportunity knocking instead of, say, annoyance or inconvenience?

With almost thirty years' experience at the New York Telephone Company, where she is now vice-president, secretary and treasurer, Grace Fippinger has had ample experience observing women being offered promotions and transfers. As she said, "Over the years in my job, I've noticed some women who didn't take advantage of the opportunities that were present. If, for instance, there was a job offer some distance away, their main thought was of the inconvenience and the added travel time. The chance for greater exposure and experience was secondary. But, in all fairness to these women, I must add that they saw little opportunity for advancement and so decided that the reward for this extra sacrifice would not be realized."

Also women often fail to recognize future opportunities because they're too busy getting things done now, too preoccupied with the immediate tasks expected of them. Men, who are game-players from kindergarten on, are constantly looking for signals, cues and openings.

Hennig and Jardim describe the case of a young woman earning $28,000 a year and in charge of an affirmative-action program for a large New York company. Her duties there included supervision of career counseling, management training and internships. She had held the job for six months when the authors visited her to talk about her job in the presence of her boss, the executive vice-president of the company.

Following the discussion, her boss said that it was time for her to write a presidential policy statement describing her work so far with the company. He wanted a draft of this by Friday so that he could discuss it with the company president over the weekend.

Dismayed, she replied that she had a conference to attend on Friday. Her boss said he wouldn't mind seeing the draft on Thursday. She then explained that she would have to spend Thursday preparing for the conference. He suggested she have it ready by Wednesday. She didn't think she had time. Exasperated, her boss finally said he didn't care how she arranged things, he wanted the draft by Friday at the latest.

After the meeting, this young woman turned to her guests and complained about his demand. They in turn asked her if she realized what her boss was really asking for. In effect, he was saying that her work with the company to date was worthy of the president's stamp of approval. The programs she had developed could now become official company policy. There existed, too, the possibility that she would meet with the president to discuss the entire matter. "My God, I never saw it," she said.

As authors Hennig and Jardim explained, *"It relates to a career concept which has to do with advancement, with growth in status and influence as well as in skill and expertise. Much more a man's career concept than a woman's, its implications for day-to-day perception, behavior and misunderstanding are immense."*[1] This young woman hadn't seen that a simple assignment—a draft describing her work for the company—was an important step in the progress of her career. She'd seen only her busy schedule and her immediate priorities.

Opportunity or inconvenience? Sometimes it's hard to see the difference. And opportunities do have a way of disguising themselves as inconveniences. They often present themselves at the wrong time, when we have other pressing priorities. Unfortunately, too, opportunities don't wait. Seeing opportunities for what they are and acting on them may mean being ready to drop everything else at a moment's notice.

Women's failure to perceive opportunities or their turning down offers clearly presented to them provide weighty evidence for those already prepared to conclude that women fear success or that they unconsciously sabotage themselves. But before writing women off as saboteurs of their own success, we need to look closely at the other priorities which conflict with career advancement. Achievers or not, women measure success according to inner values that are often of a personal nature.

The woman who missed seeing what a report to the company president meant for her career probably gave top priority to the conference. Perhaps she believed that this conference would serve the interests of affirmative action and of women in general far better than what she might do within her own company. Women who refuse offers to transfer from the suburbs to the city may be thinking of their own or their family's personal needs. Because success can mean so many different things to a woman, she may lack the clearsightedness to say to herself, "This is it, the chance I've been hoping for!"

Some women do look ahead the way men do. They picture themselves as successful or as having reached their next goal, then they let their imagination run through the various plays, moves and strategies that will get them there. They make a game of learning how many different routes could lead where they want to go, and when chances they had not previously thought of appear, they analyze these as to their ultimate effectiveness. A few of the women I spoke with obviously enjoyed projecting themselves into the future and developing strategies that would help them along the way.

The majority, however, didn't think that way. Their goals had been less specific, their strategies less clear-cut. Yet they, too, had been able to analyze certain opportunities on the spot. "Besides working hard, you learn to 'work smart,' " said one. At crucial times they'd been able to ask themselves, "Is this important?" or "Will this be important?" And sooner or later, when they were at the right place at the right time, they knew it and acted accordingly.

When writer Tracy Cabot told me she had sold a treatment for a television comedy series, I asked her how she'd managed to get the work to the right people. A writer of non-fiction books and articles, she'd met a television producer one day after turning into the wrong parking lot while looking for a magazine office. They'd chatted briefly, and although she wasn't absolutely sure he would remember her, she had no intention of forgetting him. Not long afterward her treatment, along with a reminder of their meeting, was on his desk, and after a few weeks of consideration and meetings it sold. "Was this the first treatment you'd written?" I asked. "Heaven, no," she said. "And it wasn't the first producer I'd met either. The other times just didn't work out."

We went on talking about opportunities, timing, and hits and misses. Finally she said, "Everybody misses a few opportunities. You're less likely to hear about the ones they didn't take advantage of or the times they failed. To succeed, you have to be a person who keeps on trying. When one thing doesn't work, you try it a little differently or you try something else instead."

"You create your own opportunities." Several women said something to this effect. One was another writer, Helen Colton, who sees herself as having made a lot of good things happen in her life recently, many of them after the end of a twenty-two-year marriage. Although she had been a successful magazine writer for a number of years, not long ago she completed graduate training to become a teacher of family relations and launched a new career in counseling. Also, she has a new husband and, most recently of all, has made new strides in her writing career. At first she anticipated that a small publisher would handle her book, *The Joy of Touching*. But one day, as she was writing, she noticed some of her manuscript pages lying along side tear sheets of magazine articles she'd been planning to read. One article was about the head of a very large publishing house, describing his new and aggressive policies in marketing hardcover books. "What was this doing there with the pages from my book? It was one of those rare times when I said to myself, 'This has to mean something,' " she said. That same day she sent a mailgram to the publisher himself, telling him that she sincerely believed her book was needed by millions of people who could only be reached by a publishing house with such wide distribution as this one had. Three days later she was contacted by a vice-president there who asked her to send a partial manuscript. Very shortly the book was under contract.

These women were lucky. Also, however, they were well enough along in their careers to make a careful assessment of what they were offering and to conclude that it was good, salable. Confidence in their work impelled them to act aggressively and fast. There were no conflicting priorities and there really wasn't much they could lose except the time they spent trying.

They worked hard and they were lucky. Again and again I heard those two factors mentioned in explaining success. "I believe we make our own luck," Helen Colton said, and others echoed this. They'd worked hard, they'd "worked smart" and they'd made things happen their way.

Not all women were lucky in the same way, however, nor do all regard luck the same way. For a few women, things fall into place so quickly and so well that it leaves them awed and breathless. They know the kind of luck they've had isn't the kind most women can count on.

Still there is a state of mind that enables them to know that the time and the place are right. As we've seen, it may be a matter of the right time arriving first: after a crisis, or a radical change in one's existence, a new mind-set develops from the new set of circumstances. After a serious crisis, circumstances are sometimes rearranged so that there's less to lose. And with less to lose, the dangers of risk-taking are minimized.

The story behind Virginia Carter's career is anything but typical, yet it illustrates the state of mind that gets women to the right place when the time is also right. She'd been a physicist, having graduated with a double major in math and physics from McGill University, where she was in the top 2 percent of her class, and she was one of the women who "hadn't wanted to be anything" in a professional sense but had gone on in physics because this was what she was good at. "I took the course of least resistance," she said.

Physics didn't present great opportunities, at least not for a woman finishing college in the late 1950s. Money for graduate work, even for someone with an outstanding academic record, was almost non-existent. Eventually earning a master's degree at the University of Southern California, she went to work in the aerospace industry, where she stayed for nine years. During that time she published twenty-seven papers. Her monograph on Mars prior to the first space launching summarized all the known physical properties of the planet and was then the only work of its kind. But no promotions, raises or recognition were forthcoming. "I didn't hope for anything," she said, "and that's exactly what I got. I thought I was lucky, lucky to be making all that money, while I was probably one of the lowest-paid scientists in the company where I worked."

The women's movement was an awakening for her, as it was for many others. "I saw an article in *Time* about the National Organization for Women. I remember feeling embarrassed getting the phone number from the operator—I was afraid I'd be thought of as some kind of troublemaker. Anyway, I called and talked into a machine somewhere in a closet in Beverly Hills. Soon afterward I went to a meeting that changed my life." After becoming involved in feminist activities, however, she began working all the harder at her physics job. "It wasn't considered proper there to have any other passion but science. When I got swept up by the movement, I was afraid they'd think me a dilettante, so I tried all the harder," she said. But still all that hard work didn't pay off.

Through the women's movement she became acquainted with Frances Lear, feminist, author and a founder of Lear, Purvis, Walker, an executive-job search agency for women and minorities, also wife of Norman Lear, producer of such television shows as *All in the Family*. "I didn't know for a long time what France's husband did," Virginia said. "What one's husband did wasn't something terribly important."

Not long after she finally met Norman Lear and found out what he did, she heard him asking her to become his assistant. "I thought he was joking," she said. But this was at a time when she was doing some serious thinking about her own life. The woman's movement had made her see the limitations of her position as a woman in physics. Also, she had recently been seriously ill. "I had breast cancer," she said. "Yes, I want you to mention that, because it's very important for women to know that they can have breast cancer and still be okay." She was thirty-six when it happened and there's been no recurrence.

"After having a bad thing like that happen," she went on, "you don't want to waste a lot of time being unhappy. So when Norman said, 'Come work for me,' this probably helped me make a quick decision. If somebody offers you more money, more excitement, saying, 'Come fly with me to this romantic place and do this wild thing . . . flush your physics career down the great drain'—you might want to think about it for a while. I didn't spend more than half a second thinking about it. I accepted on the spot. Most of the reason was thinking that one day I'd be sixty and if I'd stayed in aerospace I'd look back on a life's work of doing a lot of papers and research on missile systems. I'm not opposed to that sort of work; it's just that there are more attractive things, I think, to look back on."

That was seven years ago. Norman Lear wasn't joking of course, and after starting as his assistant she advanced to become vice-president for creative affairs at two of his production companies, where she now oversees the production and development of television shows.

"Success? I'm not sure what that means," she said when I asked for her definition. "I'm not sure what creative fulfillment means either. Not everybody has a creative something that *needs* to be fulfilled. If I can get the show we're working on now to reflect some of my standards, then I'll have a sense of satisfaction. And what matters most to me isn't the money—my needs don't require a lot of money—it's the people. The competitive system is such that it winnows out so many people, and those who do get through are bright, interesting and creative. Through this job I'm in touch with some of the most exciting people alive. Ideas are constantly coming at me from a hundred different directions. This keeps my brain alive, and, I think, it keeps disease away. I'm never bored, and boredom is the worst enemy.

"I was lucky, very lucky," she said, and few would disagree. But other women, too, saw themselves as lucky to have coincidentally made friends who were able to help. Rarely did I hear about "career contacts"; far more often I heard about help from individuals who were genuine friends or mentors or both.

The more women I spoke with, the more I realized that it takes a positive, unconflicted state of mind to pick up on the signals for moving ahead. While luck and chance did play a part in the development of these women's careers, more important was an inner belief that good luck rather than bad prevailed, that friends, mentors, bosses and others could be counted on and that they themselves could influence luck. Rather than the iron hand of fate, luck was more like a shining goddess who had smiled upon them in the past and would continue to do so as long as they smiled back. Despite traumas and tragedies even, they saw themselves as persons who had been repeatedly lucky and who had made wise choices in their professional and personal lives.

VI

Help from Networks, Mentors and Others

THE stereotype of the achieving woman is a solitary creature, cut off from family, friends, colleagues, everybody. Actually, it's not at all as bad as it sounds. Nearly all the women I talked with had families of one sort or another. The majority were married, and those who were single almost invariably assured me that they had close relationships with others, in some cases their parents. All of them had friends.

Yet a number of them confessed to having felt real loneliness or isolation at certain stages along the way—as a woman in an almost all-male law school or as the only woman promoted to a certain level in an organization, for example. Most felt that it was important to have good relationships with other women at career levels close to their own, and most were trying to be or hoped to become mentors. Nearly all felt, too, that close contact with professional colleagues, male or female, was vital. But even after having achieved a measure of success, not all felt they were as well connected professionally as they'd like to be.

A strongly independent nature has been almost a prerequisite for a woman getting her career off the ground and gathering momentum in the early stages. During that time, after all, there has often been far more opposition than support. More than a few women mentioned self-reliance or independence as character traits that helped

them get where they are now. As many of these same
women pointed out, however, being able to work well with
others is an equally essential characteristic.

"In the initial stages of their careers, women benefit
from being very independent and working alone," said
USC professor Dr. Judith Stiehm. "But to continue to be
successful, at some point they need to join groups or institutions where they must learn to work with others and to
become sensitive to them." Group functioning and game-
playing, which have been well documented in the business world, are mirrored everywhere people work together
—in the political arena, the universities, non-profit agencies and in many professions as well. A few entrepreneurs
and artists may reach their zenith alone; most individuals
cannot.

And learning to function in a group as one's career
progresses, according to Dr. Stiehm, "means a complete
switch in roles and in style." She said, "I've noticed some
women who were very independent and whose forthright,
insistent manner was very effective, but when it was time
for them to be brought in where they had to work with
others, they didn't know how to change. For some women,
the switch isn't possible."

Being too forthright or abrasive or insensitive is a
problem women face later, after they have survived a few
hard knocks. Before that, some women are handicapped
by being too soft or too vulnerable. Men, on the other
hand, seem to get by just being themselves. The programming they acquire on the playground suffices very well.

Male bonding begins early, and all through life men
form alliances that are different from the kinds women
make. Women seem to want deeper, more multi-faceted
relationships. Men collect business contacts, tennis friends,
poker friends, all kinds of casual associates whom they
may or may not genuinely like. As Hennig and Jardim
observe, "For men, friendship may be a valued outcome
of interaction on the job. For women, it too often tends to
be a prerequisite."[1] So it's harder for women to work with
individuals we don't like, harder for us to make career
contacts and to establish relationships that will further
our careers. Also, the occasional woman caught behaving
in an opportunistic way may be seen as phony or ridic-
ulous or both.

These apparent social differences between men and women probably result from the cultural conditioning we receive. They run somewhat deeper than mere stereotypes, and yet they may well change or disappear as more women enter the playing fields or the mainstream and as more men explore new aspects of themselves.

Already some changes are discernible. Women have recently become highly sensitive to the interpersonal aspects of the games men play and are developing some similar strategies. We're forming our own networks with great speed and enthusiasm, and we're also emulating the mentor-protégé relationships men have. The notions of "networking" and "mentoring" have both been elevated to have a certain mystique, and while the realities may not quite match the ongoing myths about them, they provide some examples of dramatic changes in the ways women are thinking and acting.

PLUGGING INTO NETWORKS

We've all heard about the "old-boy network." Connecticut governor Ella Grasso's discovery of how the OBN works is legendary. She was talking politics one day with a group of men who suddenly disappeared without adjourning. The discussion went on without her—in the men's room.

Important discussion, and decisions too, women have learned, often take place where we can't or don't go or aren't invited. The obvious examples are the men's room and the locker room, but also there are the golf course, the health club, pubs and watering places—innumerable spots, in fact, where men mingle informally. Male power plays only *appear* to occur around oiled walnut conference tables; the real moves are planned and decided in settings generally less decorous, where men feel at ease to talk their own language.

Recognizing that male power figures operate this way and realizing that it was next to impossible for women to gain entrance to their gatherings, women began forming their own networks, and there are many of them by now. The word "network" has become a blanket term for a wide variety of women's organizations with varying structures, purposes, promises and benefits.

I'd hoped to collect case histories of a number of women who'd been helped on their way by networks. But most of the women I talked to had already made considerable career progress before women's networks existed. Several of them did feel, however, that their early experience in the woman's movement was essentially that of functioning as part of a network.

One of these was Toni Carabillo. "When I went to my first meeting of NOW," she said, "I was absolutely thrilled to discover that there were other women who felt exactly the way I did—women who were angry about inequality, angry enough to do something about it. So many women felt the same way but had never talked about it before." Like many women who've worked most of their lives, she considered herself a "non-joiner." The only organization she'd belonged to since her college years was an editors' group which was requisite to her job. "No other club or association ever appealed to me enough," she said.

In a sense NOW sprang from an already existing informal network. During the Kennedy administration there was a National Commission on the Status of Women, and, subsequently, state commissions were founded which sent representatives to meet in Washington. These included women of high rank in labor unions, various professions, academia, and also writers. Betty Friedan was serving on a study group at one of these meetings when the representatives learned that nothing could be done to enforce civil-rights legislation as it pertained to women. Women began to meet in each other's hotel rooms, and on October 29, 1966, NOW was founded. As Toni said, "NOW grew out of a fantastic network of women, but it soon spawned other networks. The early members were contacting other organizations they belonged to. A mailing list was developed. All over the country, women were getting together."

She went on, "I remember attending my first National Board meeting. The setting, in San Francisco, was beautiful. It was fantastic to see that many spectacular women all in one room. I couldn't have imagined anything like this, but the following year in New Orleans it was the same, with even more women."

Besides the support and camaraderie which can do wonders for women's psyches, were there real professional advantages to women? I asked her. "I haven't used it for professional reasons, no, but I know that the many networks within NOW have been helpful to women moving around the country or moving up in their jobs. You see, wherever you go there's a NOW chapter you can call. Wherever NOW members get together, they can share common experiences."

The feminist movement made "joiners" of many women who had never had the time or the inclination to link themselves with other groups. Before the movement, most organizations of women were composed of those who did not work and who could devote considerably more time to such activities. Women with experience as volunteers and fund-raisers and committee organizers have, as some women pointed out to me, had more experience with power than have most lifelong career women. And some of the strength and leadership in the new professional women's networks comes from women who have impressive volunteer experience as well as some degree of feminist sympathy.

Elinor Guggenheimer, founder of Women's Forum in New York, spent a number of years in non-paying work to establish day care for children. She founded the Day Care and Child Development Council of America and headed its New York office for over fifteen years. As a result, she became deeply involved in urban affairs and in 1960 was appointed to the New York State Planning Commission, a paid position. In 1973 she became the Commissioner of New York City's Department of Consumer Affairs. That same year marked the beginning of Women's Forum.

Writing exactly five years later, September 18, 1978, she described the founding of this group: "I called a few prominent women on the phone and proposed that an organization that could speak for women of achievement was long overdue. The various feminist organizations were effective on many fronts, but nowhere and in no place was there an opportunity for women to communicate on the same level as male executives and male professionals. An element that is part of the infrastructure for the successful man was thus missing for the successful woman.

Also, we didn't have access to people who could facilitate business and professional objectives or growth.

"Obviously, the men's 'locker rooms' were closed to women, and because some of us felt that women at a certain level have a need to meet with each other and to communicate the way men do, we felt that such an organization would be useful," she said. Some twenty-five women attended the first meeting, and membership grew rapidly.

Today WF has over 160 members—corporate executives, elected and appointed government officials, public-relations and advertising executives, on-air and executive members of the media, artists and writers, editors and publishers and representatives of the academic world. Membership has been limited for the time being and there is a long waiting list of women wanting to join. Meetings are held monthly, with speakers from outside as well as members of the WF.

Although the group's voiced purpose is mutual support and communication, it is also known for some "quiet lobbying," which amounts to women exercising collective power. When John V. Lindsay's term as Mayor of New York came to an end, there was some uncertainty as to whether WF member Eleanor Holmes Norton would be reappointed to head the city's Human Rights Commission under the new administration led by Mayor Abraham Beame. WF members were among those who helped to ensure that she was by making phone calls and writing letters. More reecntly, they provided the same support for Carol Bellamy, president of the New York City Council.

"Women have been trained to feel that the word 'power' is somehow unladylike," Elinor Guggenheimer said. "The exercise of power and the opportunity for communication and for mutual sustaining were prime factors in the formation of the Forum. We don't take a political position as such, but when there's a need, we're there to help."

WF has assisted women in some smaller cities to form similar groups, and in many large cities women have joined forces in much the same way. The Washington Women's Network, for example, was influential in the appointment of Sarah Weddington as President Carter's special assistant in charge of women's concerns. But many women agree that achieving real power in Washington is exceedingly difficult. "Any Washington group would need to have the support of Kay Graham," one woman said. Political pressure in Washington and in the state capitals has come from special task forces within larger feminist organizations as well as from a few groups formed expressly for political purposes. So far, though, optimism about women's collective effectiveness in politics runs thin. The stakes here are high and the disappointments are many.

Eleanor Holmes Norton, chairperson of the Equal Employment Opportunity Commission, sees changes in the ways women are now organizing as positive. As she said, "Women's organizations used to have mainly auxiliary functions or they were devoted to classic feminine concerns. Today women are organizing around their own specific sets of concerns, applying their individual status to working collectively." She went on to say, "But our networks are different from the networks men have. Men don't get together in organizations to exercise power and authority. They do so by getting together informally. That's what a network is. An organization is actually the outlet of a network."

A number of the women I spoke with were hesitant about saying whether or not they belonged to networks. Some eschewed or limited involvement in organizations of any sort. As we discussed informal, loosely organized groups, however, the typical response was, "Yes, there are a number of us who get together now and then for a dinner. Usually one woman organizes these things because her dining room has enough space. I see some old friends, but also I'm likely to meet some influential women from other cities. The group consists of corporation women, professionals, some in politics and some writers or media people. I can always be sure that the person on my left and the one on my right will be interesting. And the next time I need a contact in another profession or in another city, I remember, 'Oh, yes, I met so-and-so the other week. I'll call her first.'"

Is it better for a group to remain loosely structured, without a name or a set schedule, emulating men's traditional networks? Opinions varied here. One woman said, "I wouldn't want to commit myself to the time involved in belonging to an organization—holding elections, establishing by-laws, working on committees. And I wouldn't want to have to attend meetings every third Tuesday. If our group tried to organize, I think it would fall apart!" But another woman voiced an opposing point of view: "We're all so busy. If there weren't some sort of structure and the certainty that the meeting takes place the same day every month, I doubt if we could ever get together."

Generally, although there are exceptions, the further up women are and the closer they are to the center of real power, the more loosely organized their networks are. Or they may belong to an informal network and to organizations as well. Interestingly, too, some women's networks, like men's, spring from old-school ties. One Los Angeles group, Women in Business, grew out of a seminar on business held at the UCLA extension several years ago. Also in Los Angeles, the Organization of Women Executives was founded when five women who'd gone to the same private girls' high school found that they had similar interests now that they'd become managers and professionals.

Mutual support rather than power or influence seems to be the prime purpose of most of the groups, organized or not. B. J. Kirwan, a Los Angeles attorney who was president of the Organization of Women Executives when I spoke with her, said, "I'm not a joiner and most career women aren't. There's so little time! This group provides a chance for friendship and communication. Everyone who goes to the meetings is interesting. Everyone has something to share." She went on to explain that before the birth of her first child she found it helpful to talk with other women who had balanced a busy career with family responsibilities.

Other successful women also emphasized the personal rather than professional benefits they'd gleaned from being linked to groups. The upper-level network or organization provides solace and support to those who experience the loneliness at the top that many women fear.

There's an aura of secrecy around some of the new women's groups, too, with deliberate attempts to keep a low profile. "Our group isn't a secret society," said B. J. Kirwan, "but we simply can't take in all the women who'd like to join."

"You run out of top-echelon women very fast," said another woman, "then you begin taking in mid-level women; it dilutes the group, reducing effectiveness or possibilities for power the group may have."

"It's an enormous responsibility to be a role model for other women," said another, "and there's sometimes a necessity to get away from that. To be somewhere with people who don't expect you to be perfect. Women need such places."

"We're past the stage of needing role models," said B. J. Kirwan, "and though others may need us to be role models for them, we also need each other."

It is lonely on the way to the top, too, and some women who are at an earlier stage in their ascent understandably resent the exclusivity of these sororities of achievers. The conflict has become a moral dilemma in at least a few groups. It seems only fair to admit women who show promise of future accomplishment, and yet if very many of these women join, some of the top women will feel betrayed.

But women on the way up have no scarcity of groups they can join these days, and once a woman has chosen her vocational field, there are probably several groups for which she is eligible at national, state and local levels, and within large organizations as well. Which network is best depends, of course, upon a woman's vocational field, her position within that field and numerous other factors.

The best network for a beginner may not necessarily be the one which has the most powerful women listed as members or one that has a national headquarters with famous names printed on the letterhead. Top-level role models can be found at career conferences and seminars or can be sought out when they appear as speakers or on panels. A national network should be evaluated in terms of what it actually offers. Does it have mailings such as newsletters or magazines? These may be useful in some fields. Are there local meetings? A network should provide a place to go.

"Meeting live people and being with live bodies is far better than an impressive membership card and great things you get in the mail," said one woman, an entrepreneur. "I belong to several national groups and they help me keep up with news from all over the country. But locally I can rub shoulders with real people and find out what's really going on that concerns me. Also, the local group is broader. Members are from all different occupations and this is what makes it exciting. Some successful men get awfully ingrown, I think, just being with businessmen or professors or others like themselves, and I think women are starting out on the right foot by not being so exclusive. Also, a local group is good, even if you want to become nationally visible—you have to start somewhere."

Some women mentioned, too, that through networks they'd become acquainted with professionals they needed to know as their careers progressed—attorneys, accountants, advertisers, etc. Networks of women working in different companies within the same industry have been able to exchange valuable information on affirmative-action programs and on more subtle indications of progress—or the lack of it—within their industry. Also, in some companies women are organizing into groups that loosely parallel trade unions.

Some of the local professional networks began as chapters of larger groups, but eventually broke away. The difficulty wasn't over ideologies but over the fact that membership costs were too high—well over $100—when dues had to be paid to a national organization as well as a local one. Local "networks of networks," or groups that can provide an index to the various women's groups within a given city, are springing up, too. In Los Angeles, Betsy Berkhemer, a partner in the public-relations firm Berkhemer and Kline, publishes Women's Information Network, a small newspaper about all the Southern California women's businesses, services and organizations that can be listed by name and phone number. This enables women who belong to small networks to contact many more women.

Hooking up with networks rather than going it totally alone can be especially valuable at the beginning of a career. At this time a woman needs to meet others with whom she can identify, to talk over problems that seem petty but aren't, to discuss pay problems and possibilities, to try out her image and to gain confidence in herself and her work. She is learning and changing. Old rules don't apply, and she needs to learn the new rules in an environment where she can feel safe. She needs friends.

Sheila, who told the story of her career switch in Chapter I, made a network search part of her job search, then selected the groups she liked best. "It's a real high getting to know other women and sharing thoughts and feelings with them," she said at the time. Later, with her new career in a social agency in full swing, she said, "I still belong to the same groups. Also, I have a real network which keeps expanding."

Feeling high . . . soaking up enthusiasm . . . gaining confidence . . . learning that female peers also cope with husbands and babies—the essence of "networking" is an inner experience. Fears diminish; conflicts are faced and resolved. Yes, networks can do a lot for women.

But it may also be unrealistic to expect them to fight very many of our own individual battles. New York Telephone executive Grace Fippinger said, "We're getting carried away with the idea that women must have networks." Though not a member of any formal organization, she often accepts invitations to speak to groups of women. Also, she functions as part of a very informal network of women whom she has known for a number of years, since the late New York Governor Rockefeller appointed her as one of the advisors to the women's branch of the state Department of Commerce. "There were sixty or seventy of us and many in the group have managed to keep in touch over the years. Our paths cross frequently —at meetings, business dinners and the like," she explained, but added, "I don't think networks should be vehicles for promotion. When it comes right down to it, you have to do it on your own."

Another woman, speaking as a feminist and as an executive, said, "There's a lot of mushy thinking around now; women think that because they can say 'Let's form a network' they've made real progress. But it's discouraging when you look at the numbers of women who have cilmbed to where the real power is. A network can only be as effective as the individuals in it. And so few women have any real power."

"To be effective, women's networks should be more specialized, more instrumental," said Dr. Judith Stiehm. Most women felt that the new networks are a healthy sign. Few, however, saw them as great cause for optimism.

"One thing that hasn't been solved for women is: How

do we network with men?" Dr. Stiehm continued. "Women find it hard to develop good equal relationships with male competitors, so we develop relationships with other women. It's better than being isolated, but to succeed in most areas we need male colleagues we can relate to."

Some successful women deliberately put their energies into professional organizations with male as well as female members. Daphne Bartlett, vice-president and actuary at Occidental Life, said, "I haven't been very good at helping other women so far, although I know I have a responsibility to do this." She also told me that she would "rather be known as an actuary than as a woman actuary." Having been active in the Society of Actuaries, she is now on that organization's board of governors.

Adrienne Hall, of Hall-Levine Advertising, said that she and Joan Levine never wanted their firm to be known as a "woman's ad agency." They've only competed for awards where men were also in the running, and they have carried off several prizes. Though a member of some women's groups, Adrienne has directed most of her effort toward professional organizations open to both men and women, and has achieved the distinction of being president of the three major organizations in the industry.

Belonging to trade organizations can be a boost at early stages in a career and a valuable learning experience in teamwork and getting along with peers of both sexes. Some are more social, others are more professional—and promotional—in their orientation, but there's usually a way to meet role models and people with influence. One successful woman advised, "Volunteer for a committee, ideally one having to do with membership, and even if it means taking tickets at the door, you'll get to know everybody."

As a guest of one professional organization, I spied one of the achievers I'd interviewed—at the door, collecting dinner tickets, chatting amicably with everyone who entered the room.

MENTORS—MYTHS AND REALITIES

Whether or not a woman needs a man, it's generally agreed that she needs a mentor. When successful women talk about their luck or about the various forces that helped get them where they are, they almost always mention individuals: friends, teachers, bosses, also husbands, ex-husbands and lovers. In the jargon of right now, all these can be lumped under the heading "mentors," and the help they provide is summarized by a new verb, "to mentor." The whole process is often called "the mentor thing."

Most mentors, it turns out, are men—for reasons worth exploring later. Historically, women who became great were likely to have had great men behind them, at least for part of their lives. Mary Cassatt's career as a painter was furthered by her association with Degas. Colette's first husband literally forced her to write. Margaret Mead's innovative work in anthropology grew out of the tutelage and friendship of Franz Boas.

Besides playing a vital role in the lives of artists, writers and researchers, mentors appear to be just as important in corporations, large organizations and universities. Individuals who work alone certainly aren't the only ones who need to be protégés. And men need to have mentors, too. In his research study of men's life-cycles, Yale psychologist Daniel J. Levinson concludes that the lack of a mentor may be a major developmental handicap.[2] Men who thrive in large organizations are most likely to have had the support of bosses who took a special interest in their careers. But it may be even more essential for women to be protégés. "The mentor relationship is terribly important to women," said television production executive Virginia Carter. She explained, "A mentor is someone who is older and wiser and already established in the area of your interests. This is a person who opens doors for you and who has such confidence in you that you have confidence in yourself. And by the time you're trying to climb the corporate-industrial ladder in the United States, if you don't have a mentor, others do." Others do in other fields as well.

Individuals seem to need mentors most at crisis periods or turning points in their careers: a young researcher deciding on a specialty . . . a mature woman making a career change . . . a female manager on the verge of promotion to a level where no women have been before. One's success or failure at such times greatly depends upon whether a mentor is present or not. To have a mentor is to be among the blessed. Not to have one is to be damned to eternal oblivion or at least to a mid-level status.

But few mentors will hold the net for a protégé who takes a sharp and serious plunge. And some bosses may be extremely helpful while still being very businesslike. There's some controversy as to when a boss is actually a mentor and what mentors should or shouldn't be expected to do. Some successful women believe that younger women are asking too much of men they'd like to have as mentors.

"I heard about this mentor thing at a course I attended recently. I think it's all a little absurd," said insurance executive Daphne Bartlett. "My boss isn't my mentor. He's a person I happen to work well with. He doesn't give me career advice or tell me how to fix my hair. We only discuss work problems." But when I asked her to think back to earlier in her career, she paused for a moment, then said, "Yes, a former boss helped a number of people improve themselves on the job. He once pointed out to me where my image had gone wrong, and I was grateful."

This is one style of mentoring: a good boss-employee relationship. Juliette Moran, a top executive at GAF, one of the country's largest chemical corporations, also emphasized the working relationship. "This mentor thing, I've really given it some thought because I see so much being written about it. Each boss I've had has been helpful. What is needed is to have every boss you work for be a mentor."

Looking back to when she started her career as a junior chemist, she said, "My first boss, Dr. Jack Brunn, was undoubtedly the most help, because he started me on this path. He happened to be married to a Ph.D. chemist and he was delighted to find a young female who could be useful. My being a woman didn't bother him at all."

Later, when she made the transition from chemistry to administration, she worked under Dr. Jess Werner, who is now chairman of the board of GAF. "Dr. Werner is a very bright man who took several people along as he moved up the ladder. He didn't take us along because he was trying to do us good. He took us along because we were useful!" she explained. "What people mean by a mentor, if they mean it in a healthy way, is a relationship that evolves from working well in a group. This relationship develops over a period of time. Then when there's a new opening or a challenge, the mentor tries one of the people he knows."

In a woman's slow and difficult climb to the upper levels of management, a mentor or very understanding boss may be necessary at not just one, but at two crucial stages. One is during the early phase of a career, when the woman first sees her work as more than just a job and realizes that it may be what she will be doing for the rest of her life, when the mind-set to move on and up is beginning to crystallize. The other stage is later, when it's time for the final push to the top rungs of the ladder.

This pattern appears, too, in Grace Fippinger's career with New York Telephone. Quite early she had a boss who was "a teacher in many ways," as she put it. "I remember before going to my first week-long conference out of town. He sat down with me and we discussed such things as what to wear, how to handle the cocktail hour. These little social things can be a problem, much as we don't like to admit it, and it's important to have somebody to turn to." This same boss also selected her as the best person for several promotions. "Had I worked for a different boss, I don't know if I'd be where I am today!" she said.

A second mentor supported her more recent promotions. She had been in management for some time, but no woman had ever been an officer in the Bell System. "He was strong enough to say that I was the right person for the job," she said.

The later mentor provides his "seal of approval," and this enables the protégé to gain the respect of others above and below on the ladder of command, and those outside the organization as well. For a woman, this male endorsement is absolutely essential in the corporate world. In a *Fortune* article titled "The Top Women in Business," seven of the ten women featured were the daughters, wives or widows of top executives, while the other three had had mentors who "took them to the top." There seems to be a necessity for a top man to stand behind a woman saying, in effect, "She's okay. She can do it. She belongs."

Earlier, though, a more personal, perhaps fatherly sort of mentoring is called for. This mentor is often a teacher or acts as one. In the corporations, the protégé not only needs to learn more about the job but must also be initiated into the game-playing techniques, such as building an image and learning to be an effective team member—things that are more complicated for women entering the game. In the universities, the graduate student or assistant professor learns not only academic material but also how to select viable research projects, how to apply for grants and how to publish. In creative endeavors, the mentor criticizes while, ideally, helping the protégé to find his or her own voice. Often, too, the female protégé in any field needs special encouragement to convince her that it is okay to be a woman doing what she is doing, especially if she has had no female role model close enough to learn from.

Individuals and individual career patterns vary greatly, however, and sometimes a woman passes through the two most crucial stages of a career in rapid succession. For Virginia Carter, making a radical career shift from physicist to television executive, one mentor was enough to see her through both stages.

"When you make the kind of abrupt career change I did, everything is a little unreal at first. It was all so new and I had so much to learn," she said. "Having a mentor is more than just learning and it's more than having doors opened for you. It does something for you at a deeper level. A mentor must be sure that he or she is spending time with somebody worthwhile. That does something for you, makes you stand up a little straighter. If Norman Lear is your mentor, that means something."

In certain fields, especially creative ones where such things as quality and merit are particularly hard to measure, the mentor helps the protégé fight inner battles and conquer inner fears, doubts and obstacles. When Iris Bancroft was getting ready to change her writing career from editorial work and articles to fiction, she and her husband became acquainted with mystery writer John Ball. The Balls and the Bancrofts got together on Sunday afternoons for chess and conversation. "Why not write mysteries?" Ball suggested. "I was pleased at hearing this from a man who had written one of the best-selling mysteries of all time, *In the Heat of the Night,* and so I went home and started working on a mystery." Ball, who holds classes for groups of new writers, read her material and tutored her on a one-to-one basis. "It was an excellent experience," she said, although she later realized this wasn't the sort of novel she really wanted to write. "This got me started. I knew at least that I could write fiction."

Women often mention luck when they talk about finding mentors, and some mentor-protégé stories contain elements of the miraculous, or almost. Norman Lear virtually "discovered" Virginia Carter when she was a friend of his wife, Frances. The Balls and the Bancrofts bumped into each other at a concert. And in large organizations, although everyone has a boss, the right relationship doesn't invariably ensue.

Juliette Moran had this to say to young women in management who are searching for mentors: "I tell you that if you are a useful person who makes things happen, and who isn't abrasive, not too abrasive, you will find people dying to push you up. You will establish an image of yourself in the corporation, so that when doors open, people will think: 'Why not her?' There's a terrific need for competent people. When someone is competent, he or she develops an enthusiastic public," she explained. She went on to say that women who find themselves in the wrong department or with the wrong supervisor shouldn't hesitate to make a change.

Right now, with more women moving onto managerial rungs of the corporate ladder, mentors should ideally be easier to find. But the changes that were supposed to help women can, in some cases, be a hindrance. A number of women who made their career progress before the days of affirmative action believe that the opportunities being held out to women today aren't the *real* opportunities they themselves had. "I've been fortunate to work for a company that gave me every opportunity and total support," said Grace Fippinger. "Many women are being promoted and given grandiose titles when the jobs don't have the substance or the level of responsibility that goes with those titles."

Another woman said, "I'd almost rather see people *call it as it is,* because these women may not have the genuine support of the persons who promoted them." Awhile back, a woman who was promoted knew that her boss was behind her; her position now may be far more uncertain.

Enthusiasm, the right image, working well with others— the characteristics needed to succeed are the same characteristics necessary to attract a mentor. Men actively seek men-

tors and go where they are likely to be found. And in this
situation, women can't afford to wait to be chosen. Ultimately, the mentor selects individuals to sponsor. Far
earlier, though, the wise game-players have chosen where
to work or, in a few cases, where to socialize, in order to
be at the right place at the right time.

But the mentor relationship has pitfalls in the corporate
world and elsewhere as well. Several women mentioned
having had not just one or two, but several mentor-like
relationships. "Were these people really mentors?" one
woman asked herself as she was answering my questions.
"I don't think the relationships were as deep or as strong.
They were friends, really, who gave help and support, and
yet, each time, I eventually felt constrained. Like over-
protective fathers, they were holding me back. Perhaps if
I'd found the one right mentor, I wouldn't have needed
the help of a series of individuals. But that's asking a lot.
It's very rare, I think, that another individual can know
what's the best for you for very long."

Usually the mentor figures prominently in a woman's
career life for a while, then there's a necessity for her to
break away, become independent and function on her own.
Gail Sheehy traced this pattern in *Passages*.[3] Even the best
of mentors must usually be abandoned if the protégé is to
reach full maturity.

What happens, too, is that women seeking the "right"
mentor or a profound mentor relationship end up settling
for several short-term mentors, deriving some support from
each of them. Among the women who described having
had a series of mentors, some mentioned husbands and
lovers. As Sheehy pointed out, sex is a dangerous hitch in
the otherwise healthy mentor process. Ideally, the male
mentor takes a paternal interest in his female protégé, and
whatever emotional closeness develops is along father-
daughter lines. In practice, an exciting but hazardous attraction may develop and romance ensue.

With romantic or sexual interest there may develop a
power struggle where there was none before. The male
mentor who is also a lover may instill his protégé with the
notion that she cannot fulfill her talents without him. Or,
consciously or not, she may not want to surpass her mentor
or achieve autonomy. "How many women might have been

more successful if they had not married their mentors?" questioned one woman.

Actually, some women marry their mentors and live happily *and* successfully ever after. And occasionally a husband or a lover manages to become a mentor of sorts as he sees the woman in his life becoming stronger and more independent but still in need of support and encouragement.

Several women I interviewed had been helped along enormously by men they were formerly married to or deeply involved with. These included two entrepreneurs who'd been in business with their husbands, a woman executive who is now divorced from her engineer husband, and two writers whose spouses or lovers fostered the development of their work. All these women seemingly outgrew the personal relationships, almost simultaneously needing to become independent in their professional lives as well. Most spoke with high regard of the men they'd left behind. One who didn't admitted anonymously: "I'm better in my career than my husband, and I think he knew that. The stronger I became, the weaker he got, and instead of recognizing that, he saw me as a domineering woman, a nag, and he was very threatened by the ways I was changing."

Establishing a good mentor relationship with a man can be difficult in a society that's both sexist and sexually charged. For women who work without a boss, the best male candidates for mentors seem to be a friend's husband or a husband's friend or a homosexual. One woman mentioned a gay male who worked for the same company she did, but who was only a few steps further along in the hierarchy than she was. "He wasn't in position to push me up or clear the way for me, but he was very sensitive to the interpersonal relationships within the company and very responsive to my needs at that point in my career. He became a sort of guru who suggested how I should behave and how I should dress, and who told me what plays he thought would work. I could communicate really well with him and I had a lot of respect for what he had to say."

Must mentors be male? Most are, partly because there are more males in positions to assume this role. And in many of the areas where mentors are necessary, a man has more power and prestige of his own so that he can be more effective in enhancing the prestige of a protégé. A man's stamp of approval makes a woman a more acceptable colleague or team member.

Nevertheless, many women long for female mentors. Dr. Barbara Fish, who is profiled in Chapter XIII, was fortunate to have met Dr. Lauretta Bender, a pioneer in the field of child psychiatry, just as she was nearing the stage where she had to decide how to use her training in pediatrics, general medicine and psychiatry. Dr. Bender's ideas inspired her specific area of inquiry: the antecedents of schizophrenia in children.

Anita Lands also came under the wing of a woman mentor at a crucial time. Dr. Frances Bairstow was her professor at McGill University and also director of the Industrial Relations Institute. Dr. Bairstow encouraged her to take courses in this field and to seek a job in industrial-relations research after graduation. "We've stayed in touch over the years," Anita said. "Besides the academic and professional help, there can be so much more involved in sponsorship by another woman. The female sponsor can be a role model who shows the way."

Things may not always be as they have been: females seeking support, approval, advice and guidance mainly from males. Where women have attained higher, more influential positions, they can be just as effective as males, and probably more so, in guiding other, younger women. Besides offering the kind of help male mentors usually give, they can be role models as well. Women mentoring women seems ideal.

"As women get to places of consequence," Virginia Carter said, "it's necessary that they understand the process of being a mentor to other women. I feel that I must do this for others and if I'm not doing it, then I've failed." A number of others said, in essence, the same thing, whether or not they themselves had had mentors. The women who agreed to contribute to this book were generally those who also assumed responsibility as role models and mentors. They already were, or hoped to be, helpful to other women. Why aren't more of the women who have achieved success playing the mentor role? One reason has to do with competitive feelings among women, which, much as we don't like to admit it, do exist. Women who got far when very few women were even given a chance do sometimes resent the younger women who are being given chances they themselves never had.

There are other explanations, too. As Dr. Judith Stiehm, who discussed this subject at length, said, "Women are reluctant to become sponsors or mentors to other women for several reasons. One is the feeling that they must keep their hands clean—they endanger their own careers if male colleagues think of them as being prejudiced in favor of women. Another reason is that they're working so hard in their own careers that they don't have time. Third, they sometimes think the younger woman will be better off with a male sponsor."

Continuing, she said, "Many women think of mentoring the younger or less experienced women as an obligation, and they're less likely to do it if they think of it that way. What senior women don't realize, though, is that mentoring enhances their own careers. Men who are renowned in their fields have disciples who quote them, write about them, invite them to speak. It's not just out of benevolence that they help me. It's because it's in their own interest."

She's right, of course. And would-be protégés are not playing the game wisely if they look for benevolence, from male or female mentors, instead of demonstrating what they can offer in a reciprocal fashion. Whether it should be or not, the mentor route is a two-way street, and the sooner women at all levels understand this, the further it can take them.

VII

In the Race: The Joys and Conflicts of Competing

"GETTING out into the world, being with people—it all sounds so good and wholesome and friendly. But it's not all blissful togetherness, everybody pulling together, not at all the kind of group effort you learn to have in a happy family," said a woman who started her real-estate career after her children were grown. She went on, "You find yourself in a blooming battleground, and some people are killers. You've got to be tough and competitive or you'll get torn limb from limb."

When they talked about competition, some women resorted to imagery that included the jungle, the rat race, killers, tigers and other vicious-sounding unpleasantries. Not all women think negatively about competition, I eventually found, but there is still plenty of distress and ambivalence about the subject.

What is it about women and competing, anyway? What are the real problems, and how do women go about handling them?

To say that men are naturally competitive and women are not—to assume that this has been so throughout the whole of history from the cave on down to the present time—is to ignore other times and other cultures. Agrarian societies generally have less need for competitive spirit, and in such societies, too, men and women share equally in the tasks to be performed. Societies that depend on hunting or fighting rely more on males' competing while

116

designating other duties as women's work. In some societies no one is required to be very competitive and in a few others females occupy more positions of leadership than males and are required to be more competitive than males. The taboo against females competing at all or competing against males is by no means universal. What we need to look at isn't a set of fundamental differences between men and women, but the different societal conditioning that men and women receive. Here and now, most women have received a heavy dose of conditioning against competition of most kinds. Men, on the other hand, have been trained to match strengths, wits and skills with each other from a very early age. In this sense, our own society has some anachronistic parallels with older societies of hunters and fighters.

The game that men play in the mainstream, however, is actually far more complex, more ritualistic and less aggressive than simple jungle fighting. Men learn its rules, also the joy of winning, by engaging early in team play. As Hennig and Jardim observe, women and girls usually prefer one-to-one sports such as tennis or golf rather than team sports. They point out, too, that women's involvement in sports is more likely to be for the sake of exercise than for the joy of winning.[1]

Women's experiences differ greatly, however. When looking back to their girlhood and to the factors that may have made a difference, several of the women I interviewed mentioned team activities and sports.

Grace Fippinger said, "I guess I am basically competitive. I don't like to do anything halfway." As we talked she unearthed what may have been a decided advantage as she was growing up. "I lived in a neighborhood of all boys," she explained. "I had an older sister, but I played more softball than dolls. We had a club and the boys elected me president." She laughed, then added, "Perhaps that was because the clubhouse was on our property—I never stopped to think much about it before this."

Chicago attorney Jewel Lafontant said that she had always liked many kinds of sport. "You learn to work together on a team and to take defeat," she told me. "I enjoy competing. Once you get used to it, you learn to like it. I think the fact that I was competitive all though school helped me compete in a man's world." She added that she took so many physical education courses in college that she almost had a double major.

Anita Lands, who was an only child, said, "I was introduced to sports by my dad, who had been a semi-professional baseball and basketball player. You could say that I was weaned on sports. I was always going to games and I liked to watch the Friday-night Gillette fights with my father. My mother would come in to see the commercials, which were cute, then she'd leave, but I'd stay. I also enjoyed participating in team sports such as basketball and volleyball as well as playing badminton and tennis." Theirs was a household where, as she explained, "jobs didn't have genders." Everyone helped out where help was needed. "I had friendship and camaraderie with both my father and my mother, though in different spheres, and this provided a balance that was healthy. I never felt any pressure, subtle or otherwise, to follow a traditional female route."

Judge Joan Dempsey Klein, as I have already mentioned, liked sports so much that she became a professional swimmer and a physical-education teacher for a short time. A strong advocate of women's sports, she believes that women shouldn't be deterred from participating for lack of early athletic training. "You have to start with whatever you can do and go on from there," she said. "Sports are very expansive, good for your body and your mind. All the things people have been saying that sports will do for boys, building character and so forth—well, sports can do the same for girls, too. Team sports are especially valuable in helping you learn to identify with a group. You learn to compete and you learn to share."

Competing and sharing—two concepts that males internalize at a very early age—both are valuable to success orientation and astute game-playing later on. Women's experience is generally different, but those who'd had early exposure to and participation in sports invariably felt that it was good preparation for their careers.

Both men and women who understand sports seem to know that competing and sharing overlap. There's friendly rivalry between opponents and, even more important, there's the collective spirit of team playing. Each team member knows his or her specific role and looks for encouragement as well as challenges from other team members. Successes aren't just personal victories. Successes are shared by everyone on the team, but then so are failures. Men on management teams can accept occasional failure more easily than women because men see failure as parceled out among their peers and colleagues rather than taking the sole blame as individuals. Women, however, loners that they are apt to be, too often blame themselves and only themselves.

The solitary aspects of winning and losing remain important to women even as they climb high in their careers. More than a few successful women, I found, regarded competing in a highly personalized way. Some of the comments ran:

"I guess I'm competitive. I can be tough when it matters, not for the sheer sake of being tough, but when it's expected and appropriate. Also, though, I believe in playing fair, and I'll play fair even when others don't."

"I try to do the best I can, and if I can do that, I'll come out ahead. I try to do better than last time."

"I have my own standards of excellence and I compete against those."

These women had, I realized, taken on the stiffest competition of all—the inner yardstick. It was inner satisfaction rather than external reward they were after. Fortunately, the markings on their inner yardsticks were clear enough and they were set high enough, too, so that these women were winning by objective standards as well as their own. Again and again, though, women identified themselves as "competitive" or "somewhat competitive," when what they really meant was that they believed in trying and in doing their best.

Different careers demand different kinds of competition. I talked with one writer who said she couldn't imagine herself in business because she wasn't team-oriented and didn't think she could function in a competitive environment. Not long afterward, however, I interviewed a woman in business who was awed by writers. "The competition in your field is terrific," she said. "I have a great deal of admiration for people who put themselves on the line so much of the time. Freelancers have to compete for every paycheck."

The kind of competition found in a particular career arena certainly should be a major consideration in choosing an occupation. Some fields, particularly those which involve working for large organizations—corporations, the government and the universities—require more interpersonal activity and team playing. In these settings, yesterday's colleagues often become tomorrow's rivals. While most men are prepared for this by their traditional programming, women, who've been conditioned to form strong and lasting alliances, may find shifting loyalties not only confusing but distasteful as well.

Women can change and are changing, yet they're learning that they don't have to be lady warriors and that the laws of the jungle really aren't the rules which apply in the mainstream.

Increasingly large numbers of women, however, are also doing well in independent endeavors—as writers, artists, entrepreneurs, consultants, and in other areas where colleagues are more likely to remain colleagues rather than become rivals. Women who make late career starts, after having been accustomed to spending their days at home and not interacting with very many other individuals, may be attracted to fields requiring less interaction, too.

"I look at it this way," one of these independent women told me. "My work does the competing. I'm less involved personally than if I didn't have a product to show. I'd need to be more competitive if I were paid for being someplace every day and helping form part of a group."

It's erroneous to assume, though, that all individuals who work alone can succeed simply by letting their work compete for them. Very few writers can stay at their typewriters all the time and very few researchers can remain continually in their laboratories; one eventually has to take whatever one produces to the marketplace and bargain for contracts or grants or other reimbursement. Artists or scientists who anticipated a life of working alone, away from the harsh realities of a competitive world, may be in for a rude awakening when they discover how much of a selling job is necessary for survival at a solitary occupation. When making their initial career choice, individuals not only need to consider "What do you do?" in a particular occupation, but also "What must you do to get paid?"

Competitive has another meaning, too. When we speak of certain occupations or industries as being highly competitive, we're apt to mean that there are few openings but many persons qualified to fill them. Fashion, entertainment, publishing—the so-called "glamour" industries—are competitive, and so are occupations that have to do with art, writing, music, acting, and so forth. In recent years, too, university teaching has become a very tight job market and some academic fields are almost impossible to enter. Some very non-competitive women gravitate toward tough fields for a variety of reasons but with little aspiration for success. To hope for little or to hope without realistic or clear-cut goals is to avoid competing.

Research on women's supposed fear of success and fear of competing has proliferated into an enormous body of work during the last decade or so, provoking considerable controversy. Under certain circumstances, women seem to exhibit a "motive to avoid success" which prevents them from competing in the mainstream, as Matina Horner found over a decade ago in her much publicized, often misunderstood research.[2] Subsequent studies have turned up different findings. Some of these contradict Dr. Horner's thesis[3] and others attempt to interpret it. One of the more interesting interpretations holds that women who perform less well in competitive settings are those who've been more strongly conditioned to adhere to traditional sex roles.[4] The subjects of Dr. Horner's original sample were college students in 1965, a time when sex-role conditioning was far more rigid than it is today and when the penalties for successful women were greater, too. It would be highly dangerous and defeatist, as well as overly simplistic, to assume that all women at all times shun competition and success. Horner never intended to assert this, and women in all fields today are proving that it isn't so. Even now, however, certain women at certain times can be observed not doing their best, and it makes sense to look at the reasons why.

COMPETING WITH MEN

"I was used to competing for men, not with them," said a woman who had attended an all-girl high school before entering a co-educational college. "I could speak out freely in classes with girls, but I clammed up for a while when I was first in co-ed classes. I felt I had to give the men a chance or I wouldn't stand a chance with them. Fortunately, I was in a college where being bright wasn't a bad thing, but was respected, so I learned that competing could be fun."

The message was "Give the men a chance. Remember that, powerful as they may seem, they're vulnerable, they don't like to be wrong, they don't like to lose." Between the ages of three and thirteen, many females are programmed to tread carefully in the presence of males for fear of demolishing their egos or their masculinity.

But there are other, more positive messages, too. Besides those few women fortunate enough to have been primed for competing by early participation in team sports, I spoke with some who had had boys for friends at an early age and others who had received positive programming in their relationships with their fathers.

Mothers, working or not, can also teach their daughters to enjoy competing by the example they set. Quite a few of the women I interviewed were daughters of career women or working mothers. Tracy Cabot, whose mother made a late entrance into a successful real-estate career, said, "I learned a lot about competition from her. During the years she was still at home, she was always running for president of this or president of that. I learned that it could feel good to win."

In a variety of ways, women learn that competition can be healthy, fun and even feminine rather than mean, selfish or masculine. Most of the achievers I interviewed had enjoyed and excelled in classroom competition and were not penalized by their peers for being bright or knowing the answers. In the classroom, however, especially in the lower grades of school, traditional feminine traits such as being neat, keeping quiet and waiting until called upon are rewarded. Some schools encourage intellectual assertiveness more than others, and several women felt that they were fortunate to have attended special schools or gifted classes from an early age.

Even with numerous advantages, though, women pick up mixed messages about competition. We learn that competitive behavior is appropriate for females only in certain situations and not in others. As psychiatrist Dr. Barbara Fish explains later, she felt perfectly at ease displaying her abilities in school classes and later in medical school, but found it difficult to have equal give-and-take relationships with the men she saw socially. Another woman, who thinks of herself as aggressive and competitive in business, confessed to me that she is aware of becoming a different person when she is with the man in her life. "I find myself holding back, not showing off what I know," she said.

Some of the fear-of-success research shows that women are more threatened when competing with an "important" man such as a boyfriend than they are with other males.[5] The women in Horner's original sample were subjected to a follow-up study several years later with some interesting results. Those who'd shown fear of success initially, it turned out, were most likely to become pregnant just as they were about to surpass their husbands in their careers.[6]

There have probably been a lot of women who've enjoyed getting ahead and moving up in their careers but who still have had an urge to remain number two or secondary to a bright and renowned man. Many women rise in their careers to be second in command rather than first. And, overwhelmingly, the women I spoke with described their husbands as "brilliant." These men weren't threatened by their wives' success, I was told, because the men were so far out ahead intellectually that the women offered them no real competition.

USC professor Dr. Judith Stiehm has written a perceptive essay called "Invidious Intimacy," in which she discusses the tendency of high-achievement women to select mates they see as superior to themselves. As she wrote, "Young women who do not fear success have something rather important in common. That is, an intimate relationship with a man whom they believe to be smarter (and, thus, potentially more successful) than they. These women, then, can afford to achieve because their man will achieve more."[7]

This statement carries some rather powerful—and disturbing—implications, some of which will be discussed in a later chapter. Women who succeed in their careers may still need to be secondary in other realms of their lives. Traditional sex-role conditioning may run deeper than we'd like to think. From a more positive point of view, however, it can mean simply that the woman who has a smart, successful husband to come home to has fewer conflicts about competing in her career. In tracing women's career patterns, I found several instances of those who began to take their careers seriously during the first year or so of their marriages. And a number of women indicated that their spouses imbued them with strength or courage to compete in the outside world. Although single women have been thought to have an edge over married women in careers, very possibly the married woman has certain advantages, too. Very likely, she is perceived differently by others around her and perhaps she more readily becomes a peer and a team member among males. Also, the possibility of losing may involve a smaller risk, and if she has children, her motivation to win may be stronger.

Traditional role-conditioning can occasionally make women unsuspecting victims of inner conflicts over competing. Here are two cases I learned of where ambivalent feelings made a surprise attack:

One woman had been named president of a medium-sized company after some eighteen years on the job, only to find herself suddenly overwhelmed by her new responsibilities. Actually, she wasn't handling that much more than she had before the previous president retired, and her experience had well prepared her for the spot. Consulting a psychiatrist finally, she went over her difficulties one by one. Eventually she mentioned that one of the vice-presidents, an older man who had once been very helpful to her in her career, was now cold to her and appeared to resent the fact that the job was hers and not his. Furthermore, she admitted to feeling that he might have deserved the job more than she did because of his long years of service. And finally she acknowledged her guilt at having been awarded the job.

Through therapy she eventually came to grips with the fact that she had not taken the job from him but had been appointed by the board of directors after a careful assessment of both her skills and his. She realized that the man's resentment, unfortunate as it was, happened to be his problem, not hers. Having accepted this, she began to cope with her duties efficiently and expertly.

The other instance involves a writer who'd been asked by a publisher friend to help develop a magazine, laying plans for future regular columns and feature articles. This she did while being paid by the hour for her time. Eventually the publisher began looking for someone to edit the magazine. She immediately suggested a man who was a former colleague and a good friend, recommending him highly. After the publisher hired the man, however, she began to feel considerable anxiety. During editorial conferences she attended with the publisher and the new editor, she felt embarrassed for the editor and began to fear that he might not be up to the job. Then she began taking pains to help him with his work, for which the editor gladly paid her, but both of them kept the arrangement secret from the publisher.

One night she awakened in a cold sweat. She realized then and only then that she'd wanted to be editor all along and probably should have been. She wondered why this hadn't occurred to her earlier and why she'd gone along surreptitiously and happily helping out the man she'd recommended for the job.

Ambivalence about competing, whether one is winning or losing, can impair actual performance or eat away at you insidiously. The woman executive was upset about winning over a man; the woman writer allowed a man to win, but was distressed afterward. At subliminal levels both women felt they shouldn't be competing with a man, and this undermined their confidence.

I strongly suspect that many of the negative reactions women have to competition exist on an unconscious level, making us get sick on the day of an important meeting or causing us to misplace the envelope containing a long-awaited contract. Self-sabotage takes subtle forms, triggering illness, memory lapses and sub-standard performance, also dampening one's energy level and even making one accident prone. And with new pressures for women to succeed, conflicts can be driven further beneath the surface. Today no woman wants to admit fear of success or fear of competing. But we need to be honest with ourselves, identifying our real feelings and perhaps, too, talking about them and even laughing about them with other women who understand. If we did this, we might fumble somewhat less.

WOMAN AGAINST WOMAN

One kind of competition women *are* accustomed to is the old-fashioned race to be the prettiest or the sexiest or the

classiest, and, along with this, the battle to beat out a rival
contender for a man. When I first broached the question
of competing with other women, several of my subjects
said that the only kind of competition they had experienced
was sexual competition in their personal lives. Female
sexual jealousy is probably one of the bitterest and most
insidious of all emotions, right next to male sexual jealousy
if not worse at times. Try as we may to get beyond this,
advertising continually reminds us that there's a contest
going on among women and that we're vulnerable to loss
or wounding.

Our being programmed to pit ourselves against other
women effectively prevented us from cooperating with
each other until the last decade or so. Now we're hearing
a lot about woman-to-woman cooperation, but very little
about our competing against each other for career kudos
and promotions. What is it like, I wondered, woman
against woman in the career game? Do any of the old,
familiar feelings of jealousy or envy dare rear their ugly
heads here? Has there really been a cease-fire or have
women simply put on blinders, refusing to recognize scrim-
mages here and there?

More than a few of the women I talked to claimed that
vying with other women for the same jobs, rewards and
recognition wasn't really much different from contending
with men. Having accepted competition as a condition for
success, they felt that competing is competing regardless of
who the opponent is. Generally, these were women whose
early experiences with peers, parents or others had left
them believing that women are equal to men in many
areas and that competing is acceptable for women as well
as for men. As one high-ranking woman executive put it,
"I wasn't raised to think of the differences between men
and women and I don't think of those differences now.
Winning over another woman is no different from winning
over another man."

Near the end of a long day's taping, however, Lisa
Clewer recalled what it had been like as a young female
entrepreneur dealing with large corporations less than a
decade ago. "Maybe you could get in the door because
you were cute," she said. "But once you got in, you had
to have something on the ball."

She went on: "There used to be tremendous peer pressure against women rising above a certain level. I remember the stares I'd get when I'd walk past a row of secretaries and clerical workers my own age on the way to an executive's office where I had an appointment to make a presentation. And if I entered the ladies' room, there'd be a sudden hush. Things are changing now—you get 'Right on, sister' from all sides—but I'll never forget the alienation I used to feel."

In some fields where groups of women occupy jobs at the same level, there's pressure to look alike and dress alike. Marketing specialist Marge Kinney, who also conducts seminars for men and women moving up in the savings-and-loan industry, noted, "Women who want to be managers should be dressed in conservative outfits such as suits or blazers and skirts instead of the latest or the chicest things they can find. But watch one of them change her style from frills to tailoring and the others will say, 'Who does she think *she* is?' "

Some on-the-job competition among women is thinly disguised sexual competition, according to Tracy Cabot, who writes on a variety of psychological topics. "Many women want stroking from a boss or a male authority figure on the job, sexual stroking. Look at all the so-called innocent flirtation that goes on at work and look at the sexy clothes women wear to work. But that's only part of it. Women will work very hard at their jobs and they'll give an outstanding performance in the line of duty to get that same stroking. Most women want it and need it, and men would rather stroke us than give us raises and promotions," she said.

As long as women compete for stroking rather than raises and promotions, men will continue to withhold the tangible rewards. In searching for a professional who is a mentor or in striving for genuine endorsement of one's job performance—both so necessary for women who want successful careers—a woman needs to recognize when she's competing against other women for the wrong goals, also when she's being stroked the wrong way. As Marge Kinney said, "The man-woman thing is always there. Just as you've got some guy taking your ideas seriously, he'll come up to you at the water cooler, put his arm around you and say, 'How are ya, honey?' Though you may like it, and though other women may envy you, it doesn't help you do business. You have to keep your eye on your real goals."

Could it be that women who get out ahead of the others in the race have a certain immunity to envy and pettiness that enables them to behave differently all along? Very often they do, I think, especially in business. Several women reported having felt isolated from other females as they worked their way up. This statement was typical: "I didn't dislike the people around me, but I couldn't get into their conversations very well either. They had no real stake in the business. I was bent on finding out how the company worked. I had more in common with individuals at a somewhat higher level."

A male friend and former colleague of mine observed, "Successful women hang out with the men a lot. Whatever they do, they seek the company of the finest and the best, and, unfortunately, in business a lot of those people are males. These women know this is where they should be competing."

Most women who'd won in races with males denied feeling uncomfortable among other women for having come out ahead. As one businesswoman said, "I feel that a lot of other women are glad I'm here, as proof that they can do it, too. There's more support now than there used to be. Women are recognizing that they need role models."

Winning is very different from losing, of course, and some unattractive elements of earlier programming may creep into one's feelings when one loses. There's the notion that female competition is inferior competition, which isn't necessarily the case. As one woman admitted, "I like to win. When I lose to a man, I can always figure I was being discriminated against. But when I lose to another woman, I figure I must be doing something wrong."

Another woman echoed this when she said, "I'll never forget the first time I lost an account to another woman. When I heard I'd lost it, I naturally assumed I'd been trounced by a man. That I could have accepted easily enough. But losing to a woman made me stop and think. It hurt." Being the only woman had been good for the ego, these two confessed. And the demise of the Queen Bee era left them with some adjustments to make.

There's some very real conflict, too, among women of different generations. Traditionally, women have coveted the smooth skin and slim bodies of women younger than themselves. For women more than for men, youth is a professional as well as a sexual asset. And now younger women are also being offered opportunities that these senior women never had. This makes for some ill feeling.

One of the women quoted above explained that she feels twinges of envy at seeing younger women zoom ahead in their careers. "I haven't done badly for someone who started out in the sixties. But when I meet a woman who is coming up fast without a wrinkle or a gray hair to show for it, I feel it's not quite fair," she said. "However, I have to put this in perspective. Women I really feel for are those in their fifties or older who had plenty of ability but were discouraged and didn't get very far. The world has changed, but not in time for most of them. They have a few more options now, but not many. It's sad. . . ."

Women's career success today is so much a matter of when one started. Most younger career women try to empathize with older women who had fewer chances, but they may not truly understand how these women feel except in the occasional instance where real conflict erupts. I know of one instance where a mature woman's resentment became painfully apparent. In the guise of helping a younger woman who was a friend of mine, she derided her for such well-thought-out career strategies as speaking up at meetings and putting her ideas into memos. "Between us girls," the older woman said, "this will get you nowhere." Was this conscious sabotage? My friend wasn't sure, but she politely thanked the older woman for her advice, then ignored it, and regretted that friendship wasn't possible between the two of them.

Feelings about competition are difficult to identify. Fear of losing is understandable, though it's sometimes hard to separate fear of losing from conflicts about competing. A few women can, in retrospect, identify competition itself as what they dreaded most.

Competing with women who are close friends can be so touchy that one occasionally gives up or decides to try her chances in another area. As one woman told me, "She was a very good friend. She wanted to win and she didn't even know I was in the running. I considered the consequences of losing and the consequences of winning, and I realized that either would destroy our friendship. I decided that the friendship was ultimately more important." Another woman had deliberately not entered a particular academic field because it was her best friend's specialty.

"There can be problems in the balance of power in relationships with females as well as with males," Nancy Shiffrin said. "When I sold my first book, some relationships changed. I had one woman friend who'd published in small journals and little magazines. We couldn't relate to each other from then on. Then another woman I had helped and advised got a bigger advance than I had and became, I thought, very arrogant about it. It seems that she had considered herself the victim until then, she'd felt that she was licking my boots. Now she was out to get even with me. But what's good," Nancy concluded, "is to admit these feelings, get them out in the open. With my best friends I can do this. We talk about them and laugh about them."

These days women are counting on other women to be loyal and supportive. We may not be more sensitive to the disloyalty of friends than men are, but we're apt to be shocked and surprised when good friends behave like rivals. It's perhaps for this reason that some woman build strong dividers between their personal and professional lives, trying to keep one as separate from the other as possible.

Partitioning off one's emotions may not be easy, and it may not always be appropriate either. Different job situations dictate how much emotion one dare show, a subject to be discussed in the next chapter. Where women colleagues are also close friends, as they are in many types of career, airing competitive feelings honestly and openly seems wisest.

Women know that life isn't fair, but we usually believe that it should be, especially when competing with people we like. "Women are so imbued with the idea of merit," said USC professor Dr. Judith Stiehm. "You have to be wise enough, however, to see that human judgment is exercised in any decision. People want to believe that merit counts; even the judges want to believe it. We all pretend there is such a thing as honest, meritorious selection. But merit is very hard to define and it is not decisive. When somebody succeeds or is hired or is honored, it's merit plus: plus politics or peers or influence or a sponsor. At some point it might be more honest to draw names out of a hat. After all, there's a great deal of capriciousness in human judgment."

The capriciousness can be very apparent when we're competing against males. In contests with other females as well, the race is not always to the swift. Being young, attractive, charming or all of these enhances a woman's chances in almost any career. Men seem to be able to capitalize without guilt on their youth, good looks, good family or whatever advantages they have. It's all part of the game they play. But for many women a conflict remains: they want to make the game fairer than it is, and that attitude can diminish their chances of winning.

VIII

Images of Success

PACKAGING yourself, creating an image, developing a style —it sounds phony, even superfluous. Haven't women heard enough about how to walk, talk, dress and behave? Whole generations of women were trapped into preoccupation with superficialities, and now there's a lot being said about the images we need to succeed in our careers. The soundness of the current advice varies. Some of it stops just short of telling us to feign interest and enthusiasm we don't have, to fake what we can't feel.

"Be yourself!" was the advice most women gave when I asked them about images. Some of these women were highly conscious of using packaging and marketing concepts as tools to get ahead, while quite a few others hadn't given much thought to the subject of image-making. Overwhelmingly, though, they stressed being real and not faking it.

"Know yourself, be yourself, sell yourself," said Anita Lands. "First you have to assess your strengths and weaknesses, but as you get to know yourself better it becomes easier to be yourself, and you begin to exude a certain amount of confidence, too. If you sell something you're not, it's going to come out after a while. Image doesn't mean façade. It's a genuine expression of who you are."

The most important components of an effective image develop naturally, even unconsciously, from genuine enthusiasm and commitment. They can't be calculated or fabricated. Lisa Clewer explained, "If you've picked your career and your industry well, it will matter to you when

132

one little widget falls off the assembly line. You'll feel a flutter in your heart over that one little widget. If you don't and one day it falls off wrong, you won't be able to think fast on your feet and deal with it. A phony image can fall apart at crucial times."

She went on, "It has to be *the real you* in there playing. If you don't care about the widgets or whatever your career is about, you won't be consistent either. Occasional brilliance is nice, but people value consistency far more. They want to know they can count on you every time."

When your career has been well chosen, and when the things and the people you are working with are "right," then the correct image should just grow naturally. The trouble is, however, that it may not form fast enough, and this is one reason some women's careers don't progress fast enough either.

THE IMAGE IS THE MESSAGE

You want to move up and move on. Do you tell the boss or the senior partner that you want his job? Some career fields tolerate more blatant ambition than others, but usually smart players do not hit their bosses or models or mentors over the head with their intentions. Instead they perceive how the winners in a particular playing arena look and act, and they plan their moves accordingly. They pick up on the the signals that have been agreed upon to communicate "I want to be in your game" and "I want to win." They get these messages across in many different ways, carefully calculating the effect of what they transmit and evaluating how their signals are received. Others see them as someone on the way up.

Much of the career game is played on the level of subtle moves and surreptitious plays. To many women, it smacks of compromise and, worse, deceit. Also, it seems childish. "The men around me were always seeking recognition and then showing off their rewards and their trophies. They were like little boys showing off! When modesty was called for, of course, they'd act that part, too. It was a little nauseating to watch," one woman said, smirking.

Most women don't want to play a game of duplicity in

order to succeed, and my impression is that most successful
women haven't played this sort of game. But, besides being
a person who cares about what she is doing, the woman
who does well is extremely aware of her individual situation, the people as well as the things. And she probably
calls this "sensitivity" rather than "game-playing." She has
a keen eye for all that is going on around her, for what is
expected and what is appropriate. She knows that others,
especially males, may see her as having joined their game
only temporarily and without serious intentions. To get
their help and support, she knows she must convince them
that she is in the game for keeps and is playing to win.

Her programming probably hasn't prepared her for this.
Also, the specific cues and markers of the game, even the
uniform and the jargon were developed for men rather
than for women. Often she must try to get her message
across without rules that apply to women and without role
models. To do so without some conscious effort is difficult,
almost impossible, and yet she may feel some conflicts
about directing her attention toward appearances.

"We may wish we didn't have to package ourselves,"
said entrepreneur Toni Carabillo. "When we think of
images these days and realize that our leaders may not be
real people but instead are artificial creations of the opinion
polls, then we appreciate those who want to be accepted
as they are. But if you're going to do well, you have to put
your best foot forward. And you have to determine which
is your best foot. We all have multiple images to choose
from. You have to choose wisely."

Women sometimes wish their career packaging didn't
have to be so opaque, hiding what's really there. Total
transparency may be the ideal in the intimate relationships
of our lives where we want those we love to accept our
strengths and our weaknesses, everything. But the people
who surround us in our careers don't necessarily love us,
not at first anyway, and maybe not at all. Different career
settings permit varying degrees of transparency and of
intimacy, but very much naked emotion can be too ex-
plosive even the most hang-loose, casual sort of atmo-
plosive even in the most hang-loose, casual sort of atmo-
harmoniously with the images of others around us.

We can be many things and still be ourselves, but our
prior programming and our other roles may make it hard

to put our best foot forward in our career. Many women must make some very sharp transitions—emerging from home to career, switching from one career to another, leaping to job levels where women haven't been before. Some stumble and fall by the wayside because what *was* their best foot is definitely the wrong foot now. At transition points especially, women's images need some conscious nurturing.

But too much advice to women, I think, focuses on formulating the right image or decorating the package. These things alone aren't enough and can't possibly be. Even the perfect image straight from central casting won't compensate for lack of real substance or real commitment. And too much preoccupation with surface detail can dilute the concentration and energy that must be directed toward one's craft or one's industry. We have to remember that the packaging is something extra, the trimming that supplements and enhances the rest, but that it's no substitute for substance.

No, the right image won't make your career. But the wrong one can break it. A number of women said something to this effect. "It's the little things that can do you in," said Lisa Clewer. Daphne Bartlett put it this way: "One wrong word can ruin a brilliant career. When people don't know you, the image you have is the one thing they think of whenever your name comes up."

Even when you care, your image can go wrong. To show others that you are someone who wants and deserves to move ahead, you have to look closely at what you're doing and what external effects you create. You have to watch your step and make sure that it is your best foot you're putting forward.

WRONG IMPRESSIONS

Consciously or not, we constantly project some kind of image. Lisa Clewer said, "I look at it this way—starting at day one, when somebody put a pink ribbon in our hair instead of a blue one, we were packaged." The wrappings and trappings we carry with us mark us as helpless, sexy, classy, earthy, artsy, efficient, studious or ambitious. Although we didn't choose the pink ribbon, we do choose the rest of it, and we all have different images in different phases of our lives.

These vestiges from other roles may be hard to shed. They're terribly adhesive and they still show when we let them. Gestures, habits of speech, instantaneous reactions, things which seem small or insignificant by themselves may nevertheless make us appear to be incompetent, an inferior team player or less than serious about our career.

And it's the little things that can cause someone to seem inconsistent and therefore not quite real or entirely trustworthy, as Lisa Clewer explained. "What if you show up looking like a refugee because it's raining or because you don't feel good one day? They'll say to themselves, 'What if she looks like that on the day of the national conference? We'd better not send her.' Or, just as you're hoping to convince a client that you can do a neat, professional job, you happen to wheel into the parking lot at the same time he does and your car is heaped with coat hangers and fried-chicken buckets. He may picture you surrounded by all those things every time he sees you. He may never get that image of you out of his mind," she said. "You can lose a lot for the lack of a little—and you may never know what cost you the job or the contract."

Little things can add up to something bigger, too. One successful woman described another who is less successful for obvious reasons: "She's naturally very sexy, but instead of playing it down, she plays it up. She flirts a lot and wears clothes that are too sexy for business. So, everybody thinks she's going to bed with everybody else. She may not be, of course. But the point is, she's not going any further, and I don't think she realizes it yet. She has an attitude of 'not caring what people think.'" It seems almost unbelievable that there are still women who don't realize that a sexy image only *seems* to help and that it can really hurt. The more conservative the career or the organization, the more it hurts. And, almost anywhere, sending sex signals scrambles the message a would-be achiever wants to send. In retaining the images from our outside roles—from the discothèque or from the kitchen or wherever—we're reminding susceptible males of other times, other places and other women, too. And we're inviting them to play other roles—maybe Don Juan, maybe the disapproving priest. They may quickly go back

to being the team members they always were, but they'll
be less likely to see us as equal players, and they'll make
it harder, not easier, for us to be in the game.

More than a few women are hampered by an image of
being too soft, too pliable, too bent on pleasing people.
They're waiting to be chosen and hoping that hard work,
merit and tenure will bring good luck. Traditional programming is holding forth, and when it persists, it can
hold back well-qualified women. We've all seen some very
bright, responsible secretaries and assistants whose bosses
think they are happy because they never complain or
step out of this role.

Some women who've become successful can now look
back on an earlier phase when they were quite different
from what they are today. Daphne Bartlett, who confessed
to having been shy, also said, "I grew up believing that I
should behave in such a way that everybody would like
me. After I was married and began taking my career more
seriously, I realized that not everybody is going to like me
and that there's nothing I can do about it." It was after
her marriage, too, that the progress of her career accelerated.

The too soft, compliant, traditionally feminine image
can be remedied. Usually it's an inside job: with increased
motivation, assurance and enthusiasm begin to show, convincing male players that the sweet young thing in their
midst has grown up. But for the woman who has been
doing the typing, getting the coffee and taking care of endless details, it may be necessary to change jobs and make
a new start in a different setting for others to see her as
someone on the way up. Some women have had to pretend
that they couldn't type or make even instant coffee in
order to dispel the traditional "office girl" image.

Yet it's possible to carry this too far. I suspect that
women imagine themselves as appearing somewhat more
compliant than others perceive them to be, and that they
may be far less aware of having given the impression that
they are tough, hard-headed, abrasive and hard to get
along with. The brittle exterior may develop after a woman
has been involved in her career for some time. As Dr.
Judith Stiehm pointed out, it may result from the independent nature a woman needs for early survival, but to
advance beyond a certain point she must alter her style,

loosen up a little and learn to function compatibly in groups.

Nearly every woman executive I spoke with pointed out that some women trying to create an image of toughness for themselves quite early in the game have only ended up giving the impression of pettiness. Grace Fippinger said, "I'm all for women getting ahead, but women do themselves a disservice by making too much out of little things. Recently a woman was upset because a man called her 'dearie.' I'd recommend ignoring it, but if he persisted, I'd just say, 'My name is Grace,' and let it go. Also, I've seen situations where the coffee is getting cold because the women are deliberately waiting for the men to serve them. Now, that's silly, too. I serve men sometimes and they serve me at other times. It depends on what is easier or what comes naturally. It really doesn't matter who serves the coffee. Handling these small things is really a matter of common sense. I think more people fail for lack of common sense, no matter how brilliant they are."

Daphne Bartlett noted, "The younger women come in, having read all the books, and they anticipate trouble from males or sexual harassment on the job. They're full of fears and traumas and worries. Maybe it helped not to know about these things. At any rate, maturity helps. You need to be able to put things into perspective."

The women who've made it aren't siding with the men. The experienced managers assured me that they themselves would never tolerate real rudeness from men and that they felt that sometimes younger women's complaints were entirely justified. But they felt that the beginners gave the impression of being negative or nit-picking, and they emphasized using discretion in selecting what to complain about so as not to project the image of a person who complains about everything. One woman supplied this somewhat more positive outlook: "It's hard to get so involved in the work that you forget who is male and who is female. When this happens, everybody just pitches in everywhere. There's a spirit of everybody helping out." The good team player, of course, pitches in.

Don't be too traditionally feminine on the one hand or too ardently feminist on the other—avoiding the wrong impression entails treading a very thin line. And the answer isn't to try to be "one of the boys" either, although one must become part of the team. It can be hard to be oneself and play a smart game.

And yet, focusing on the problems and the polemics makes it all seem harder than it is. In actuality, women who've decided that making it is worthwhile take their cues from the individual setting, keeping a keen eye on the style of other women, if possible, and picking up on men's reactions, asking advice now and then of potential mentors.

When you slip, or when you sense that you're giving the wrong impression, it may be that your image does need doctoring. Or it may be more serious. Lisa Clewer cautioned, "When your image ceases to fit, this may be your clue that something is really wrong. It may be a signal 'Do not pass Go! Stop, look around you, think!' It may be time to think about who you are and what others expect of you. Maybe you've outgrown your old image, maybe it's time to move on. But stop and think before you do."

RIGHT IMPRESSIONS

"What are they like, these successful women?" friends, relatives and other writers would ask me as I was doing the interviews. I usually responded that they weren't much different from other women. They certainly weren't formidable, although perhaps the women who didn't wish to be interviewed were.

I realized that I'd have to consider this question if I was going to extract any practical advice to hand on to would-be achievers. I'd been asking women what characteristics they themselves thought had helped their careers most. I thought about what they'd said and also looked back to my own first impressions of them. Above all, they were enthusiastic, committed, dedicated, and these internal characteristics were expressed in what they did as well as what they said.

None prided herself on her efficiency as such, although a number of them said that they had more energy than most people they knew. Nearly every woman struck me instantly as being very good at not wasting time. I'd call for an interview, and if the woman was interested, she'd want to know when and how long it would take, pausing only long enough to check her calendar or to have someone else check it for her. Almost invariably the first conversations were short, matter-of-fact and quickly ended. Only rarely did I hear women describing the various demands on their time—what had to be done when and how difficult it was—until later when I questioned them about it.

And this is important. I imagine that when a boss or a client wanted something by Friday, they didn't stop to explain what they were doing Thursday or the next Monday. If something is worth doing, it's worth scheduling, and women who succeed must be experts at placing personal and professional matters in prearranged time-slots.

But it wouldn't be accurate to describe these women as always in a hurry. Although some spoke rapidly, relating a lot of facts and feelings in a short period of time, there was a leisurely aspect to most of the interviews. They took time to provide thoughtful answers, usually with their telephones and buzzers shut off. An occasional interruption was usually postponed or referred to someone else. One woman answered a buzzer, excused herself for half a minute, went on with the interview and finally said in a very calm voice, "Excuse me, but there was a crisis going on and I'd like to make sure it has been taken care of." She quickly ascertained that it had been and resumed her train of thought.

Researchers, executives, attorneys, writers—they all seemed to maintain a calm, collected demeanor while a lot of things were going on around them. Several mentioned that being able to concentrate on the matter at hand was either part of their style or one of their assets.

Esther Shapiro said, "When I'm doing something, I have the ability to shut everything else out of my mind. Right now there must be about fifty phone messages on my desk. Some of these I'll have to take care of myself and some other people can handle. But I'm not thinking about those phone calls now," she explained. And indeed, there was no indication that she was thinking of anything other than her responses to my questions.

As it turned out, a number of the interviews ran longer than planned, and the women didn't seem to mind giving extra time. Sometimes other appointments had just been canceled, and other times they simply decided to take longer. They seemed to believe that if something is worth doing, it's worth doing well. I'm not sure what this did to their busy schedules, but I didn't see anyone glancing anxiously at her watch.

And I had a definite impression that these women— not just the executives, but all of them—were decisive. Those who didn't want to be interviewed said no at once, apologized and wished me luck, and the others just wanted to know when. Also, the occasional interruption or crisis that I witnessed was always quickly as well as calmly handled.

Several volunteered that decision-making capacities were important to the success they had achieved, and others readily responded to my questions on the subject. "Whether you think of yourself as a decision-maker or not, other people think of you as one," said one woman who admitted that her job demanded a lot of fast, on-your-feet thinking. "If you have an image of not being able to make up your mind, you'll get stuck where there aren't any big decisions or responsibilities."

I'd always wondered about decision-makers and what makes them different from others who vacillate, question and postpone. What some of the women had to say was enlightening. "Half of it is sheer gall!" admitted one. "Some women fear decisions because they think you have to be right all the time, but it's not true," she went on, shaking her head. "You'll be right a lot of the time if you know what you're doing, but nobody is ever going to be right all the time. You have to decide that you're going to decide by a certain time, usually the sooner the better, and then you just decide."

What others said was similar. "Being decisive means being able to decide quickly," said another, adding, "and it means taking the responsibility for what you decide, too. You're going to be wrong sometimes, and if you are, admit it. Never defend something to the death once it turns out that you were wrong." I detected a lack of ego involvement here, and I saw this same quality in many of the achievers. Being proven wrong now and then wasn't a crushing experience; it was something they could accept in themselves and in others, too. Being effective doesn't mean being superhuman or perfect, they'd realized.

Also, individuals who aren't afraid of sometimes being wrong can be themselves more easily. And they can take certain kinds of risks.

Were these women risk-takers? I'd been reading about how important it is for women to learn to take risks, and so I was hoping that they would demonstrate or describe certain fearless qualities. In a sense, all women risk some degree of personal serenity in having careers, although the risk in not having a career at all may be greater. But the majority of these women weren't gamblers. When I asked them how they looked at risk, a few viewed their past accomplishments in terms of possible losses and ultimate gains. For a number of them, the biggest risk had been starting their careers, changing direction or switching jobs. Only a few had ever risked their security by putting their entire career or bank account on the line, and none had done so without carefully calculating the odds. Generally, and not unexpectedly, the entrepreneurs were the biggest risk-takers.

"Risk can be creative or destructive," said Anita Lands of the National Association of Bank Women. "Plunging into a no-win situation where the cards are stacked against you is destructive. In a creative risk, you've weighed the odds. You've asked yourself, *'What's the worst that could happen?'* You know it could go either way and you know that you can handle whichever way it goes."

Not many careers demand that you be a person who is willing to go out on a limb, and most women probably shouldn't worry if their basic personality prevents them from projecting such an image. Being a person cautious enough to calculate the odds inspires considerably more trust.

More than a few interviewees were leery of the way risk-taking is portrayed in current advice to women. Said one executive who has had fairly long tenure with the same corporation, "What does it mean, anyway, not being afraid to take risks? Taking a job you're not qualified for?"

She went on, "Not all risks are good. I think it's important to distinguish yourself in the job you have, and when you come up with a new idea, tell people about it.

Some women are shy about doing that. It's not an enormous risk, but it can make a big difference."

"Be a person who has ideas," echoed Daphne Bartlett. "You should always be searching for better ways of doing things. When you come up with something that's different, try it out on somebody." One of Daphne's own ideas was a new type of life insurance: Adjustable Term. It was adopted by Occidental, sold very well from the beginning and now, several years later, still accounts for as much as 20 percent of the firm's total volume.

This was the kind of risk I heard mentioned most often: being creative and innovative, coming up with new ideas and making them known. Some women were obviously able to be more daring than others.

"Don't hide your light under a bushel," said still another, quoting the old proverb, then adding, "I haven't! Once in a while I get laughed at. So? There are worse things than being laughed at."

"What's the worst that could happen?" I could imagine most of these women asking themselves that, then shrugging if the worst was being laughed at. They knew that it was okay to be laughed at and even to be wrong occasionally if that's what it took to get their ideas across and to get things done. Their style—firm, decisive, assertive—paralleled the assets they'd developed as part of their career growth. And all of this related back to their motivation and their commitment to careers where they could bring their own values into play. It was anything but a shallow game.

THE LOOK OF SUCCESS

Clothes don't make the woman, but they can make or break the woman manager. Also the woman entrepreneur and very possibly the woman in law or government. Supposedly, dress matters far less for academicians, researchers, writers and certain others, but I didn't see any women anywhere who looked careless or sloppy or who were more than a very few pounds overweight. They all looked different, of course, but if there is a look of success, it's simplicity. Their clothes and their offices as well are uncluttered. This doesn't mean that women who do well are necessarily neater or more orderly than other mortals. However, their lives must be arranged so that time and things don't get lost, and often others do the arranging for them. Part of success is getting beyond minor details and distractions, pushing away little things to get to the bigger things.

It's no wonder that women who've made it are amused at the plethora of advice on how to *look* successful. Unless their careers are directly involved with the fashion industry, they don't have time to contemplate the latest nuances in sleeves or skirts. Many of them do devote time to tennis, swimming, jogging and other exercise for relaxation as well as for fitness, and the results of it show. The look of success is healthy, fit. But most of these women don't have time for shopping, certainly not for the preoccupation with *chic* that women have always been encouraged to develop, because, though they might enjoy fashion, other things interested them more and took higher priority. As a career progresses and as priorities and rewards fall into place, there's more money than time to spend on clothing. Dressing expensively is a mark of rank for men and women who reach a certain level; also, for women especially, it's a matter of practicality. Spending money on quality and on the care of clothes can make up for time you don't have to spend studying styles, shopping, matching colors or making alterations.

Marge Kinney pays a single visit to the same designer season after season, each time selecting jackets, blouses, skirts and pants in two colors which go well together. The result is a well-coordinated wardrobe which is easy to travel with. Mercie Butler, who modeled high-fashion styles before becoming an account executive in a brokerage house, now chooses very classic designs, including mostly tailored suits in very basic shades. The first time I saw her she wore a black suit with a white bow-tied blouse. On a cold, rainy day when we met for lunch, she had on a medium-gray wool coat, a suit of the same shade and a deep maroon blouse. "Most of the high-fashion styles just aren't right for business," she said. What she wore was perfect for the world of finance, where the male uniform is still conservative, but would have been striking almost anywhere. Daphne Bartlett alternates between good-quality suits and simple, classic dresses which she can slip into quickly and easily.

Business, more than most other careers, demands a tailored look. At the time I was interviewing, the fashion industry had just ushered in broad-shouldered blazers and skirted suits. I saw women in various career fields wearing this sort of thing. Those I talked to were happy that fashion had, for once, responded to the career woman's real needs, though some lamented the difficulty of finding comfortable but attractive shoes. At about this time, too, stores were featuring blouses and dresses with big, droopy sleeves and some very full skirts. I saw fewer achievers in these styles, which somehow make the wearers look frail and helpless. Add high-heeled sandals to the ensemble and a woman is indeed helpless, and quite literally unable to keep up with sensibly shod male colleagues.

There's something about a jacket that invites friends and adversaries to take us seriously. A man's jacket is his "mantle of authority," as Betty Lehan Harragan notes in *Games Mother Never Taught You,* which includes other excellent tips on dressing for and understanding the business world.[1] Marge Kinney explained her own preference for blazers and jackets this way: "When the men in a meeting all decide to leave, if you have to go to the other end of the office to get your coat, you're going to be left behind," she said.

But jackets may not be right for all women in all situations. "Even in business," Lisa Clewer said, "if the suit or the blazer isn't right for you, you shouldn't wear it. You have to find your own style, and once you do, you'll find things every season that are somehow right for you and right for what you're doing. You can't look successful if you look outdated." Lisa's wardrobe includes a variety of things from tailored suits to soft dresses. As an entrepreneur doing business with widely divergent industries, she explained that she changed her style of dressing accordingly. "I check out what the men are wearing. If they're all in pin stripes, then maybe I'll wear a simple suit and a silk blouse."

Other women, too, recommended studying the male "uniform" of a particular company where a job or a contract might be pending. "Station yourself somewhere and spy on them before your interview," said another woman. "Every organization has its own uniform that the men conform to. The women who want to be on their team don't dress too differently, although it would be a mistake to try to look like a female version of them or like a psuedo-male." Clothes that are too mannish can be intimidating or—as Marlene Dietrich has always known —on some women they can be very sexy. Either effect can mar the success image.

Jobs that don't require the classic, tailored image will require an alternative that's just as costly, perhaps more *au courant*, perhaps more casual. Either way, women are required to have an aura of being upper middle class, as John T. Molloy makes clear in *The Women's Dress for Success Book*. This is the real command behind the advice that tells us to wear real silk or wool or linen or to wear classic styles in blues, beiges and grays or, in some careers, the latest fashions in the latest shades. Men who are bosses and would-be bosses, regardless of their origins, take pains to look well bred and rich, and they're apt to be more comfortable around women who do the same. Women used to try to look as though they didn't have to work, and today's women, wisely enough, want to project the image of being accustomed to earning a lot of money. In some cases, the actual clothes of yesterday's "Real Ladies" and today's successful women are very similar.

It's hard for women on the way up. Although men don't have it easy either, their salaries at apprenticeship levels still make it easier for them to dress well. "Dress for the job you want to have," Marge Kinney advised. "If you dress for the job you have now, that's the image you'll have and that's where you'll stay."

How can women possibly afford to dress for a salary level above their own? I discussed this with Marge. She felt, and I agree, that most women already spend a lot on clothing without serious consideration of where they spend it or what their clothes really say about them. They dress to compete with their peers rather than to impress those who decide their future. Some concentrate on quantity rather than quality of clothes. Also, as Marge has observed in the financial institutions where she offers seminars to employees, women in beginning jobs foolishly choose current fashions and fads rather than making a practical investment in classic clothing that won't go out of style so quickly.

Women who have more time than money will find John T. Molloy's advice on cross-shopping helpful.[2] Basically, he advises visiting the expensive shops and looking at the items you need, then going to a cheap store and studying the same items there. Finally, go to a medium-priced store and purchase the items that come closest to the expensive ones. I used to do something like that in New York and also in San Francisco. When I settled in Los Angeles, I found that it took too much time getting from store to store. Also, like many other women, I reached a point where I had far less time to search out clothes but still didn't have the money to buy things with the kind of fabric and detail I'd learned to appreciate. Time and money—these are the trade-offs for striving women, and a little excess of either one goes a long way in solving the dilemmas of dress.

Dress somehow shouldn't be so important. Clothing makes social statements now as it did in Marie Antoinette's day or in Jane Austen's, though the statements have become more subtle. It can separate the "haves" from the "have-nots," and, to some extent, women who work from women who don't. But dress also reflects aspirations. Not only does it say something about where we are but it signals what we're trying for. And it does this so clearly and instantly that it becomes a very important part of the total package.

WHY THE SUCCESSFUL WOMAN ISN'T MORE LIKE A MAN

Women concurred in the belief that the qualities a woman needs to succeed are the same ones a man needs: firmness, decisiveness, assertiveness, ability to calculate risks. And there's not much disagreement that certain traditional female characteristics, such as passivity, blind obedience and dependence, hinder a career rather than helping it along.

As women change their thinking and change their images, though, the adversaries of women's equality believe we're losing that much-prized but hard-to-define quality:

femininity. They charge that women are becoming more like men.

Absurd as this sounds, it's not so different from wishing that men would be more like women. When we talk about being "like a woman" or "like a man" we're resorting to cultural stereotyping. As Dr. Cynthia Fuchs Epstein has perceptively pointed out, "Even feminists share the culture's assumptions when they defend women's rights to be emotional and ask that men be allowed to be so too. They also sometimes insist that women are kinder, more caring, and more nurturing. The defense too often rests on the same biased assumption as the attack: that women are emotional whereas men are not, and that the capacity to work, or love, is sex-linked."[3]

A great many of the characteristics we've attributed to one sex or the other turn out to be results of what our culture expects rather than of hard-and-fast biological or chemical differences between the sexes. This means that both men and women can change and can adapt better to the changes in society. But it also means that some very important issues become extremely difficult to talk about. It's hard to look at the differences between male and female images without constantly identifying what is stereotypical and what isn't, and constantly examining what is cultural and what isn't. The stereotypes remain part of our thinking and our vocabulary on an everyday level. And we ourselves, of course, retain parts of our cultural programming.

The woman making it in a man's world today keeps some of the best of what it means to be feminine in this society. Consciously or not, she selects from her early conditioning which elements to keep and which to cast off.

Many of the values which she learned through her own experience are worth keeping. These may provide the major motivation in her career, and they can surface in subtle ways, influencing her approach to people and problems.

"My style isn't tough," said writer turned network executive Esther Shapiro. "But I'm prepared to make changes that are needed. I believe I can be direct, yet tactful. It's possible to disagree without destroying another person. I know what it's like to be on the other side of the desk. The hardest part of this job is rejecting writers' material. It may be very important to them, and, after all, they're human beings." Working with writers, however, also provides great satisfaction for her. "If I can give them something—you might call it stroking, you might call it love—then maybe they'll have a sense of enthusiasm they didn't have before. If I can help them find a new voice that is still their own, then maybe they'll do ten times better than they've been doing," she explained. Working this way, she hopes to bring new and better material to television.

"There is nothing magic or wonderful in being like a man. Or like men are supposed to be," said attorney Jewel Lafontant. "It's not supposed to be manly to show emotions, but I don't feel that it's important to be tough or unbending.

"Women bring a high degree of sensitivity and compassion to whatever we do, and I hope we never lose those things. We can be more effective by not denying some of the values we've acquired through our lives as women, through suffering perhaps or through whatever experiences we've had. I also feel that being a full human being includes having compassion and sensitivity toward other people. The men who are most successful are those who have these capacities. If you can relate to other human beings and understand their problems, you'll do better in handling those problems. You'll do better in trying cases or doing business or anywhere," she said.

Empathy, compassion, sensitivity—the same characteristics that supposedly fitted us for nurturing families or for the "helping" professions such as nursing, teaching or social work can also make us better lawyers, judges, doctors or executives. Not necessarily better than men, but better than we thought we could be. Women of future generations may be quite different, for all we know. Or men may be. Perhaps we're less likely to lose these characteristics if we think of them as human rather than as feminine.

Emotions can be an asset or a liability. They can provide the energy to get things done or they can stand in the way of getting things done. They can upset the existing order of things, sometimes for better and sometimes not. "We ought to be concerned enough to have real feelings about certain issues," Jewel Lafontant asserted.

Women are presumed to be more emotional than men are, and most women think of themselves that way. Advertising executive Adrienne Hall thinks that "women bring a lot more to a business relationship that isn't strictly business. Men tend to leave their personal lives at the door when they walk into an office." She went on to explain that when she and Joan Levine started their agency, they expressed their emotions and talked about how they felt about a lot of things. One reason for this, she thought, was the fact that they both had small children whom they sometimes had to think about during the working day as well as afterward. "It was very healthy," she said, but she added that there can also be problems when emotions are allowed to come too close to the surface.

Emotions can complicate working relationships that are already anything but simple. Are women any more adept than men at functioning in settings where emotions are revealed rather than concealed? Some are.

Some women find it easier to be themselves in work situations that are somehow more "like home." It used to be, though, that many women who went to work bent over backward to be "businesslike." They never displayed pictures of their children although the men around them did. They might not even say a word when a crisis occurred in the family. But this sort of style is rarely demanded or even appropriate now.

Also, career settings differ in how much emotion they can tolerate. For example, in putting together a television comedy, individuals must draw upon their feelings in order to create the final product. Certain individuals will be far more at ease in this kind of atmosphere than they would be in the worlds of law or finance or government where more formality still prevails.

Women are fitting in, however, in places of many kinds these days, including those where expression of feeling is still pretty much taboo—which are some of the same places where women themselves were once taboo. "When expressing emotion can be taken as a sign of weakness, then you'd better not show it," Jewel Lafontant went on to note. "My father used to say, 'If you're winning, you don't need to get angry. If you're losing, you can't afford to!'"

Sometimes the career game is like a poker game. Sometimes you can't afford to show your hand or how you feel about it. Nervousness, excitement, various emotions must sometimes be held in check or kept in the reservoir for later. Women cope with their emotions in various ways.

"Something I've learned that's very effective," Lisa Clewer volunteered: "Lower the tone of your voice. When some people, especially women, are angry or excited or nervous, they raise both the volume and the pitch. And it doesn't work. It doesn't even get kids to listen. Speak softly in a low tone and only after you're ready. Then everybody listens."

When she told me this, I remembered an occasion shortly after she'd hired me to write a story for a company magazine she'd contracted to edit. I was to interview a man who was corporate vice-president of a financial institution, and she was there to introduce me and explain what the magazine was all about. Awed by a top-floor office that could easily have housed a family of sixteen, I heard the nervousness in my voice. From the instant Lisa opened her mouth, however, she seemed assured and controlled. I sensed a certain effectiveness, and at the time I thought of it as power, feminine style. Looking back, I recalled that her voice at that moment had been a whole octave lower and several decibels quieter than mine. And the man behind the big desk had been listening very carefully.

One woman anonymously confessed that her very worst fear was that she would someday burst into tears in front of a group of men. "They'd go absolutely berserk if I did," she said, "but I'm a person who cries easily if I'm upset or tense or gravely disappointed. It doesn't mean that I totally fall apart. At home I can fix things or handle the crisis with tears rolling down my cheeks."

There are people who cry more easily than others for reasons having nothing to do with their emotional stability, and some of them are women. One, an achiever in a high position, confessed that she does cry now and then at work. "It's out of tension," she said. "This is a very high-pressure job and my staff knows that I cry easily. I try not to do it where I'll dusturb anybody else. I usually shut the door to my office and I cry for a little while. Then I'm okay. Very few men would allow themselves this. But it's better, I think, than having an ulcer or a heart problem."

Crying may not be a problem for many women trying to make it, but when it is, the best policy would surely be to let co-workers know so they won't be upset by it. Yes, we wish our packaging could be more transparent. It might be better if individuals of both sexes could cry more openly, but, for now, there are far more important issues to defend than their right to do so.

In recent years, just as women have invaded more job areas, the atmosphere of the places where people work has been changing, too. Men dress more casually in offices now. Floor plans are less likely to be designed for maximum intimidation. Desks are no longer huge wooden boxes to hide behind, more often they are antiques that look like tables or they've been replaced by real tables, usually glass and chrome. Offices seem more like living rooms, and visitors are treated more like guests. First names are used more often, too.

Are women responsible for these changes? In some places they undoubtedly are. More accurately, though, letting women in and creating friendlier atmospheres are both part of the same trend. The once rigid hierarchies ruled by fear are beginning to crumble, and although much of the same structure remains standing, there's a discernible move, however slight, toward democracy. Industries and organizations are beginning to alter their images, and in time this may mean that men and women won't have to worry quite so much about theirs.

Women are often blamed for more things than we're really guilty of, but we're also given credit sometimes when credit isn't due. There's quite a lot of talk about "women's intuition" as one of the assets we bring with us to the working world. But just what is it? Is it a kind of sixth sense that depends on some different level of awareness? Or is it perhaps the result of a desire to keep things simple rather than cloaking one's ideas in long-winded explanations and rationalizations?

Women don't succeed on intuition alone, but there are times when a woman can astound male game-players by going directly to the point or by taking an over-all glance at something and predicting a probable outcome. We'd be kidding ourselves, however, if we refused to recognize that men do this, too. There are times when anyone who is aware, alert and concentrating in a relaxed way will instantaneously grasp something very complex. Zap—they just *know*. More than a few men, especially those who are successful, are aware of their own intuitive responses, though they may call them by a variety of names. They know which product will sell, which play will be a hit, which person can do the job best.

Whatever this quality is, it has to do with looking ahead and not being too entrenched in the here-and-now of things around you. It's maintaining perspective even when game-playing.

"Keep your eyes on the bird's-eye view, see the overall picture," Lisa Clewer advised. "If, when somebody tosses out the ball, you pick it up and play with it without looking around you or looking ahead, you can be manipulated by the situation itself. Your game-playing can contribute problems. The great thing that you get off at today's meeting can come back to haunt you in six months if you aren't aware of what's out there six months from now."

Always looking ahead can be one of the costs of success as well as one of its essential ingredients. Perhaps women are more comfortable focusing on the future when this goes by the name of woman's intuition rather than some other label taken from the jargon of the game. Intuition by any name, however, is a highly marketable asset, especially for someone who also has logical, rational explanations ready to back it up.

Daphne Bartlett told me, "A very distinguished actuary paid me what I consider to be a great compliment not long ago. He said, 'You have a talent for seeing the big picture.' I was very pleased and I thanked him, of course. I wonder, though, what is it really? Is it woman's intuition?" She thought about this for a moment. A mathematics major who reached her managerial position through the actuarial side of life-insurance work, she finally said, "You know, it might also be the result of having a logical mind."

It could be both. Or neither. Whatever it is, it's an asset —and an image—that can be used effectively.

IX

Getting It All Together–
Balancing Career and Family

Not all women want careers, and most of the achievers I spoke with were adamant in their belief that not all women should feel they must have careers. But nearly all women who do want to work and to become successful at it also want the rest, and they apply their energies feverishly to getting it all. Women's definitions of success emphasize not only achievement in their jobs but also relationships with their mates, children and others.

Perhaps more than anything, this is what makes women's success so difficult. We're almost never content to play a hard and tough career game and let it go at that. Success to us is the total picture of our lives. Other individuals are important to us; relationships are important.

"No matter what marvelous and exciting things you do, eventually you have to go home," said advertising executive Adrienne Hall. "Eventually, too, you grow older," she added.

Toni Carabillo put it this way: "There has to be a balance between career and caring. Without that, you can't have success."

What's really tough is the timing. The very phase of our lives when society expects success-oriented individuals to devote their attention almost exclusively to work is the same period of time we're told is best for bearing children. This is also the time when we're most interested in forming relationships and have the most opportunities for doing so. There's only so much we can do between the ages of twenty and forty.

It's no wonder, then, that until recently many women saw career vs. marriage as an either/or choice. Dr. M. Elizabeth Tidball, professor of physiology at George Washington Medical Center, randomly selected 1,500 achievers from several editions of *Who's Who of American Women*. After earning their undergraduate degrees, they had devoted an average of seven consecutive years to building their careers.[1] Only slightly more than half were married. In Margaret Hennig's original study of twenty-five women corporate executives, all had seen marriage as an either/or choice when they were in their twenties. They'd opted for a career and deferred close relationships. When they were about thirty-five, their more conventional feminine interests emerged. About half of them then married, and those who didn't greatly expanded their social life at that time.[2]

The women I talked to, representing many different kinds of achievement, had fitted their careers into many different life patterns. Almost none had seen marriage and career as an either/or proposition. Yet there's a lot to be said for launching a career first and marrying later, and not all the advantages are professional ones. Very likely, we'll be seeing somewhat more of this pattern in years to come. Devoting five or seven or even ten years to their careers before they marry, more women will advance to higher levels in careers that demand long periods of training or apprenticeship. It might mean more solid marriages, too. The woman who has established herself professionally and who has also gained some emotional maturity will probably have a better perspective from which to choose a compatible partner. And the man will know what sort of wife he's getting. It sounds ideal—get the career under way, find out who you are and then find the mate who accepts the individual you've become.

But for many women it doesn't happen that way. Women in general seem to choose their life partners even more haphazardly than they choose careers, and the results are apt to be as disastrous in one area as in the other. Many of us were programmed to believe that marriage and childbearing would be the most significant events of our lives, and programmed as well to wait to be chosen—or for

Cupid's arrow to strike. For many women, a chance to marry was an opportunity to be seized before it was too late, and by the age of twenty-five it might seem to be too late.

The women I talked to who were both happily married and successful in careers had almost invariably regarded marriage and close relationships as matters over which they had control. Some knowingly suppressed romantic and nurturing instincts at times when an exclusive commitment to their careers was necessary. "For several years I simply didn't dare become involved with a man," said one woman. "Of course, I was still attracted to men, but I'd have to say to myself, 'This is just my hormones talking. Get back to work!' It wasn't easy." Others said, too, that while a career might co-exist with a firmly established, stable relationship, they didn't see how any woman could manage the early and often tumultuous stages of a romance or an affair at the same time she was coping with a crucial phase of a career. Those who had postponed romance or marriage had done so by choice, believing, seemingly, that men were, as the old saying goes, like streetcars: there would always be another one along. And often there was.

Successful women sometimes make unwise choices in the personal side of their lives just as other women do, although I doubt that they are *more* likely to err than other women. The more strongly motivated they are or the closer to success they come, however, the more carefully they choose their marriage partners or those with whom to form close relationships.

Although women have great difficulty getting all we want in the time we have, and although we cannot reproduce indefinitely, we must remember that at various stages along the way we do have options. We decide when to embark on intimate relationships or when and whom to marry. We don't always get precisely what we want, but we can, through our attitudes and intentions, exert great influence upon this sphere of our lives. This may sound cold and unromantic, but in actuality it needn't be. As women told me the stories of their careers, they interwove some real love stories too, and many of these had happy endings.

Although my investigation wasn't a statistically sophisticated study, the intimate lives of the women I talked to were to say the very least, encouraging. Over half—twenty-eight of the forty women I spoke with—were married or had been widowed after long-term marriages, or else, though single or divorced, were involved in on-going, long-term relationships. Most of the married women and widows had only been married once. Most of those married for the second time had now had the same spouse for ten years or more. The relationships described to me, different as they were, seemed to be stable, secure and healthy, and although I had only what these women told me to go by, I'm convinced, from the way they talked about their husbands, lovers and companions, that they were telling the truth. I could see, hear and feel their emotion, and I could tell, too, when some subjects shouldn't be pursued. Divorce was a subject I didn't pursue, although some women volunteered details. Among the forty, ten had been divorced and five of these had remarried. Whether the woman's career or her success was a factor in the divorce, I couldn't be sure, but in most instances the couple had separated before the woman's career was well under way or even started; her unfulfilled need for a career and a new life may have been a factor.

All in all, my impression is that women's success doesn't disrupt the home as severely as defenders of the *status quo* predicted it would. But then the home isn't quite what it used to be either. Marriage is becoming a more flexible institution, allowing individuals somewhat more room to meet independent needs. And the single life, too, affords somewhat more opportunities than previously of meeting the need for intimacy.

Ten of the women were single; they hadn't married or remarried "yet," as they usually put it. Those who had never married had devoted considerable effort to their careers while they were in their twenties, and these efforts were now paying off. But, whether they were divorced or single, in their thirties, forties or fifties, they had active social lives, were dating and had by no means given up the possibility of marrying. What this woman said was typical: "I expect I will marry someday. When I look at my friends who have children, I think that, yes, I have missed something even though I have a life that is wonderful as it is. I enjoy other people's children and I would very much like to marry into a ready-made family. I imagine that I will, because most of the men I meet these days are divorced." One woman mentioned that she was signing up for a Big Sister program in order to satisfy a nurturing urge.

Although these women saw being single as one of the costs of their success, they didn't see the price as too high, and they were optimistic about their futures. Had I talked to more women, I might have collected some stories of bitterness, but I suspect not many. Just as very few women will talk about fear of success these days, few, too, will talk about fear of being single. The social pressures for women are changing. Success is admired and so is the single life, and the two together are beginning to constitute a new ideal. I heard only one woman say, "My career comes first," but she acknowledged that it hadn't always come first and that right now she was undergoing a transition which made heavy demands on her time and energy. The other single women took pains to point out that, while they had worked very hard in their careers and had at certain times given their work top priority, their definitions of success, their ideas of life, were not based exclusively on work.

The bad news here would be easy to ignore since it involves women I didn't interview. These are women who had given their careers priority over their personal lives and who have been disappointed on both counts. I'd almost forgotten such women existed until Dr. Judith Stiehm told me of a group who had recently visited her in her home. All, she explained, were in their mid-thirties and single, having decided to become professionals rather than to marry. "Not only had they given up families in order to devote themselves to their work, but now they find they aren't winning in their professional roles either. They're competing against men ten years younger than themselves and losing," she explained. "The sacrifice wasn't enough. These women had paid the full price—and they still weren't successful. They'd now like to meet somebody to marry and they were discussing at what age to foreclose the possibility of having children."

These women's careers might still flourish. And in their mid-thirties they still have a good chance of marrying. At this age, women's suppressed instincts surface and demand to be heard, but now, too, the biological time-clock is racing toward an ominous point of no return. Very shortly one of life's options will be gone forever. It's a high price to pay just for being in the game.

It's often supposed that it's easier to have a successful career if you're single. It is almost certainly easier to launch a career that becomes successful. And it's a lot easier today to be single if you're successful than if you're not. Whether it's getting any easier to be married and successful, though, is another question.

PRIORITIES

Theorizing on women's dilemmas, one researcher, Monique de Meron-Landolt, drew an analogy with playing the parlor game "Puss-in-the-Corner." The career is in one corner, the husband in another and the children in still a third. Winning the game entails keeping the whole situation in balance by charging frantically from one corner to another.[3] A great many women don't win in all three corners, but those who do seem to have an acute sense of timing which propels them to the right corner at the right time.

How do they manage? Consider these for timing. Edna Alvarez gave birth to her first child the very day she finished law school; Marcie Carsey went into labor while screening a television pilot. And such events were only the beginning.

Successful women's careers pretty much follow a logical and believable sequence of events, and even when they weren't planned, they seem as though they might have been. But bring in the other facts of their lives, consider the very things that these women have in common with other women everywhere, and their stories take on an element of unpredictability, suspense and even surrealism. Just when successful women should be seen at their most human, as individuals all women can identify with, they became superheroines. They do cope, but not easily.

A note from Dr. Cynthia Fuchs Epstein informed me that she was currently involved in an attempt to teach, do research, write a book, fix up an apartment in New York and a house in the country, all in addition to being a wife and mother. "There are times when I wish I could be married part-time!" she said. Many other married professional women know that feeling.

Yet these women manage by setting priorities and resetting them, by acquiring a kind of tunnel vision that nevertheless can be shut off at will, by losing sleep, by trying not to worry about the things that didn't get done and by trying not to feel guilty.

Adrienne Hall married young, worked while her husband was in graduate school, then centered on advertising as her career field. When she and Joan Levine, who was a copywriter and a friend, started their own agency, both women were pregnant. The business grew rapidly and so did their respective families: two children for the Levines and four for the Halls, including a set of twins.

When Adrienne was in labor with the twins, an emergency call came from *Vogue*. One of their ads was scheduled to run, but the client's name had not arrived with the ad. *Vogue* was approaching a deadline and so was Adrienne. She handled the crisis by telephone before being wheeled into the delivery room.

Because Adrienne and Joan began working out of their homes, both the Hall children and the Levine children were at times clamoring around the drawing boards and typewriters. "We couldn't risk spoiling the artwork or scattering the invoices. It was obvious we would have to do something differently!" Adrienne recalled. All this time her husband had been extremely helpful—she credits him with being a better cook than she is. But once the agency moved to a small office, a housekeeper became a necessity.

Adrienne said that after they'd set up the office, "I think Joan and I went through some of the conflicts, some of the guilt that most women feel when they leave small children to go to work. I worried that I might not be spending enough time with them. Although I'd chosen to give high priority to my life and my identity, I wanted my children to have everything children should have." The children are now grown or nearly so. "We resolved the conflicts along the way. And I think today when we look at our children compared to those of mothers who were home all the time, there aren't any discernible differences. Perhaps ours have gained a greater sense of independence. I've been lucky in every way," she concluded, "and without an unusually supportive husband I never could have managed."

In *Passages* Gail Sheehy notes that it is a rare woman who can integrate marriage, careers and motherhood in her twenties "and it's about time some of us who have tried said so," she states, because, as she explains, "the personal integration necessary as a ballast simply hasn't had a chance to develop."[4] Besides the ballast, it's necessary to have an understanding husband, as much help as one can get and babies who quickly learn to sleep all night.

Those who try covering all three corners come up with some unique solutions to everyday problems. Even so, it's a difficult game and they don't score on every possible point.

Entrepreneur Marge Kinney helped her husband start a company and worked in the office with him during the years their four sons were born. She kept the first baby in a desk drawer she'd converted into a crib. "I'm a great believer in breast feeding, so I wanted him with me all the time," she explained. "Whenever the phone rang, I'd pick him up and hold him to make sure he wouldn't cry. Our clients might not have liked that." Several years ago, when the boys were all well into their teens, she was divorced. Besides wrestling with personal problems, she had to disentangle business interests so that she could have her own marketing firm. Today she has all four boys and a growing company of her own. A much-valued live-in housekeeper assumes responsibilities Marge herself no longer has time for. Also, she and the boys have developed systems of their own to take care of household chores more efficiently. For example, each boy's clothing is color-coded to make laundry-sorting easier. Like several other mothers with children at home, she doesn't feel that she has time for activities other than career and family. "Business and the boys are enough," she said. "Any free time I have I'd rather spend with them, and there isn't much free time."

It's not simply a matter of marriage, career and family requiring superhuman efforts—or even the added maturity of being in one's thirties. Rather, it's that any one of these responsibilities can take more than half of one's energies and waking hours when they are new and unfamiliar or when special problems exist. Trying to *adjust* in all three areas adds up to a near-impossible challenge. Having a new job and a new marriage and babies coming right away can be too much for even the most energetic and well-integrated woman. One or maybe two of the corners of her life should be stable and settled before she can meet the demands of the third. And it's far easier to make the adjustments in a somewhat leisurely sequence. Daphne Bartlett worked for six years in the insurance field while still single, but only made a firm commitment to her career once she was married. She waited another four years before having her first and only child, a daughter, and then stayed at home for only three months before resuming her career. Various other patterns are possible. I know of another woman who married, had a child, then quickly divorced, all while still in college. She then worked for several years, supporting her child and eventually meeting her second husband. When they'd been married for a couple of years, she went to law school.

Babies, whether they're born early or late, change a woman's life, especially if she has a career or is planning one. There seems to be no ideal time for having them. Although modern contraceptive methods make it easier to postpone child-bearing, motherhood can't be postponed indefinitely. There's a lot of anxiety right now among career women about how late still isn't too late to be giving birth. And at meetings of career networks, women who haven't yet had children are asking those who have what it's really like to be a mother and have a career, too.

Looking back at her decision to return to her job, Daphne Bartlett said, "Once you make that transition, once you spend that first day away from the baby but realize that you still get to be with the baby, well, it becomes easier than you thought it would be." But she also put in, "I wish more books and magazines for women would get to the nitty-gritty things so many of us face: How do you hire a sitter? What do you do when the kids get sick?" Others agreed that practical advice was hard to find.

Marcie Carsey was another woman who felt that most of us ought to be better prepared for parenthood. She seems never to have pondered the dilemmas of working vs. career that have plagued so many women. When I asked her if she'd even had a crisis in her life, she replied, "No." I persisted, "Weren't you ever scared or threatened by anything?" She responded thuoghtfully, "I've never been scared about work, no, never. About decisions, no. The one time

I was scared was when I found out that I was pregnant for the first time. This was something I hadn't imagined really happening. I talked it over with Johnny. When a career woman decides to have a baby, she'd better make sure she's married to the right man. She'll have to say, 'Now, dear, if we're going to do babies, there are certain things that have to be taken care of.' We decided to do babies. This meant Johnny and me sharing responsibilities, and it meant having a full-time housekeeper."

These two share parenting to a degree that isn't possible for most other couples. "Johnny spends about half the time at home writing or working on some project of his own. Right now he's at home, working on a new movie. He loves what he's doing, loves being at home and it's terrific!" she said. They now have two children.

It used to be motherhood that women took for granted. So many of the women I talked to had—both those who made early vocational commitments and those who stumbled haltingly into careers later on. Increasingly, though, women make an early career commitment and, even though some of them also marry early, the decision to become a mother is left hanging. Often enough, chance still intervenes and nature makes this decision for us. As for the prophecy that "liberated" women will be bred out of existence in a few generations by not reproducing—it seems unlikely. Career women are also having and raising children.

What of the woman who marries and has children first, fulfilling the nurturing role before embarking on a career? Late emerging has been a familiar pattern in recent years, and it's one we'll keep seeing for some time. For a decade, maybe longer, a woman's family has counted on her for maintaining the home and taking care of myriads of things, large and small. Then, one day, probably after much soul-searching and inner growth, this woman makes a new commitment outside the home.

The challenge is integrating her new role with her old one, which means that priorities have to be shuffled and rearranged. Some things that used to be of crucial importance don't get done. Social events and perhaps school events may have to be missed. Other members of the family must assume new responsibilities and new roles too, and they may resent this at first. But she forges ahead, coping with internal and external conflicts as best she can.

Elinor Guggenheimer, whose career in public service evolved from her volunteer work, became, in 1960, the first woman on the New York State Planning Commission. It had been over two decades since her graduation from Vassar. She then decided to earn a degree in Urban Planning at Pratt Institute, and her career in city and state government continued to develop. More recently she has also been a moderator of radio and television talk shows, a teacher, writer and lecturer.

"Every woman who is married and has children must overcome some obstacles in working full-time," she said. "My husband has been extremely supportive, but there have been times when he had to sit down and talk about how he felt about my involvement in a career. In particular, I think he used to resent my coming home later than he did, and it isn't possible for a woman to continue in a career if her family doesn't adjust to the hours she must keep.

"It's important for a husband to understand that your career is as serious for you as his is for him. It's hard to avoid feeling guilty when your career interferes with plans he makes. Without the right kind of understanding between the two of you, I don't think a career is possible."

Others who'd made late career commitments agreed. It was absolutely essential for a husband to understand.

Mercie Butler, married and the mother of three children, was a full-time homemaker for only a few years. On the other hand, though, she didn't make a commitment to a full-fledged career until her children were nearly grown. When the children were small, her husband taught at Dartmouth, where women couldn't teach or even attend classes, and where there was no job open to her. "Books from the local library were my only escape," she said. "And this was at the time when everybody was saying that women needed something to do after the nest was empty. I wondered what I'd do." She became so depressed that she put on weight. But after the family moved to Southern California, she quickly slimmed down to a size eight and found jobs as a fashion model. She also taught art classes at a community college, worked on paintings of her own and even saw her work displayed in art galleries. "It still wasn't enough," she said. "It wasn't quite me. I didn't think of myself as an artist, and I knew modeling, which was fun, couldn't last forever."

The Butlers were accustomed to Mercie's being away some of the day, but the real adjustment came when she decided that she wanted a career in investing. This entailed six months of intensive study before she took and passed her exams. "It was hard work, but I knew I could do it if I really tried. And I couldn't have managed without my husband." In her new career she has to be at work by seven in the morning and often comes home exhausted, especially on days of heavy trading.

Her priorities, of course, have changed and some of the things she used to do remain undone or aren't done as often these days. "I like to have my house neat and clean with things in place," she said, "but I had to realize that I can't be perfect. My housekeeping standards aren't those my mother had when I was growing up. If she could see the dust! But I have to do what's important to me. Fortunately, my husband and children understand this. I'm a better person now, I think, a better wife and mother." Other members of the family have taken on certain chores, and they manage with an occasional visit from a housekeeper.

Other women, whether they'd emerged from their homes only recently or had had careers first, echoed Mercie's remarks about housekeeping. They couldn't keep up with *House Beautiful* or with the standards their own mothers had laid down; they'd had to put their priorities in different places. "It's not easy if you grew up during the fifties and thought you had to be good at absolutely everything," said Daphne Bartlett. "I used to feel guilty about the dust or about eating meals out. I've stopped worrying. I do the best I can and my daughter is perfectly healthy."

It's the little things—dusting, dishes, laundry, grocery shopping and cooking—that add up to a lot of time. Since so much of the caretaker role is comprised of routine household tasks, hiring a maid or a housekeeper would seem to be an ideal solution. And in some cases it is. But even this isn't always as easy for women to do as it seems.

"If you can afford a maid, why not?" quipped one woman.

"Do you have one?" I asked.

She shook her head. "No. There are enough of us around to see that everything gets done."

Dr. Barbara Fish didn't have household help even when she and her husband were raising his children from an earlier marriage. They were nine and thirteen when they moved in, though, and were able to help with chores. "It didn't occur to me to hire a maid," she said. "Lauretta didn't have one." Dr. Lauretta Bender, her mentor, had been left a widow with three children under the age of four and somehow managed. "By the time Max and I considered hiring somebody, we asked ourselves: did we really want someone around the apartment? We decided that no, our privacy was more important," she explained.

Space—and privacy—are apt to be prime considerations when it comes to hiring household help. But other, less tangible factors create internal conflicts for many women.

Esther Shapiro, who employed a housekeeper-babysitter while she was writing television plays at home, appreciated this assistance even more once she went to work as a network executive. She confessed, however, "I have trouble with this, with hiring someone else to do what frees me to do other things. Some people who worked for me in the past didn't really enjoy what they were doing and I was concerned for them. Sometimes I overpaid them. Also, I feel it's important for my daughters to have a sense of being able to do things for themselves."

Part of the reluctance to hire someone seems to be political. Women who see themselves as lucky to have a career may empathize strongly with other women not so fortunate, and consequently they don't want to play the role of slavemaster. Some career women, too, have a backload of experience in the kitchen and the laundry room that has convinced them that this work is demeaning, and, much as they themselves would rather not do it, they have trouble asking anyone to.

And then there's that part of traditional programming which engrained in us the idea that housework really is womanly and satisfying in itself, that a good wife and mother does it herself and does it well. Dr. Judith Stiehm pointed out that many urban middle-class women somehow equate the preparation and serving of food for their families with giving love and emotional support. Magazine advertising and television commercials still reinforce these notions in women's minds and get the message across to our children as well.

Women I talked to who still had young children at home, however, evinced little if any conflict over employing help, usually a babysitter who also contributed to housekeeping tasks. Most of these women were younger than the others, too, and they had either missed the messages about being Supermom or else ignored them. They'd been busy with their careers since before their marriages and had never been full-time homemakers. Their careers weren't afterthoughts.

THE BEST KIND OF MATE
FOR A SUCCESSFUL WOMAN

Nobody laughed when I asked what characteristics the ideal mate should have. Discussion of the topic evolved quite naturally out of women's descriptions of their home and family lives, explanations of their career patterns or details of the ways they'd been lucky. "I couldn't have done all this without my husband's help and support," so many women said. In a few instances the person mentioned was a partner in a long-term relationship rather than a spouse.

The achievers volunteered that these individuals were variously kind, understanding, compassionate, soft-spoken, good-humored, liberal-minded, flexible. The adjectives I heard most often were "supportive" and "brilliant." What paragons they seemed to be! I began looking at what else, if anything, they might have in common.

Five women were married to professors. What the professor husbands seemed to have in common with the attorneys, businessmen, writers and others was that they were very busy.

Being busy didn't necessarily mean being away a lot. Some men were, but a few had offices at home and more than a few had flexible hours. The professor husbands often left home later in the morning or returned earlier than their wives. The writer husbands wrote at home. Nobody had a house-husband, though a few half jokingly said they wished they did. What these women did have, however, was a partner deeply committed to his own career, involved in it and enjoying it. As Carolyn See remarked,

"A successful woman needs somebody who is happy enough with his own life not to resent what you do with yours. The best kind of mate is somebody who is content enough running his own life that he doesn't want to run yours. If each of you have your own projects, then the relationship doesn't become a project."

Most of the men were, by outside standards, too, successful, although they were often less visible than their wives and in some cases probably earned less money. Most of the women specifically said that their husbands were extremely satisfied with their own working lives and were secure in themselves. Given this much, they were often able to do more than simply "help out" with home and children. They understood their wives' needs outside the home and they assumed some very real responsibility for what went on in the home. Or, at least, they tried. Their hearts were in the right place, and what they felt and what they believed mattered very much to these women.

A number of the men were now married for the second time and, seemingly, had analyzed what had been wrong the first time around. Said one woman, "My husband used to work night and day, never seeing his first wife or his kids. He wants something better this time around."

While, apparently, it worked fine for some couples not to see a lot of each other, there were also couples who were closely involved in every aspect of each other's lives, and this worked beautifully, too. What made it work were the very unusual attitudes these husbands had. Being able to share many things was an added plus.

Marcie Carsey explained that her husband, Johnny, is twenty-three years older than she. "By this time he has weeded out what's important and what isn't," she said.

"Lots of men talk liberation," she went on. "They'll talk up a storm. It's what they do that counts more than what they say. It's the kind of person they really are that counts. Johnny is a man who started out believing—as I did— that deep inside at some inner level, men and women are really very much the same. Men and women both want the same things and fear the same things."

How marvelous, I thought, to be able to determine this much before marrying someone. Did she really know?

"Falling in love is easy, marrying is something you do very seriously," she said. "People think that when you get married you just 'know' it's right. Well, you don't just 'know.' But, besides being in love, I realized there was something about him that would let me—no, not just let me, giving permission isn't enough—*make* me be anything I wanted to be!"

The husband as mentor?

"Yes," she acknowledged. "He's like a Jewish mother, in fact. He'll say to friends he hasn't seen in a long time, 'You wouldn't believe what Marcie's doing!' And then he'll tell them." She went on to describe how she usually shares all the details of her day with him, sometimes taking home pilots for him to read.

Dr. Barbara Fish's career was well under way when she married. "Until then I'd met only men who didn't make me happy, and through the help of my own analysis I discovered that the only consistent part of this pattern was me," she explained.

"Max didn't fit the stereotype," she went on. "He wasn't athletic, didn't care for dancing, but I could see that he appreciated me for being myself. I could be competitive, aggressive, bright, whatever I am. I could holler or be furious and he wouldn't fall down dead. I could finally put together all of me and feel perfectly safe. And if he hadn't liked how important my career was to me, he wouldn't have hung around. . . ." Although not quite a mentor, he has encouraged her and has been involved with her career at various stages.

During the years she worked at home as a writer, Esther Shapiro collaborated on many projects with her husband, Richard. They would work as long as eighteen hours a day together, something few other couples would dare try. When I asked her what sort of person he was, she responded that he was "witty, quiet, understanding, non-judgmental, a brilliant writer, a writer who handles conflicts through writing, the quintessential writing personality." Not only that, she went on to say, "He really believes, and he once said to me, 'Your liberation isn't really my gift to you. It's your due as a human being.' And I think it takes that kind of relationship for a woman to pursue her own fulfillment. The best mates are people who first know who they are, as Richard does. Then it's ideal if the person you choose sees you the way you yourself want to be seen and if he helps you achieve whatever fantasies you have for yourself. I've been very lucky."

But the mate as mentor or as collaborator can be less than ideal for some women. Not every relationship thrives on so much togetherness. Many women, in fact, warned strongly against mixing love and work. One told this story: "For a while I lived with a man with whom I was also involved in a business relationship. The first two years progressed very much along egalitarian lines, personally and professionally. But he wanted me to need the support he gave me. As I developed professionally, my needs changed and power plays developed. He had a need to dominate, after all, but he was unable to recognize it or to take responsibility for it. He couldn't 'own' these feelings, couldn't admit to having them," she said, adding, "I've come to believe there's often a power dimension with sexuality."

The subject of sex and power needs more exploration, I think. Meanwhile, though, there seemed to be another power dimension that the women themselves were seemingly unaware of even in many otherwise egalitarian relationships. Typically, women told how their husbands had been supportive, helping their careers along in many ways. Then they'd go on to say something like this: "He has no need to be threatened by my accomplishments, because he's far more brilliant than I am." Or "He has a far keener mind; he's much brighter." Whether the men had played a mentoring role or not, whether or not the couple worked in closely related or competitive fields, these women almost invariably described those men as having greater mental or intellectual capacities.

I wasn't surprised to hear this once or twice or three times. I agree that superlatively bright men are more interesting. They keep one's mind alive. And intellectual stimulation at home might well be an asset to a woman with a challenging career. But I hadn't expected nearly *all* of the married achievers, themselves very bright women, to describe their husbands as "brighter," "much brighter" and "far more brilliant."

When I talked to Dr. Judith Stiehm, I found that she had already spotted this trend. In her essay "Invidious Intimacy" she writes that women usually choose husbands who are taller, stronger, better educated and richer than themselves. This much isn't surprising, considering the relative sizes, education and wealth of men and women. But she goes on to say that women who achieve much tend to choose husbands who are brighter than they and who will achieve more. Even after competing rigorously and winning in her professional life, the achieving woman wants to come home to a man she can look up to as her intellectual superior.

"In what is presumably their most absorbing and significant social interaction—that involving their husbands—our society's superior women find themselves in second place," she wrote. This can mean, she explained, that women will undervalue their achievements and, consciously or not, defer to their husbands. The husband's interests will come first.[5]

The women I spoke with didn't see themselves in this position. In many instances, their own careers and interests had been put first. Often, too, their accomplishments exceeded those of their spouses. But surely many women do achieve less because they fear surpassing their husbands or out of the conviction that it would be impossible to do so. And the attitudes beneath the surface here have the potential to affect women's attitudes toward the men they encounter in their careers and, more seriously, the ability of men to perceive women as equals. Surely this is another underlying cause of the waste of many women's talents.

I wondered, were these husbands really brighter? Did they consider themselves more intelligent, or was this something that only their wives believed to be true? It's not hard for women to find men who are stronger, taller, richer and even better educated than themselves, but are enough of them brighter, too? The point is, though, that the wives have a necessity for seeing them this way and for seeing themselves as intellectual runners-up. Here is another trace of the old programming that resists erasure and that may persist for generations to come, because children can't very well be prevented from picking up on it.

While some of the women I interviewed worked in fields very similar to those of the men in their lives, making it possible to share a lot and eliminating the necessity for a drastic role change between home and work, a number of couples had vastly different professional interests. As perfect as it might sound to be able to share everything with a partner, this doesn't seem to be a necessity. The very lack of togetherness, the fact that there is a divergence of outside interests, seems to enhance certain relationships. Adrienne Hall, for example, is married to a land-developer. Mercie Butler's husband is a professor and scholar. Lisa Clewer's fiancé is an international rare-stamp dealer. Another business woman has been dating an airline pilot for some time.

Most of these women, as well as certain others, emphasized that their personalities were diametrically opposed to but complemented by those of the men they loved. "What I need in my life is stability, organization, order," Lisa Clewer said. "George provides all these things and more." Some of these men were also described as more retiring and many of them as more intellectual. These women, most of them involved in endeavors where there was a great deal of pressure and competition, seemed to need a safe harbor to come home to. It was perhaps coincidental, but certainly surprising, that no less than three of the women were now either involved with or married to men they had known as far back as high school. One pair got together in college, another after twenty years and another after an even longer time. And in all three cases the couples' career interests diverged widely, but there were other things to share.

When the careers of a dual-career pair are greatly dissimilar, there may also be the advantage that their accomplishments resist comparison and there's less chance for competitive feelings to emerge. One woman, now divorced, volunteered, "There may be room in a marriage for one competitive partner. There usually isn't room for two and certainly not when the two are competing at the same thing." Two people can be involved in the same thing and not be competitive, but this requires a unique sort of relationship.

Different kinds of relationship, also different kinds and degrees of sharing, can provide the home base a woman needs to make her career successful. An individual woman's needs depend upon her career and her own psyche. But her success also depends greatly upon the psyche of her partner. It's not enough for him to do the dishes or "talk liberation." He must believe in the equality of human beings of both sexes at some very deep level. When he does, he can be supportive, above and beyond power games in the home. And he can recognize that a woman has ability, drive and ego. He can share responsibilities and even spur her onward. Choosing this sort of man is crucial for any woman contemplating a career, as the achievers I talked to agreed.

"There aren't many such men," said Judge Joan Dempsey Klein, who echoed the comments of other women I'd talked to while also saying that her own husband was one of the unusual ones. "When we find them, we should have them cloned!"

X

A Woman in Public Life–
Eleanor Holmes Norton

WHY would any driving career woman want to work extremely long hours, subject herself to public criticism and stand the chance of losing her job every few years? It's not hard to understand the reluctance of women to enter public service or politics, but there are those who care enough about what they believe in to take the risks and the flak. I wanted to understand the thought processes, the attitudes and goals of a woman who had chosen this path, and in doing so, I hoped to discover something that other women who might want to follow in her footsteps could understand and identify with.

"Was it my goal to become the chair of the Equal Employment Opportunity Commission?" mused Eleanor Holmes Norton. "No. Although all my life seems to have been leading toward this. I can look back at when I was at Antioch and first made a commitment to the principle of justice through law. Or when I learned to practice law as a civil libertarian. Or when I went to the New York Commission on Human Rights, where I learned to administer law. And now I'm at EEOC. But this wasn't my goal. I just regard it as a kind of organic process. I believe that we are always in formation. I would say that I'm essentially an existentialist. The meaning of life is in the struggle. This keeps me from understanding life in terms of a static concept like success. Today's success is tomorrow's failure.

"I think we should all have goals. If it works, fine. For some people it may work better than for others. And yet this can be a very mechanical approach to life. This formula would not have worked for me," she said. "I believe life has to do with becoming rather than with having become."

It was her lunch hour, and we were talking long-distance. Twenty years before, though, our paths had crossed when we were both Antioch co-op students at *Parents' Magazine.* Like other cooperative employers, the magazine kept a full-time job open on a year-round basis to Antiochians. When one student left after a few weeks or months to return to classes in Ohio, another would arrive to assume the same position. Sometimes there'd be a few days when students would overlap at a job; the outgoing one would train the incoming one. We'd met during that brief overlap. As Eleanor was phasing out of the job, I was phasing in. It was she who showed me around and briefed me on magazine-publishing protocol as well as explaining my job duties. I remember her as very bright, conscientious, and able to use words in a way that was precise and often witty and entertaining. Her journalistic aspirations had already begun to dwindle, though, and she now saw law rather than writing as her best means of contributing to needed social change.

It was like her, I thought as we spoke on the phone— also like an Antiochian—to be questioning my questions.

One reason why specific goals or five-year plans haven't been necessary in her career is, as she said, "I may have had certain built-in advantages." She explained, "I'm a first child in a family of three daughters. From the time I was very young, I believed that life is the pursuit of excellence. That probably caused the formation of an ego and a super-ego that accounts for being striving and ambitious. People like me may not need to operate with a five-year plan as much as those whose circumstances make their life patterns different."

The advantages she perceived were, however, mingled with some clear-cut disadvantages. A black girl growing up in Washington, D.C., she attended segregated schools. Department stores in the city granted charge accounts to black customers but wouldn't let them use the restrooms.

Seats on the city buses were the only thing blacks and whites were allowed to share.

She was the daughter of middle-class parents who took considerable pains to see that she didn't grow up feeling inferior to whites. Her mother was a teacher, and her father, who worked in civil service for the District of Columbia, took law courses at night. From them she developed an early awareness of civil-rights issues. "I had a finely honed social consciousness at a very young age," she said.

While she was in high school, she'd thought of becoming a teacher, then found that she liked to express ideas in writing. Attracted to Antioch College by its liberal reputation and its work-study program, she enrolled there in 1955. As a first-year student, she considered becoming a scientist. Shifting career interests isn't unusual for Antioch students, who work in several different fields before having to choose a major. By her second year she knew she wanted to become a lawyer.

"The civil-rights movement was then taking off, and Martin Luther King, Jr., had emerged. The posture of the movement was oriented toward seeking justice through law," she recalled. "My own strengths seemed to lie in analysis and advocacy. These were brought out by the Antioch educational experience. I didn't know if I could be a fine attorney, but these are abilities that are associated with the law."

Teachers at Antioch have often been mentors to students, I knew. Had she had a mentor?

She reeled off the names of professors and administrators, all of whom would be familiar to anyone at Antioch during the late fifties. Then she stopped herself. "I'm reluctant to mention specific individuals. Education there was so intimate that I have a warm feeling about any number of my professors and others I knew there. There was a very strong commitment to developing a student's intellectual capacities."

Free speech was much discussed at Antioch in those days, even in classes not devoted to political issues and outside the classroom as well. The continuing thread in Eleanor Holmes Norton's career has been her profound devotion to the right to freedom of speech as provided by the First Amendment. As she stated in another interview,

"I'm in love with the First Amendment because I think it's such a beautiful, flowing mechanism. Most of my studying was in history, and I've studied with some great people. All were impressed with the importance of the First Amendment in promoting almost every social change, at least in the twentieth century. There's the labor movement, the women's movement, and the civil-rights movement—all these began with protest. When you think about it, you just have to cherish the First Amendment."[1]

After graduation from Yale Law School and the traditional apprenticeship as a legal clerk for a judge, she became a lawyer for the American Civil Liberties Union. There, her belief in free expression was put to the test on several occasions.

The first time was in 1966. The National States Rights Party (NSRP), an avowedly white-supremacist group, had held a rally in Princess Anne, Maryland, where derogatory remarks about blacks and other minorities were made in "caustic language." Violence had not erupted, but authorities feared it might if the party met again. An injunction barring the party from holding another rally in the county during the next ten days was upheld by the Maryland courts. Taking the position that the injunction was unconstitutional, Eleanor argued the case before the Supreme Court and won.

In 1968 the city of New York denied George Wallace permission to speak at Shea Stadium on the grounds that his presence was a threat to civil order. Wallace took his case to the ACLU. "We ought to assign him Eleanor," the ACLU director joked. As it turned out, she wanted the case because the First Amendment was again at stake. Again she won.

When I asked her how she had felt defending the NSRP and George Wallace, she said, "Like a lawyer. Yes, like a civil-liberties lawyer. I felt that I had a perfect—a virtually unmatched—opportunity to make the point of why the First Amendment is so important. This was during the height of the civil-rights movement, you'll remember, when so many people were bewildered by the outspoken militance of some blacks such as Stokely Carmichael, Rap Brown and others. Many Americans would have shut them up in an instant. I could defend those who were my comrades without ever bringing home the point of the First

Amendment. I could bring it home best by defending people whose ideas I abhor, the NSRP or George Wallace."

She went on to explain, "Blacks were enormously receptive to this. When I'd apear to speak, I'd be introduced as the sister who defended George Wallace. They'd say, 'It shows that George Wallace needs bright black women to get him out of trouble!' And whites who were either lost in racism or bewildered by the social changes became more thoughtful about what was going on in the world around them."

She also prepared the brief for the defense of a Klansman who had been convicted of criminal syndicalism—advocating overthrow of the government by violence. The Klansman had invited newscasters, then explained that the Klan planned to march to Washington and several surrounding states in order to make its views known to the President and to Congress. Since criminal-syndicalism laws had previously been invoked mostly against left-wing activists and protesters, she felt that winning would ultimately benefit them as well. Underlying this reasoning is the belief that all individuals, regardless of their ideas, must be allowed free expression.

There were also opportunities to help or represent persons whose ideas she admired, as in the Muhammad Ali case. She helped draw up the brief for Julian Bond's defense after the Georgia House of Representatives voted to unseat him because he had spoken out against the Vietnam war and the draft. Bond was a friend with whom she'd worked in the early days of the Student Nonviolent Coordinating Committee (SNCC).

She refused to believe at first that New York Mayor Lindsay was considering her for the job of Commissioner of Human Rights. She had opposed the mayor on the Wallace issue. Also, as she once said, "I never thought of myself as a person on the inside of government." She had always worked for the people rather than for the bureaucracy, and although she was becoming increasingly visible, her career was developing out of her own system of values and not according to any grand master-plan. Deciding, though, that this position represented another opportunity to work for the people, she accepted.

Taking the job in April of 1970, she became the highest-ranking (and the highest-paid) woman in the Lindsay administration. Just three months later she and her husband, lawyer Edward Norton, became parents of their first child, Katherine. Their son, John, was born twenty months later. Each time she took a four-week leave of absence, then resumed her official duties.

During her seven years in city government Eleanor Holmes Norton worked for equality in housing, jobs and services, making it clear from the very beginning that she would combat discrimination against women as well as against racial, national and religious groups. She obtained maternity benefits for women in various jobs. Also, she forced the fashionable "21" Club to serve women and ordered the Biltmore Hotel to change the name of its Men's Bar. Horrified to find that almost no members of minorities worked as teachers or administrators in the New York City schools, she investigated recruitment and hiring practices, then demanded immediate change. Subsequently she offered a census of all city employees to uncover discrimination in hiring. Another of the many projects she was involved in during that time was the Neighborhood Stability Program, which effectively prevented white flight from neighborhoods where blacks were moving in.

With a change in city administration, both blacks and women's groups, including Women's Forum, supported her reappointment, and the new mayor, Abraham Beame, announced that she would continue in her post.

All along she has remained deeply committed to the concerns of both women and blacks without allowing either group to diminish her devotion to the other, although she perceives differences in their problems. In 1973 she helped found the Black Feminist Organization, and in a speech she made shortly afterward, she emphasized that the problems of black women have not yet been understood. She concluded this speech with the words, "No one writes about black women—what's in their heads, what's in their hearts."

When President Carter appointed her to head the Equal Employment Opportunity Commission in 1977, she made plans at once to increaes its efficiency and to improve its effectiveness as a policy-making arm of the federal government. Charged with enforcing Title VII, the job-rights clause of the 1964 Civil Rights Act, the commission had had seven directors in twelve years. "EEOC had lost

power, and an enormous backlog of cases had built up,"
she explained. It had been taking two years or longer to
resolve complaints, no less than eighteen separate government agencies were attempting to fight discrimination practices through some forty laws and regulations under two
different sets of guidelines. The challenge she faced was
enormous.

Her first day in office she started working on uniform
guidelines. The President has since strengthened the commission. It now sets standards for other agencies to halt
discrimination in both public and private employment.
Anti-discrimination functions and authority previously
spread out among several government agencies have been
consolidated under EEOC. Age discrimination has been
brought under its jurisdiction, as have equal-pay provi-
sions formerly administered by the Department of Labor.
The federal work force of 2.8 million people has also been
brought under EEOC authority, and Eleanor Holmes Norton has the President's assurance that the commission will
be reviewed again in 1981 to see if there are any ways it
can be made even more effective.

In what she calls an "extensive overhaul" of the agency's
organization and procedures, she has also stepped up its
efficiency impressively. Under the new system now being
put into effect, when a complaint is filed, staff members
immediately collect data that can be used by lawyers and
that determine if EEOC has jurisdiction. Thirty days later
a hearing is held, and a settlement may even be possible
at that time. The backlog of old cases has already been
considerably reduced. New procedures, too, make it possible to handle more complaints at one time instead of individually. Also, EEOC has begun monitoring employers
and stands ready to file class-action suits even before individual complaints come in. "We've developed strategies
against systemic discrimination," she said. "We're now able
to help far larger numbers of people than before."

WHY THERE AREN'T MORE WOMEN
IN GOVERNMENT

There's a lingering belief that woman's place is in the
home—not in the House, the Senate, the judiciary or in

top-level government appointments, and certainly not in the White House.

Queen Victoria once remarked, "We women are not made for governing." Nevertheless, she ruled England for sixty-four years.

Cleopatra, Isabella of Spain, Elizabeth I and Victoria of England, Golda Meir, Indira Gandhi, Margaret Thatcher —a few women have wielded great political power, though none in the United States, at least not visibly. Historically, people have more readily placed their trust in one woman, *singular*, who could be considered different from the rest of her sex. Women, *plural*, and women as a group have been greatly mistrusted. Jeanette Rankin, the first woman elected to the United States Congress, took her seat in 1917, two years before the Nineteenth Amendment granted women the right to vote. And yet during the next half-century and longer, most women who advanced to policy-making positions in government did so as the widows of politicians who'd paved the way for them. The few who made it on their own somehow managed to gain the acceptance of bourbon-and-branchwater circles and old-boy networks. These women had to develop an image that made them seem "not like other women" in order to elicit trust and respect.

We're hearing that there's been progress. True enough, whole legions of women have descended upon Washington and certain state capitols to do somewhat more than transcribe and process the ideas of men. And, significantly, there are a few women in government who actually can be said to represent the interests of women.

But, considering that women make up over half the voting public, we are not well represented in places where important decisions are made. As of the 1978 elections, there were fewer women about to take seats in Congress than there had been sixteen years ago. There are only two women governors and only six women lieutenant-governors. No woman has ever been appointed to the Supreme Court and only five have ever been members of the President's Cabinet, two during the current administration. As of 1978, women held only 9 percent of the seats in state legislatures, 2 percent of state judgeships, 3 percent of county commission offices and 8 percent of mayoral and local council offices.[2]

No woman has even come close to being President. Yet a 1976 poll showed that 73 percent of voters would cast their ballots for a woman if they liked the candidate.[3] First, though, the voting public would have to know the candidate.

Getting the votes is only the last in a series of necessary steps to public office. A newspaper cartoon showed two women discussing an election. "My candidate lost by several million!" one announces. "Votes?" asks the other. "No! Dollars!" to which the second replies, "Blitzed by TV!"

To get elected, it is first necessary to make contacts and gain visibility in order to raise the money for a winning campaign. It's a double bind. A candidate needs visibility initially in order to get backing for more visibility. Many qualified women candidates haven't made deep enough inroads into the labyrinth of male political networks to raise the kind of money needed for an all-out media blitz. Some have had to run for office twice, the first time to become known to voters and the second time to win.

Also, party machinery has encouraged women to run mainly in those races where the party anticipates chalking up a loss. According to former New York Congresswoman Bella Abzug, "Most women who do get backing are running in districts that the party feels are impossible to win. If the race begins to look winnable, prominent male politicians move right in."[4] This is what happened when Massachusetts State Representative Elaine Noble ran for the Democratic nomination for the Senate. As Edward Brooke began to appear less likely to win, three male Democrats were suddenly challenging her. She lost.

Would-be women politicians have been blamed for lack of game-playing savvy and fund-raising ability. Also, women's action groups have been accused of spending too much time confronting issues instead of maneuvering strategically to gain necessary support. Undeniably, women need to be better organized than they've been so far. Strictly women's issues, however, do not often garner large political donations because they aren't seen as constituting a winning platform by the people who make such donations. And women as a group don't have the financial resources to make large enough donations. Where women have had big money behind them, not only money from women's groups but from other interest groups as well, they've been able to campaign aggressively.

Political visibility is sometimes attained gradually. Winning local offices has traditionally been a solid steppingstone to state and national elections. Connecticut Governor Ella Grasso, the first woman to become governor of any state without having a husband precede her in office, is encouraged by the number of women winning small races and predicts that numbers of them will progress from there to higher office. But there are differences of opinion. Susan Hone, Vice-Mayor of Berkeley and president of the California Elected Women's Association for Education and Research (CEWAER), is not optimistic about the future of local officeholders. One reason is that local officials now have a harder time than ever satisfying their constituents. "What was once a breeding ground for a political career is now a graveyard," she said recently. New networks of women in politics such as CEWAER are urging committed women not to make the mistake of starting too small.[5]

Women candidates must also tolerate a kind of intrusion into their private lives to which male candidates would never be subjected. Voters still want to be reassured that their husbands and children are not being neglected. When asked how she managed being both a mother and a politician, Colorado Congresswoman Pat Schroeder replied, "God gave me a brain and a uterus and I intend to use them both."[6] Women who eventually do go to Washington or to their state capitols may be forced to uproot their families or spend a great deal of time away from them. Pat Schroeder's husband and children made the move from Colorado to Washington. Former California Congresswoman Yvonne Burke maintained two homes, one in Washington and one in Los Angeles. The Burkes commuted cross-country on alternate weekends. And women appointed to key governmental positions face the same personal hurdles if not the same public inquiries into how they manage to cope.

On the surface, it may look as if public service through appointment rather than election is a smoother route for women. In his first term, California Governor Edmund G. Brown, Jr., appointed women to over 30 percent of high-level posts, but many states still have very few, if any, women in upper-echelon appointments.[7]

On the national level, women have fared better during the Carter administration than before, but not as well as they might have. Carter's campaign organization collected women's résumés by the thousands, thus defying the myth that qualified women are hard to find. When the President began making appointments, however, it soon became apparent that he was tapping the old-boy network, asking the advice of men he knew well. And the only names these men suggested were those of other men.

Women sprang to collective action, impressively but too late. The National Women's Political Caucus organized the Coalition for Women's Appointments, which met personally with President Carter and with members of his administration. Urging that more women be appointed, they offered a list of specific names. The Coalition did not, however, have enough staff members to work closely with every department. Some were more responsive than others, with the Department of Commerce under Juanita Kreps ranking highest: thirty-six women in key-level jobs. Agriculture followed, then Housing and Urban Development.

Many women feel that more presidential intervention is needed if women are to take their places in such bastions of male power as the Department of Defense and the Department of the Interior, but it may take another administration—and a very different sort of administration—to achieve this. Although heartened by a few significant appointments such as those of Juanita Kreps, Patricia Harris as Secretary of HEW, Eleanor Holmes Norton at EEOC and Nancy Teeters as the first woman governor of the Federal Reserve Board, Frances "Sissy" Farenthold points out that women are still discouraged by the lack of commitment toward women and women's issues at the presidential level. What gains women have made, she goes on to say, have been in response to pressure rather than out of commitment. And that pressure has been applied repeatedly.

The parallels between industry and government are strikingly clear. Women have captured a good number of mid-level jobs; about a third of the mid-echelon White House staffers are women. There is clearly a new breed of woman in Washington, as there is in the corporate world and elsewhere, but the victory has been "more in numbers than in power," as Sissy Farenthold puts it. "The doors are open, at least." There's a chance that more of these women will advance to higher posts as they gain experience, but there's no guarantee that they will be permitted to do so. The fact that so few women now hold key policy-making positions when there are already many qualified for these posts is discouraging.

What are the new women in politics and public service like and what does it take to join them? An article in *The New York Times Magazine* described the typical "New Wave woman" in Washington as being in her thirties and having a track record that includes work in a congressional office and active participation in a few political campaigns. Her educational credentials usually include a law degree, most often from an Ivy League school, or else a doctorate in economics or in one of the physical sciences. "In short, this New Wave woman is highly qualified, probably more qualified than her male counterparts," the article stated.[8]

The law degree has long been considered a prerequisite for a public career, and a number of women have found it a kind of passport to this male-dominated territory. Chicago attorney Jewel Lafontant, who held three appointments under President Nixon and was finally the Deputy Solicitor General of the United States, said that as a young black woman she saw law as the best way to effect social change and that she still thought it an effective way for females to gain respect and trust.

I asked several other women with political experience what background they thought best for a young woman aspiring to a career in politics or public service. Sissy Farenthold responded to my question by saying that "In electoral politics we are so tradition-bound that a law degree is helpful," but she went on to point out that graduate work in public administration can also be valuable for women who seek other kinds of public careers.

Former Commissioner of the New York City Department of Consumer Affairs Elinor Guggenheimer said that "Many public jobs depend on legal knowledge," adding, "Public life offers intermittent employment, so it's absolutely necessary to have a profession to fall back on." However, her own background as a volunteer in support of day care for children demonstrates another viable route. As she said, "It was impossible to remain interested in the children we served only for the eight or ten hours a day that they were in our centers." Consequently, she became involved in housing and social-welfare issues as well. Although holding volunteer administrative posts may seem less suited to the goals of many women today, such positions can yield the experience, contacts and visibility essential for a career in public life.

Yvonne Burke was another of those who mentioned the usefulness of a law degree. She added significantly, though, that "A career in public service, especially in politics, is for the serious-minded and not for the faint of heart or spirit."

There always exists the danger that too many women will go into law, a field that is already overcrowded. Eleanor Holmes Norton said, "I think it would be a great mistake to look at any particular occupation as the key to power in society. Men haven't gained their power just by becoming lawyers. We're seeing more women in law school now and we do need more women lawyers, but we're not seeing the same attraction to other fields that are also very important."

A firm base in business or industry or the academic world can also serve as a springboard to public life. Most of the female names appearing on lists of suggested government appointees are the same names that appear on the lists of possible corporate board members. There are many routes open to women, but no sure and direct ones.

Although the role models we have now will surely motivate more women to aspire to public lives, it would be overly optimistic to assume that women will be able to compete for public careers on an equal basis with men for some time to come.

XI

Climbing the Corporate
Ladder and Loving It–
Marcia Carsey

FOR a long time women simply went to business, handling the plethora of paperwork and routine details which freed men to do the more important and more creative work. Men made the decisions, and they made the real money, too. Business just wasn't considered appropriate for women, even those who were career-minded. Today, though, more and more women want to be in business as officers and executives. Some industries welcome them more than others, and there are still numerous problems, but women are discovering what men have known all along, that the greatest enjoyment is where the greatest challenges and the most important decisions are: at the top. Now that women know, business will never be quite the same.

"I love television," said Marcia (Marcie) Carsey, senior vice-president for comedy and variety programs at ABC Entertainment. "I love to watch it as well as work with it. I want to make it as good as it can be. I see my job as bringing certain standards to television and seeing that it gets better."

Television isn't a typical industry by any means, although it is certainly one that affects great numbers of people. There's fun, but there's also a swift pace and considerable pressure, and nothing here is very direct. Arriving for the first time at the ground floor of ABC's futuristic Century City headquarters in Los Angeles, I couldn't find an entrance. I learned that to get in, one must take the escalator two levels down, then an elevator five floors up. ABC's congenial public-relations man had arranged the interviews —after carefully screening my credentials. When I told him I had written books that were feminist-oriented, he replied, "You couldn't exactly call Marcie a feminist. She's not anybody's anything. She defies categorization or labeling. She is, well, very much herself."

Somehow I expected to meet someone brash or formidable. Instead, here was Marcie Carsey, firmly shaking my hand, making me comfortable, chatting easily and warmly, asking about my book, sitting cross-legged in her chair, sometimes bouncing out of it to make her point clearer. A recent magazine piece had made her sound "like a hayseed," she said. A hayseed she's not. A cheerleader maybe. As she fiddles with the dials of the television set in her office, there's the instant impression that here is someone who has just been turned loose with a favorite toy and who may possibly have to be dragged away from it in order to eat or sleep. But she exudes calm competence and even fearlessness as well as exuberance and enthusiasm. She knows what she's doing, and knows, too, that a complex array of concerns can best be brought together in an easy, relaxed atmosphere.

In many ways she's very like the new breed of woman executive we've been reading about recently. She's in her early thirties, happily married with two young children. She grew up assuming that she'd always work. "Working never scared me. Working hard never scared me," Marcie said. And quite early she acquired an immunity to notions that women couldn't or shouldn't do certain things. "I grew up believing that men and women aren't all that much different." She laughed, then said seriously, "What counts is what you can do as an individual. I've always believed that. My parents never gave me the impression that there were certain things I shouldn't try."

Growing up in New England, she let herself dream of becoming an actress and she also found that she enjoyed writing. Majoring in English at the University of New Hampshire, she also appeared in summer stock productions. Her early interests were fortuitous, as it turned out, but she didn't focus on a career in television until after finishing college. "A girlfriend called me from New York and asked me to join her there. Her father had agreed to put us up in a hotel for a brief stay. We agreed that this was a perfect chance to find ourselves apartments and jobs," she said. It's not like her to hesitate.

She went to work as a tour guide at NBC, although there were other jobs that offered more pay. "Find out where you want to be—then take any job where you'll learn more. That's my advice," she said. Where she really wanted to be was at the *Tonight Show* with Johnny Carson, so she found a job there answering fan mail, among other things. "I knew then that I'd never find anything else that could excite me as much as television did," she said. She worked her way up to production assistant and also met the man who would eventually become her husband, who was then the producer of the show. "With my husband, it was 'like' at first sight," she said, and her eyes lit up as they do whenever she mentions him. "I admired and respected him. From the start I knew that he was a very unusual person. But he was older and he always went out with gorgeous women, ones with great legs. . . ."

They began dating and she switched jobs to become a program supervisor for an advertising agency. This new position gave her the chance to work closely with television networks, studying shows in development and recommending certain ones to prospective sponsors.

After about a year John Carsey had an offer to write for *Laugh-In*, which was produced in California. "He really wanted to move to the West Coast, although it meant a tremendous cut in pay. And I wanted to come along," she said. "At that point we had to talk about what to do and decided to get married before leaving. A quick decision, but I couldn't have been more right," she said. For her wedding she wore a borrowed dress, and the ring was "the quickest thing we could find."

There was never even the faintest suggestion that she leave her career to become a full-time homemaker, "not for one minute," she said.

In Los Angeles she was first involved in making commercials, next she became a story editor at Tomorrow Entertainment, and then she decided that ABC was where she most wanted to be. "ABC had—and has—the reputation of being the gutsiest network, the one eager to try new things," she said. "I like being where the action is. In the thick of things." She soon found herself in the thick of things as a program executive.

Promotions came quickly. In less than two years she was vice-president in charge of comedy and variety development, and two years later she became senior vice-president. Some of the shows she's been deeply involved with are *Soap, Barney Miller* and *Mork and Mindy.* "I loved *Soap* from the start, but so did ABC. The difficulties we encountered were with the outside world, with people who'd never seen the show. The network was behind it all the way," she explained.

Program executives—whose jobs, she says, provide rigorous training—now report to her. "You throw somebody in and let them learn the tanglements and complexities—how to coordinate with the press department, with business affairs, standards and practices, the legal department, with every department. This person has to connect with all these areas and iron everything out. He or she is on the line, responsible for that half-hour getting on the air. We tell new program executives that it's going to take a couple of months before they start to feel competent. We tell them, 'Give yourself two months to be miserable!' But they know they can come to me or someone else here and say, 'What's going on here? How do I handle it?' It's okay to be confused at first," she said.

I asked about those times it didn't work out. How did she feel about firing people? "I take forever *hiring* people," she began. "It isn't good to take somebody off a project, so we try to arrange things so we never have to. We hire program executives who have good relationships with the producers. We pair off people who've worked together before. Everybody cares about what they're doing and wants to do their best. And then—if there's a mistake, it's simply *human error.* You just take the person aside and say, 'Hey, look at what just happened,' and that person will say, 'Yeah, I really messed that up.' You make sure the person knows it's important and will take steps to see that it doesn't happen again. But you know it's not a bad person you're dealing with, just a person doing a terrific job who just happened to make a mistake." She went on, "The atmosphere here has to be very relaxed and open and —what else?—simple. That's the only way creativity can flourish, I think. At some jobs I've had to explain that the minute you put lids on people and try to suppress them, or when you resort to petty office games or cadginess, well, creativity doesn't thrive. In this sort of atmosphere we have here, there's warmth and supportiveness in all directions."

I asked her if she'd ever sensed competition from men or women. "I don't see much difference between being a man and being a woman as far as work is concerned. Certainly not here. I've never been in a one-to-one competition with a man or a woman for a job. My jobs were just a natural progression," she said.

ABC Entertainment has not just one but three top-level women. Besides Marcie there's Esther Shapiro, mentioned in previous chapters, and Pam Dixon, senior vice-president for talent. "Pam and I work in some overlapping areas, and if either one of us got territorial about it, the creative process would be destroyed. We all work well together," Marcie explained.

So many things happening all at once, so many decisions to be made—the pressures of television are very intense. I asked her about how she handled the decisions and the pressures. "I make hard decisions awfully fast sometimes," she said. "You may not be one hundred percent sure, but you're pretty sure and you have to decide. So you do."

She went on, "I once described this job as being like balancing plates on sticks—you know, like those guys used to do on the Ed Sullivan show. And I can get overloaded sometimes. It's as though every circuit has been going all at once all day long and by six o'clock we'll all of us become pale and we'll look at each other and say, 'Okay, this day is over! Done! Right now!' Because any further decisions would be dead wrong. This isn't anxiety. It's just feeling frazzled. And sometimes I get frazzled. Pressure that's among friends you can survive." She shrugged laughed, then went on. "But there are two kinds of stress, I think. When the basic work situation is positive and people are working well together, I can take as much stress as anybody can dish out. The worst that can happen is that I'll get frazzled. But when the relationships with people are askew, then the pressure is negative. Then stress really gets to you."

One of the hardest things about the job she has now,

Marcie acknowledges, is maintaining objectivity. "With new material—and I spend about half my time developing new shows—you can get too close to it. I mean, you've read eight drafts, you've seen the rough cuts three times and you lose your perspective altogether," she explained. "It happens to the best people in the business, especially with those projects you really love.

"What's terrific is having Johnny as a sounding board at times like this. He loves the whole business, loves what I'm doing and is a terrific comedy writer himself," she said, speaking animatedly. "So I'll discuss a pilot I've been working on with him and I'll come up with a whole new perspective. This way I don't have to erase the whole day when I get home. I can be a network executive here and a network executive at home, too, as well as being a wife and mother. Think of it!" she exclaimed. "Being able to share it all, even the slightest detail. It's such a release—I can't tell you how good it is—to be able to go home and not have to forget about work."

Her typical day might begin, as she described it, with "Johnny feeding Petey at six so I can get another hour and a half of sleep. I always get up a little late, just manage to get dressed and throw some scripts in the car. I get to work around nine, and if I'm lucky, there'll be a breakfast meeting at the Sports Deli downstairs. I like to schedule breakfast meetings, because that way I get to eat and because I try to get the most important work done before noon while I'm still fresh. Anything can happen in the afternoon, more things than anybody can imagine. I usually leave here between six and eight."

But not for dinner with the family. "We don't have dinner. Not in the usual sense," she explained. Their dining room, in fact, has been converted to a playroom—one large expanse of carpet with a thick pad under it and toys everywhere. "When I get home, it's kid time. It's go on the floor and play with Lincoln Logs," she said, gesturing. "Depending on what time it is and what schedule the housekeeper has, maybe Johnny and I can sneak out and get a hamburger a couple of times a week just so we can look at each other and talk—and that's terrific, just being together," she said, quietly now and smiling. Other nights, though, the kids go to bed and out come the scripts.

Rising in the television industry demands not only talent

and hard work, but more commitment than some hopefuls are willing to give it. "People come to TV to make money," she said. "I've been going to pitch meetings for four years now. People put out ideas they think TV uses." She shook her head. "Can't do it that way. It never works. You've got to have passion. We tell them, 'Give us your favorite idea. If you had to stick with television for the next five years of your life, what idea would you want to work on? What idea would you want to work on even if nobody bought it?' And you know something? These are the ideas we buy—people's favorite ideas.

"Regardless of what you do, that same measure of commitment is necessary. The whole notion of putting together an image that you think *they* want doesn't work. Either you're good or you're not. Either you care about what goes on here or you don't. Either you're nice to work with or you're not. Relationships count here. Relationships with people are at least half of what goes on when the competition is this stiff. Forget the superficial things," she said.

HOW WOMEN SUCCEED IN CORPORATIONS

The way women succeed in business is by really trying. I've heard men apologize for being in business, and perhaps men can get by without real commitment and dedication, but I'm convinced that women cannot. The enthusiasm that Marcie Carsey has for television is by no means unique. Other women executives I interviewed in vastly different industries—a public utility, an insurance company and a chemical corporation—all expressed an intense involvement with what they were doing .

The individual backgrounds and the interests of these women varied as greatly as their industries. Their ages represented different generations, too. But they were all where they wanted to be, doing what they wanted to do. Thy relished the complexity, the demands and the responsibility, even thriving on the stress and the pressure.

None of them started out wanting to make it big in business. They got caught up along the way.

Juliette Moran has always thought of herself as a chemist although she began assuming administrative duties early in her career at GAF and eventually rose to become one of two executive vice-presidents and one of the highest-ranking women in any American corporation. "I'm still involved in chemistry," she pointed out during our conversation, mentioning that until a few months earlier she had supervised research and development. "It was reluctantly that I changed my job description on my IRS form from chemist to chemical-company executive," she said, adding that she still reads chemical journals and keeps her membership active in the American Chemical Society.

I had been intrigued by what I heard of Ms. Moran. She is one of very few women to have reached the top level in American industry without family connections. Also, I had heard she was a person with a wide range of interests—books, music, art, theater, good food, bicycling and gardening. It was because of these many things that I wrote to her asking, among other things, what she had to say to women who think they would find business dull.

When we talked about it, she admitted, "I had to laugh at your question. This is a great delusion, this is the horror of what is being said to women, that 'business is dull.' Business is one of the least dull things there is, especially for a person who doesn't have specific professional training. Any generalist—anybody whose mind covers art, books, science, people—couldn't find a place more fascinating. I find myself giving it so much of myself as a human being although I do have outside interests, too. I would be bored to tears if I were in some corner somewhere, doing the same thing over and over, better and better. . . .

"Did I ever think when I was a junior chemist here that one day they'd ask me to run a classical-music station? As part of my work here, I've also written technical treatises, press releases and speeches. I've traveled to foreign countries. I've put together teams of people to do things. I've also been involved in graphics from an aesthetic point of view. You name it, I've done it!"

A technical specialty in the sciences or engineering or math gives women a foot in the door, also enabling them to command higher starting salaries. Studies show, however, that most such technical specialties do not constitute a facile springboard to top management even for men.[1]

Actuarial work in the insurance industry is one notable exception. Through complex mathematical processes, often with the help of computers, actuaries determine what will earn money for an insurance company and what won't. Because their decisions so directly involve profits, actuaries are line rather than staff executives, and many insurance executives have actuarial backgrounds.

Daphne Bartlett was the daughter of an actuary who suggested that she might find work relating to actuarial studies interesting as a summer job. Born in Scotland, she had attended schools in England, then majored in math at Vassar during the fifties when most of her friends were studying English or art or history. Although she has always enjoyed math, she is glad to have had a liberal arts education. "If I'd stayed in England, I'd have probably specialized in math or science and I wouldn't have had the liberal education I got here," she said. "To be an executive, you have to be able to write well, communicate with people at all levels. I'm not sure if I'd have learned to do these things without liberal arts."

Actuarial work suited her better than teaching or dealing with pure mathematics, she realized. "I like problem-solving. I don't like chasing the square root of minus one. I have what I call a 'crossword-puzzle mentality.' I like to get an answer, and the satisfaction is in filling in that last box, in finishing something." Working in the public-relations end of life insurance right after college, she became a student actuary at the John Hancock Life Insurance Company in Boston several years later. Student actuaries may work while studying for exams which they take at their own pace. She married, moved to Los Angeles and continued her career at Occidental Life Insurance Company, but she stayed at home three months when her daughter was born.

"This may be the reverse of the usual pattern, but when I got married, I settled down and began taking my job more seriously," she explained. "I got through what exams I had left a lot faster than I had the first ones. Although I was lucky in that I didn't suffer as much as some women do in their careers, I worked very hard. I'd go home, put the baby to bed, then crack the books. For any woman who has a career, there are sacrifices to be made."

In Daphne's case those sacrifices were rewarded. Today, as vice-president and actuary, she is now the highest-ranking woman in her company and one of the few women officers in the insurance field. Still fascinated by math, she

is pleased that her career has broadened to include involvement with people as well. Also, she feels fortunate to be
working for Occidental, a company known for its innovative management practices.

Grace Fippinger became the first woman officer in the
Bell System, a company of about one million employees,
when she was elected vice-president, secretary and treasurer
of the New York Telephone Company in 1974. She started
as a representative in the business office there after graduation from St. Lawrence University with a degree in English.

"I hadn't planned to stay more than a few years," she
said. "It was an interim job until I decided what I really
wanted to do. There were few role models then and none
at the vice-president level, so I never thought I'd become
one. It was the furthest thing from my mind. I simply did
every job as it came along." She was studying interior
decorating in her spare time and planning to be married,
but a severe personal setback made her aware of the
genuine concern of the people she worked with. "It was a
difficult first job, especially because of the personal strain,
but the attitude of the people around me was so warm and
considerate that I felt a great deal of admiration for a
business which valued employees so highly. It was then
that I decided to stay with the Telephone Company. I soon
received my first promotion, and then the promotions just
kept coming." Although she did obtain her decorator's
license, she said, "My decision to stay with the Bell System
is a decision I haven't regretted for one minute."

Grace plays cards, loves to read, is learning to play golf
and enjoy summer sports at a house on the water which
she keeps in addition to an apartment in New York. Also,
she manages the real estate she has bought over the years.
"I'm very busy," she said, "I have a very full life."

Like Marcie Carsey, the other three businesswomen had
not only chosen their industries well, but had found the
specific company and the specific department which provided the opportunities they sought. Becoming an executive
wasn't so important as being given a chance to do the
things they enjoyed doing, and they did so well that they
were promoted onward and upward.

But besides having enthusiasm for the work itself—the
numbers on the page or the chemicals in the lab—they

also found that they fitted in naturally and easily with co-workers at various levels. Job knowledge was important, but leadership and supervisory ability became even more so as chances for advancement opened up. And these qualifications were noticed by individuals further up the ladder, especially their bosses.

The support and encouragement of one's immediate supervisor is crucial to advancement for both men and women in management. All three of these women found themselves working for bosses whom they described as helpful, whether or not they thought of them actually as mentors. Early in their careers, their bosses provided special guidance which assisted them in launching those careers in earnest, and later on other superiors stood behind their promotions to the top management level. They didn't see themselves as protégés who'd been specially singled out, however; they stressed that these supervisors had aided others, too, and would have helped anyone who demonstrated hard work and potential.

The traditional way women have succeeded in corporations—other than being the boss's daughter, wife, widow and/or being a co-founder—has been to start at the bottom and work hard without great expectations. In 1978 Heidrick and Struggles, Inc., a management consulting firm, investigated 1,050 leading businesses in the United States and found 416 women officers, to whom questionnaires were sent.[2] Of the 235 women who replied, two thirds had started working for their present company in a clerical position. The age breakdown is significant. The clerical workers who had advanced to the top included 84 percent of the women fifty years of age or older, 65 percent of those between forty and forty-nine and only 46 percent of those under forty. A majority reported having had mentors, though not as high a percentage of the male officers also investigated. Women who had mentors made significantly higher salaries than those who did not. And those higher-earning women are more likely to be mentors, too, usually to other women.

The profile of the woman officer is changing. The "typical" woman officer, according to this Heidrick-and-Struggles study, is over fifty years of age, has had some college, is from a low- or lower-middle-income background, works for a non-industrial firm and earns less than $30,000 per year. The younger officers, the study found, are from more prosperous origins, are more likely to be college graduates, more likely to have mentors, and are more supportive of women's issues. Women under forty cited their own "lack of aggressiveness" as the most serious impediment to their advancement, while women who were older cited "discrimination." The researchers theorize that younger women may be more likely to see equal-employment-opportunity programs as effective.

The climate for women in corporations is also changing. When Heidrick and Struggles conducted its 1977 study, only 325 women officers could be found. Just one year later the number had increased by 28 percent. Some women may not easily remember that only a little more than a decade ago job openings were listed in major newspapers according to sex, and women were routinely turned away when applying for management or management-trainee positions. No women were admitted to Harvard Business School until 1963, and the first graduating class to have as many as 5 percent women was in 1973. The figures for other prestigious business schools are similar, although by the fall of 1978 Harvard, Stanford, Wharton and the University of Chicago all had more than 20 percent women while Columbia had 35 percent.[3]

The good news is that there are more opportunities for women in corporations. Fewer need to start at clerical levels and those with real motivation and ability should be far less likely to find themselves stranded outside the promotional hierarchy. Increasingly, the M.B.A. is a woman's passport to better starting positions, and, like the law degree in politics, it is a badge which enables a woman to gain the respect of her male colleagues.

Although the M.B.A. gives a woman an edge in many large organizations, much of management is not "credentialed," and those who can demonstrate personal qualifications still have a chance, too. Women who major in subjects other than business and who can somehow learn about a particular industry will find openings. The job search is crucial here, and it is somewhat more complex than for individuals seeking other types of career. So much depends upon matching one's skills and interests to a particular industry, and then upon finding an organization where one can fit in and begin to move forward.

Catalyst, already mentioned, and other career-search organizations are now working with women and with employers in an effort to match individuals' skills and backgrounds to specific industries.

In business as in politics, though, women's progress must still be seen more as a matter of numbers than of real commitment. Businesses are hiring women but not promoting them. Or they're promoting them and giving them titles rather than the responsibilities or the salaries that are commensurate with those titles. This phenomenon may partially account for the increase in women officers among the major companies studied by Heidrick and Struggles. Although responsibilities were not analyzed in that survey, salaries were. The range was from less than $10,000 to more than $100,000. The majority earned under $30,000, with one fifth earning even less than $20,000. Fewer than a third were earning as much as $40,000. It would be hard to avoid the conclusion that tokenism has played a part in the promotions of women to officer rank.

Money may be a major motivation for men embarking on careers in corporations, but it would be highly unrealistic for very many women to go into business for the same reason at the present time. Of the few women who advance to the level of real power in corporations, fewer still are well compensated. The real motivation has to be something other than money. Those women I interviewed described their work with the same unabashed enthusiasm as women in academia, the professions and even non-profit organizations. They loved what they were doing and felt that it was important.

There need to be more women in business for women to become real participants in the major decisions affecting the country: to help determine what products, services and entertainment are to be produced and how they are to be produced. The decisions of large corporations as well as the decisions of government affect all of us.

XII

A Woman in Higher Education– Judith Stiehm

I'VE heard women who'd been stalemated in professional or business careers express regret that they'd left the academic world, where, they assured me, they'd done well for as long as they'd stayed. They look back with a certain nostalgia, remembering senior male academicians as mild-mannered intellectuals who tried at least to make objective judgments. They may also remember an occasional female professor or administrator who seemed extraordinarily content in her work.

Outsiders to higher education, though they may be products of it, are often ignorant of the rampant sex discrimination found behind ivy-covered walls. Women who've tried to carve out careers for themselves in academia, whether they've succeeded or not, know better. They know that the academic world thwarts the aspirations of many able women. Here, no less than in business or politics, each subject field has its own system of networks and patronage. And without mentors to provide ties to the network, young scholars find many, perhaps all, doors to their specialties closed.

Dr. Judith Stiehm knows well the consequences of women's isolation in universities and colleges. "I never had role models or a mentor or a network along the way," she said. In place of these almost essential ingredients, however, she has drawn on firm determination, an abundance of energy and considerable flexibility. Since her late thirties she has been an associate professor of political science and director of the Program for the Study of Men and Women in Society at the University of Southern California. She is also the author of books, articles and scholarly papers—and attends frequent conferences—on women's issues.

I knew when I first telephoned her at her Santa Monica home that this was a dual-career family, because when I asked to speak with Dr. Stiehm, a young voice answered, "Which one? Mr. or Mrs.?" The voice was that of her third and youngest daughter, and the other Dr. Stiehm is a medical doctor and researcher specializing in pediatric immunology. I learned this later when Judith Stiehm and I were seated in the spacious but informal living room of her two-story house on a quiet street in Santa Monica. "We didn't always live like this," she explained. "In fact, until my husband was thirty-eight and I was thirty-five we lived in two-bedroom apartments.

"But marrying a man who is in training to become a doctor is not a bad idea for a woman who plans to become an academic," she added. "For one thing, there's time. There isn't money right away, but there's potential. You get used to accepting 'deferred gratification'; you know that someday things will get easier. And another thing, a lot of women have a problem when their kids get sick. Well, when you're married to a doctor and the children get sick, they're *his!*" She laughed.

I asked her more about what had made it all work for her, what her motivations were and how she got started.

There wasn't always much money. She managed to earn her Ph.D. while her husband got his medical training and served in the military. There was very little money then. They were moving around the country, babies were coming and she often worked full-time as a teacher while pursuing her studies. All this without a life plan, although she is now a firm believer in women having long-range career goals.

Looking back to her childhood, she said, "My basic ethic was that I should do something well and worthwhile. My mother thought 'everybody should be good for something.'

"Although I was a first-born daughter with two siblings, my father didn't take a major role in my intellectual training. He was an engineer who built highways, a nice man who didn't talk much," she went on. Her mother had been raised in a ranching community where she had cooked for hired hands. "The role of women is somewhat different in a rural milieu. Everybody works, everybody must be competent, everybody learns to fill in where they can. But as a result of having the mother I did, I never learned to cook. She was willing to teach me what I wanted to learn and there was never a time that I wanted to learn. So I was spared the kind of feelings that urban middle-class women have about preparing and serving food. Cooking has never had connotations of emotional satisfaction or giving support for me. It has never been connected with my identity," she explained.

We agreed that this attitude was a decided advantage for a woman with career priorities. She explained, too, that she'd developed a sense of independence at an early age. "I never had the pressure or the bad advice many people get from their parents. I got very little advice, really. I was left to make my own choices. But I was never a loner. I was very social," she told me.

One early choice she made was to attend the large public high school rather than the small, more intimate university school in Madison, Wisconsin, where she grew up. "Most of my friends were going to the university school and at first I decided I'd go there too. At the last minute I changed my mind. I wanted to be where there were new people and a wider range of activities. I wanted new experiences. My parents let me think this through without trying to push me one way or the other," she said.

Although she didn't yet realize it, she was establishing a pattern that was to stay with her. "Whenever choices have presented themselves, I've selected whatever appeared to be an opportunity for branching out, being with new people, doing more things," she said. When it came time to go to college, she decided on Oberlin, where she was offered a scholarship. "I'd wanted to get away for a year and go to college in the East, but when I got to Oberlin, I met all these people from the East who'd thought they were coming West to school. I had a marvelous time there—was in a play, held a class office and did well academically—but I was disappointed to find myself in the same Midwestern intellectual environment I'd left. It's an environment that has roots in the abolitionist tradition. I can appreciate that, plus the fact that Oberlin was the first college to admit women. And yet I felt I could have had that same cultural climate plus much more back in Wisconsin," she explained. So after a year she was again living at home, and attending the University of Wisconsin, where she belonged to radical groups, a sorority and church groups as well as being active in women's intra-mural sports. As she said, "It was like being at several colleges all at once, and this is just what I wanted."

She majored in Far Eastern Studies, another attempt to branch out and broaden herself. She said, "I wanted to learn the most I could about everything, so I chose the thing I knew the least about. I wanted to know more about other kinds of cultures and what it meant to be a part of them."

She didn't know what sort of career this might lead to, but when the CIA offered her a job after college, she turned it down. "We didn't know that much about CIA activities then, but this was definitely not my idea of what I wanted to do." Just before her graduation in 1957, the Dean of Women invited the top fifteen women seniors to her office one by one to talk about future plans. "When it came my turn to see her, she suggested that I go to library school. I thought, 'If she thinks I'm so great, why does she say that?' Afterward I found out she'd suggested library school to all fifteen of us!" Also at graduation time the university held "Women's Day," a statewide event for college women. "We were lectured on how important it was for us to leave the university and go out into the world, where we would take responsibility and do things. I was getting swept up in this. I was ready to run for governor! And then I realized they were talking about joining the PTA. No, I didn't understand the full implications of this at the time. All I knew was—this wasn't for me."

She continued, "So I took what savings I had and did what so many young women from the Midwest or South do. I headed for New York to find adventure." She found it at the Institute for International Education, where she screened Fulbright applicants and helped initiate the first student-exchange program with a country behind the iron curtain, Poland.

Following that first year in New York, she married Richard Stiehm, whom she'd begun dating in college. Actually, they'd known each other since her high-school years when they'd belong to the same church group. Also a native of Madison, he'd lived across the street from her aunt and uncle in the house where her father had grown up.

She felt confident that there wouldn't be any conflicts between marriage and the other things she wanted to do. One reason for this was the sort of individual she knew her husband to be. As she pointed out, "He was the son of a widowed mother with four children. He'd never been catered to and didn't expect to be." Also, she was aware of her own unusual level of energy. "I already knew that I could do not just one thing but several things at the same time," she said. But she still had no long-term career goals. "It was always a question of 'What can I do next that's interesting?' never 'Where am I going in the long run?' " she explained.

The Stiehms spent the first year of their marriage in Madison, where she earned her teaching certificate at the University of Wisconsin. For the next two years they lived in Philadelphia, where she taught in secondary schools and took night classes at Temple University, earning a master's degree in American Government. "I still hadn't mapped out any future career plans," she explained, "but I was already involved in the study of different 'world views.' I'd done that in Far Eastern Studies, now I wanted to have a closer look at our own culture."

She was pregnant with their first daughter the same year she finished her master's. Her husband by now had been drafted, and the week before the baby was due, he was sent to New York and couldn't get back until a few days after the delivery. "I really didn't mind his not being there because, you know, it works both ways. He has never expected me to take care of him and I've been very independent, too.

"Only after I had the baby did I do some serious planning," she admitted, going on to explain, "There were two things to be taken into consideration. One was that I now had a child and the other was that, although we would now be in New York for a little while, we would be moving to a different place every couple of years while Richard was in various stages of training. Since I couldn't build a career in any one place, I decided to continue in school. A Ph.D., I figured, is portable. You can take it anywhere you go."

Haphazard as all this may sound, her academic direction was already decided, built on the foundation of her previous work in Far Eastern Studies and American Government. "You could call it intellectual history or the sociology of knowledge. It comes under different headings," she said. While working for her teaching certificate, she'd taken a course in history of education which was actually much broader, encompassing the history of philosophy as well. "I realized then that what interested me most was the ideas people have and how they can possibly believe them," she said.

At first she thought her interests came under the general heading of philosophy, but when she applied for admission to New York University, philosopher Sidney Hook interviewed her, asking why she wanted to study philosophy. She explained her curiosity about different sets of ideas that are fixed in the minds of people as a result of the culture they live in. "Finally he looked at me and asked, 'But don't you want to know *the truth?*'" It wasn't the absolute truth she was seeking, but rather a better understanding of the truths that men and women live by. As it happened, the political-science department at Columbia University offered a better opportunity for this kind of study, so she enrolled there. Actually, she'd never had a course specifically in political science, although she had studied related subjects.

Her husband was on duty at the hospital for long hours, as many as thirty-six out of forty-eight, which left her time of her own. Also, they were fortunate to be living in a housing project where the neighbors were eager for baby-sitting jobs. But attending Columbia was still an expensive proposition. "Richard was only getting paid a couple of hundred a month in addition to living expenses," she remembered.

She'd read in the Columbia catalogue that graduate students with good academic records would be given student loans, so she applied for one after her first semester. "I went waltzing in asking for money, only to be told, 'We don't give loans to married women!'" This was in the early 1960s, and instead of challenging the system, she explained, "My concern was: 'How do we get what we want out of the system?'" Her husband, then a resident at Columbia Presbyterian Hospital, approached the university loan office. "He went in saying, 'My wife and I are here from the Midwest and too poor to take advantage of the wonderful cultural opportunities New York has to offer without more money.' He got a loan. They were willing to lend him money to go to the theater when they wouldn't lend me any to get a degree."

Time after time, she adapted her plans to take advantage of whatever loopholes she could find, although this usually meant doing several things at once. While she completed the course work for her doctorate at Columbia, her second daughter was born. The family left New York soon after that, but all there remained for her to do was a rather vast amount of reading and, eventually, the writing of her thesis—things that could be done elsewhere. She often carried a heavy teaching load as well as studying and having two children at home. One year at San Francisco State, for example, she was hired as a lecturer. "I was teaching four courses, had two children twenty-two months apart and was studying for the doctoral exams," she recalled. "That sort of schedule was typical, and I think about it now with some disbelief!"

She didn't mind working as only a lecturer at universities until after she'd finished her dissertation and had her degree. Then, upon applying for an opening at the University of Wisconsin, she was told that two men from Harvard were already to be interviewed. "I asked, 'You mean I'm not going to be considered?' and was told that I wouldn't have sufficient visibility in my career." She can laugh now, for she has become extremely visible in her field. But when she first got the message that a woman from Columbia—or from anywhere—was no competition for men from Harvard, she was shocked and dismayed. It wasn't just the prestige of Harvard; it was clearly sex discrimination.

She added, "The fact that I'd done everything I was supposed to do in the same amount of time and that I'd done it just as well, too, should have indicated that I was a better candidate. But no, it was still negative proof. There really is no sure way of proving yourself once and for all if you're a woman. You end up having to prove yourself again and again, every time you compete for something."

She and her husband ultimately moved West, not because of either career but because she had an asthmatic condition. He joined the faculty of UCLA, where she worked as a lecturer for a year. Finally she was hired at the University of Southern California, also in Los Angeles, to direct a special program for gifted high-school students on campus. Several years later she became an associate professor of political science.

USC salaries, especially hers, aren't high, and there's considerable pressure to publish; nevertheless, she conceded, "This is an atmosphere where individuals who are motivated can do what they want to do. There's a certain *laissez-faire.*"

Judith Stiehm has always functioned well in an ambiance of *"laissez-faire,"* without support, structure or advice. Although this has generally worked for her, she acknowledges that there have also been disadvantages. "In college I applied to Yale and other graduate schools. I also applied for a Fulbright. Later I learned there are ways to enhance your chances of winning these things. But I had no advice, no help whatsoever. I was admitted to several fine graduate schools, but I wasn't offered any money. And I had no idea I was being discriminated against, no idea at all that there were quotas for women at that time. Just being admitted was, in fact, doing very well."

When she was a graduate student at Temple and again at Columbia, her academic work was almost entirely self-directed. "At some graduate schools where very few students are admitted," she said, "each one becomes a precious object. Once you're in, you're adopted and cared for. People see you through. Columbia admitted a lot of students and left them on their own. A lot of the women who got their Ph.D.'s in the sixties were at Columbia, and it's fortunate that we were given the chance. Generally, however, it is far better to be adopted because then you have mentors who are part of a larger network. Yet there's another side of this, too. I have colleagues who had superb training, but they still think of their former professors as very exalted individuals they can never compete with. They may have been more thoroughly trained in the con-

ventionally defined subject matter, but they still think
hierarchically; they don't think independently. So I don't
exactly envy them. I didn't have gods who prevented me
from growing up."

The greatest satisfaction in her work now is "in doing
things that otherwise perhaps wouldn't have been done,"
she said. "Especially in doing something for somebody
who might not otherwise have had help. I derive a lot of
satisfaction from helping women students who perhaps
wouldn't be where they are if it weren't for me. There
are men students I like very much, and I have helped them,
too, but somebody else would have picked them up. With
women, you can't be sure what would have happened
otherwise. My effort might mean their winning instead of
losing."

Something else which she feels no one else would have
done, at least from the same point of view, is her book
*Bring Me Men and Women: Mandated Change at the U.S.
Air Force Academy*, soon to be published by the University of California Press. Instead of studying the women,
as others have done, she studied the men. As she explained, "I wanted to know why it is the men were falling
apart, why they are so upset about having women around.
After I wrote my book about non-violence [*Nonviolent
Power: Active and Passive Resistance in America*], it became clear to me that nobody was very interested. Few
men take non-violence seriously and women aren't interested because they're *de facto* pacifists. So I decided that
I wanted to understand those people who believe that
violence is the right way to solve things. Whole govern-
ments are built around this idea. The state is, after all, an
institution which has a monopoly on the use of force, and
keeping women out of the military is, in effect, exclud-
ing women from participating in the real function of the
state."

Her field of inquiry permits the exploration of broad
and varied topics. "This is a field where you make your
contribution late," she explained, "because you don't get
to demonstrate your capacity as a generalist until after
you've tested your way through a specialized field. It's
hard to get anyone to let you start as a generalist."

Most of her publishing has been done in the last few
years, and she has no regrets about only starting now.

"I look at my male colleagues who've spent twenty years collecting empirical data in some very narrow area, and I can see that some of them are growing stale. They don't have the enthusiasm they used to," she went on. "As for me, I've just gotten started and I have maybe forty years left to write. You can keep going in intellectual history until the day you die. You don't even need research funds!"

Like so many other women, she is enthusiastic and optimistic about her own future, but not for the future of women generally. As she also said, "I'm concerned about the waste of women's talents."

FACING THE OBSTACLES IN ACADEMIA

Success for the academician ought to be, as Dr. Stiehm put it, "doing things that otherwise perhaps wouldn't have been done"—discovering something through one's research or someone through one's classes. But for the female scholar today, success may be obtaining tenure or even simply being hired. It can be an enormous hurdle just getting to do what one has spent seven or eight years training for, after surmounting many obstacles to obtain that training.

Education, particularly higher education, has hit on hard times because of predictable but steep downward swing in population growth. With enrollments dropping, the competition for jobs in educational institutions has become fierce indeed. Far more individuals have trained to become teachers and scholars than can ever hope to find positions now. Many of the victims are men, but many more are women.

The academic system is one which permits enormous waste of talent. Without the necessary advice, endorsement and sponsorship, would-be scholars go unnoticed and are set adrift, jobless and embittered. While not all of the academic cast-offs are women, many are, simply because senior academicians are more often men. Although these men may not be avowed chauvinists, they are accustomed to working with other men and have difficulty recognizing that women are serious about their work.

Even under the best of circumstances, women academics

are made aware that their sex is a handicap. Sociologist Dr. Cynthia Fuchs Epstein noticed when she was a graduate student at Columbia in the sixties that able women students were hired as research assistants but were not steered into the better jobs after graduation. "I began to hear at professional meetings how professors asked each other about who their bright young *men* were as if bright young women didn't exist. The women were never asked to think ahead the way their male peers were and managed not to think about it themselves," she wrote in a recent paper. As a result, these bright young women "felt a generalized sense of insecurity which drove a number of them, including me, into therapy to find out what was wrong."[1] Her own analysis, which she undertook as a graduate student and wife and mother, was a process of isolating what she herself could change from what was wrong in society itself.

Like many other women, she started without having clear-cut vocational objectives. "I wanted a career, didn't know what, but I thought I would do some socially useful thing," she said. Although she fully expected to marry, too, she was urged by a practical-minded mother to be able to make her own living "in case things should go wrong," and somehow picked up the message that "things might very well go wrong." Fears as well as rewards may be motivational factors, she realized later. "My goals were all short-range," she wrote recently. "To be a good student. To do a good job for the professor. To pass my oral exams. To get my dissertation written. All seemed like barely passable hurdles beyond which I could scarcely permit a fantasy."

After one abortive semester in law school, she worked as a secretary, an editorial assistant and a publicity writer while attending political science classes at night before finally entering the doctoral program in sociology at Columbia. "Why Columbia? Because it was in the neighborhood," she wrote, looking back. "I didn't know it was one of the best graduate sociology departments in the country, although I did know that the names of the professors were the same as those whose books I had been assigned at college, and so I figured they must be good." She continued in part-time jobs out of the feeling that she should carry her share of the financial responsibility. Her husband was struggling in his own career at the time, and her father, who hadn't been in favor of graduate school for a married daughter, helped out with some tuition money. Her future career began to take shape when she became a research assistant and enjoyed the work immensely. While still a graduate student at Columbia, she was hired as an instructor at Finch College. Only then did she realize that she also wanted to teach.

In Dr. Epstein's case, other factors made up for the lack of goals or plans. She was unique in having had role models and mentors at several crucial stages. The first was a teacher in the New York City schools' program for gifted children where she was enrolled. Later there was a female analyst who was also a teaching professor at Columbia, and a wife and mother as well. Also there were male mentors. During her undergraduate years at Antioch, political scientist Dr. Heinz Eulau stimulated her interest in the analytical methods of the social sciences, encouraging her work along these lines. Later, at Columbia, she had the opportunity to work with Dr. William J. Goode in a study of cross-national, cross-historical approaches to the sociology of families. Another Columbia professor, Dr. Robert Merton, known for his work in role analysis, was instrumental in helping her form the basis of what was to become her specialty: the investigation of women's roles.

She is now professor of sociology at Queens College and a research associate in the Bureau of Applied Social Research at Columbia University. Widely published, she is the author of several books and numerous articles. She has testified before various government committees on discrimination and has traveled all over the world to lecture and participate in conferences on women's issues. When I spoke with her, she was writing a book comparing what happens to women in different political systems and under different ideologies, investigating why women can become doctors and enter other professional fields quite readily in some countries but only with great difficulty in the United States.

Other female academics I've spoken with had matured intellectually, mastered their subject fields and embarked on their research, still without knowing what place, if any, there might be for them in the research-and-teaching establishment. They were bright, over-achieving, did well in school and felt at home there, making an easy transition from student to teacher or researcher. They seemed to have been so engrossed in their work that they hadn't devoted much thought to furthering their careers. Their conditioning, perhaps, had not prepared them to look ahead. Also, it's possible for scholars, male and female, to indulge in solitude to the extent that they ignore certain practical and pragmatic considerations. Few academics today, however, allow themselves this luxury.

Many women, too, were initially led by male colleagues to believe that the research which interested them most was either not valid or else not very important in the larger scheme of things. Not until after they had experienced the consciousness-raising of the sixties or plugged into one of the newer networks of academic women did they realize that they'd underrated themselves or had otherwise been victimized by the very system in which they'd placed their loyalties. Often it was a harsh and dramatic awakening.

"Higher education is a slow learner," said "Sissy" Farenthold, who went from politics to being president of Wells College. The facts and figures bear her out.

The proportion of women in college and university teaching positions is now around 24 percent. Compared to the percentages of women who are lawyers and legislators, this figure doesn't seem shocking. But, placed in the context of over a decade of supposed progress against sex discrimination, it is very low. In 1920, women accounted for about 26 percent of the faculty in colleges and universities, and by 1930 the proportion had risen to 27 percent, where it remained for several decades, dropping to 24 percent in 1960 then to 22 percent in 1970. For the year 1975–76, the proportion had returned to its 1960 level of 24 percent.[2]

A closer look at what women are actually doing in colleges and universities is equally disheartening. As of 1976, only 9.6 percent of full professors and 17.1 percent of associate professors were women. The proportions are about the same as in 1960. Most women are in the lower positions: assistant professors and lecturers.[3] At all levels they earn lower salaries than their male counterparts.[4]

Also, the highest percentage of women are on faculties having the least prestige: 34 percent in junior colleges, but only 17 percent at universities. The percentage of women faculty members at some of the more outstanding universities is 5 percent or even lower.[5]

Women are also effectively excluded from administrative, policy-making positions. According to one study, only 6 percent of all accredited institutions of higher learning have women presidents.[6] As of early 1979, just three women were presidents of large universities.

By now many charges of sex discrimination have been brought against institutions of higher education—more than against any other industry, according to the Association of American Colleges Project on the Status and Education of Women. But funding has never been denied to educational institutions because of this discrimination, and furthermore, there exists the tradition-bound belief that education should somehow be above and beyond the legal system. Judges ruling in discrimination cases have, in several instances, voiced the opinion that the courts should not interfere with hiring practices in institutions of learning.

Women will never come into their own in higher education, however, until there are role models who can point the way for younger academics, helping them set their career targets early, and establishing networks that have an effective power base. College and university women have been forming a veritable maze of overlapping networks in recent years. Some are local and some, rooted in specific subject fields, have a broader geographical base. It's not uncommon for a woman to belong to several networks, perhaps one in her department, another local one devoted to bettering conditions on a university-wide scale and another, perhaps national, composed of women in the same subject field.

To make needed changes, women students are speaking up where women faculty members and administrators are afraid to do so because of jeopardy to their jobs.

"The energy in university networks often comes from the women graduate students," Dr. Stiehm pointed out. "University faculty members who are women are too likely to be over-extended and exhausted." There's strength in the numbers of women students. Almost as many women as men now earn master's degrees, and very shortly women are expected to outnumber men at the undergraduate level.

Meanwhile, however, the lack of women in the upper reaches of academia means that women have not shared in the power that academia exerts upon the society at large. Academic power, while differing from industrial and political power, nevertheless has broad influence in ways that are subtle as well as direct. The popular media are filled with the assumptions and assertions of certain visible and verbal academics. Journalists wishing to prove almost any point can find professors or pop-psych authorities to back them up, and too often a quotation from a Ph.D. passes as fact whether it is or not. Such ideas filter down into conventional wisdom and everyday folklore. Often the public is fed information that is erroneous, and some of the serious errors stem from the strong male bias that has dominated certain academic fields. In psychology, for example, some assumptions about what constitutes male and female behavior have long been accepted as *a priori* and are just now beginning to be challenged.

Dr. Epstein has noted that until recently sociology did not address itself to women as a group to be studied, and that women sociologists have been discouraged from studying women because this is not a subject which will enhance their careers. She does not believe female perspectives in sociology to be necessarily different from male perspectives. "One should not study only women," she warns. "The good social scientist studies either sex in the context of the other."[7] But, she wrote, "It is clear to me that to the extent that the profession's work *has* been *male*-oriented, it has been skewed and therefore wrong; the same would have resulted from work done from a 'female' perspective."[8] Sociology has not yet documented women's 'unseen' roles in politics, for example, nor has it examined the subjugation of women as a factor in the maintenance of power by elite groups. Furthermore, investigations by and about women are not frequently reported in the journals having the most prestige, and studies having to do with women, children or families are still dismissed by males in the field as topics of lesser importance.

Women in other fields are uncovering parallel discrepancies when they have the chance to do so. It's very apparent that knowledge about the world and its people, past and present, has been distorted and even suppressed by scholarship that has been male-dominated. There's exciting work to be done now in many academic fields, and the few women who are doing it know they are fortunate to be where they are. They are dismayed, however, that more women cannot join them. A few will, but many would be well advised to try to make their contributions elsewhere.

XIII

The Professional Life–
Barbara Fish

For generations there have been women who've wanted to become doctors, lawyers, architects and professionals in other fields where the training was long, hard and specific. Until recently only a few managed to squeeze past quota systems and discriminatory practices to attain professional status. Of those who survived and became professionals, fewer still reached a position where they were able to make original contributions to their fields and to challenge existing assumptions.

Not all of women's contributions are in areas that couldn't have been dealt with by men. But women, even while struggling against far greater odds, have been able to do important work that men simply hadn't yet done.

"Why did you choose to study childhood schizophrenia?" I asked Dr. Barbara Fish. A professor of psychiatry at UCLA she is now well known for her twenty-five-year study of this disease, but her recognition was late in coming. Her conception of schizophrenia as a neurobiological disorder met with hostility from the psychiatric community in the 1950s, when notions of castrating mothers and bungled toilet training were more popular as explanations for mental illnesses. But, tracing the development of twenty-four children from birth to early adulthood, she persisted even when there was no grant money or private funding.

Although well aware that women are often willing to

work extremely hard, I wondered why she'd been willing to persevere independently year after year at a task that would normally take a whole team of researchers and a generous budget. How had she coped with the difficulties? What satisfactions had there been along the way?

We were seated on the patio of her suburban house overlooking a green, rolling meadow. When she opened the door moments earlier, I hadn't been sure that this very small and lithe blonde woman in a blue slacks outfit was really the Dr. Fish I'd read about. She seemed far younger than I'd imagined, also far more attractive, casual and relaxed than I somehow thought a psychiatrist had any right to be.

She had offered to meet me at UCLA "if it would help you to see my very cluttered office," but since she was then taking a sabbatical year, she suggested that we might meet at her house instead. The atmosphere there was comfortable and pleasant, with files and papers filling a wide bookshelf near the door to the patio. Outside, too, was a table with more work on it.

She began: "Schizophrenia always intrigued me from the first time I worked on the wards with mental patients. I was fascinated by people who could be so normal, functioning at such a high level one minute and unable to function at all the next. It was the most challenging puzzle in psychiatry for me." Her enthusiasm was apparent in her voice.

"It seemed to me that maybe I could get back to the very beginning to the roots of schizophrenia. Of course, there's much more work to be done. But—it all gets to the heart of what makes people *feel* the way they do, *think* the way they do, *behave* the way they do," she said.

"The real fascination is in the possibility of learning what makes for normal behavior, what are the various biological mechanisms which contribute to individual differences. I've always been interested in people, in what makes them different." As she spoke, she smiled and her eyes flashed.

Here was a woman who entered college before the onset of World War II and who went directly on to medical school. Why, I wondered, had she decided to become a doctor at a time when very few women wanted careers and almost none gained admission to medical schools?

What got her started? I asked her about her original career decision.

"I always wanted to be a doctor," she said. Her father, she explained, was a mechanical engineer. "I was an only child and he enjoyed explaining things to me. You know how it is when you're a kid, you want to know about bugs and animals and trees and flowers, what makes this and what makes that. My father would tell me if he knew, and if he didn't know, he'd get out a book."

She remembered watching an eclipse of the sun with him when she was five. Her father had demonstrated what would happen, using a grapefruit, an orange and the kitchen light-bulb. "I think he was one of those fathers who would have treated me the same whether I'd turned out to be a boy or a girl," she said.

A lucky beginning, having a father who stimulated her intellectual interests! Her early background, though, like that of a number of achievers I spoke to, included disadvantages as well as advantages. Her father's own career wasn't then financially successful and the family was quite poor. Also, her parents separated when she was nine. But, living with her mother, she still managed to remain close to her father. "He was someone I could escape to," she said.

She managed to get an exceptional education, with scholarships from kindergarten on. As it happened, the class in the local public school in New York City was full when she was ready to start kindergarten. "I made a terrible fuss—which was very unlike me—because my friend a year and a half older could read and I wanted to be able to read too. My mother went to one of her friends. 'She's having a tantrum, what should I do?' she asked."

The friend told her about the Ethical Culture School, which had scholarships. "I was tested and they took me in right away, although classes had begun ten days earlier. It was a fantastic school. Art, music, dramatics, science—everything was there. They encouraged us to be independent and creative. School was exciting and I loved all of it. I was supposed to be very good in art, especially sketching faces. One day the art teacher came down to the chem lab and found me. 'Barbara, what are you doing here?' he wanted to know. He was shocked. I told him I liked chemistry, too," she said.

I wondered how she'd sustained her resolution to become a doctor once she discovered she had so many other interests. The liberal arts can be so seductive to women. Had she never been tempted to pursue some other sort of career?

"I loved all those things—art, dance, theater," she responded. "I realized, though, that in the arts or dramatics you have to be really original and creative to accomplish anything. I thought to myself, 'Even if I'm not that outstanding as a scientist or a doctor, I can still do some good.' Looking back, I guess I was quite modest about my abilities."

When it was time to go to college she chose Barnard in New York, although she could have had a scholarship to other schools. "My mother insisted, 'You have to stay home with me!'" Recalling this, she imitated her mother's plea, then smiled and shrugged. "So I stayed."

She didn't waver from her original decision to go into medicine, though. "I was still going along on my own track," she said. "I guess I was somewhat shy socially. In high school the scholarship kids were not in the social clique. I went out with a group and didn't date until I was seventeen. I knew boys as friends, because if your interests are in science, that's who you talk to. But two of my girlfriends in high school also went on to become doctors."

After graduating *summa cum laude* from Barnard, she went on to medical school at New York University. Although men had gone off to fight the Second World War, there was still a 10 percent quota imposed on females.

"I remember having two close girlfriends in med school, Renée and Sylvia. But most of my friends were men," she said. What she'd learned in high school about getting along with men applied here, too. Intellectual abilities were appreciated, it seemed to her. Medical students chose their own teams or sections which worked together, and, as she remembered, "They wanted you in their section if you were bright. The fellows came up to me saying, 'Barbara, we'd like you to be in our section. But you can't have any special privileges just because you're a girl.' So I said, 'That's fine—I'd love to be in your section.' They were a great bunch of guys. We went all the way through med school together. I liked the camaraderie and the fun. I learned a lot from them." When she finished medical school in 1945, she was awarded the Alpha Omega Alpha prize for the highest scholastic rating in the four-year course.

Although she dated a lot during the years she was in medical school, she realized that she was a different person when she went out. "With my classmates I could be as bright and competitive as I felt and as aggressive as I wanted to be, but I resolved not to go out with any of the guys in my class because I felt that with men socially I had to be sweet and compliant. I'd try to be. Then—wham —something would happen and the other side of me would pop out. And the guy would run. I wondered what sort of neurotic problem I had. I went into analysis and wondered, 'Why did I have to suppress what I felt was the real me?' "

She never planned to forgo marriage for a career, but had already completed several years of residency training when she met her husband, Max Saltzman, a chemist, who'd been married before and who was the father of two children. He'd been looking for a "bright, scientific girl," he told some friends. They thought of Barbara Fish, and arranged a dinner. "I came as a hungry intern and sat down to this beautiful steak dinner. 'What, steak again?' came this booming voice from the other end of the table. I thought, 'Who is this character?' But he took me home and we started going out. For once I didn't have to worry about being aggressive or bright," she explained.

He took a serious interest in her work from the very beginning. Renée, her good friend from medical school, wasn't so fortunate. Her husband insisted that she drop out of training when they were married, and she was unable to finish until her children were grown.

Before Barbara Fish was married, she'd already met her mentor, Dr. Lauretta Bender, whose ideas inspired her life's work. "I'd planned to go into medicine to take care of people," she recalled. "As an adult, I never thought seriously of doing research until I worked with her." This was in the final stage of her training at Bellevue, where, in 1935, Dr. Bender had founded the Children's Psychiatric Service.

"Lauretta Bender had a very creative mind," she said. Contrary to the psychiatric theories then popular—especially among child psychiatrists in this country—Dr. Bender viewed schizophrenia as genetic in origin and believed that the roots of the disorder were neurological. "While I was there, she was analyzing the 'baby books' of twelve schizophrenic children. She found signs of disordered neurological maturation that began in infancy. I remembered infants I had seen as a resident in pediatrics who had puzzled everyone, and I thought it should be simple to test her theory."

No one had ever traced children with these characteristics to see if they might become schizophrenic in later life. This is what Barbara Fish set out to do. "It was a fascinating problem, but it had to wait. The Children's Psychiatric Service had over three hundred and fifty kids admitted every year, and I had to take care of those kids first.

"Lauretta kept encouraging me to start some research." Dr. Fish did do some small clinical studies before completing her training, but never wrote them up. She remembered finding out what children were afraid of when given shock treatment. "They would wake up half an hour afterward in a sort of clouded state. The hallucinatory material would come back in a half-waking nightmare. I found that if I sat with them and held their hands, it got them through it. I guess I could have written this up for the journals, but I wanted to write about how schizophrenia started!"

Laughing at herself, she went on, "Yes, I wanted to solve the whole puzzle. I had this 'Madame Curie complex,' as I call it. I wanted my first paper to be something really important. I began in 1952, just out of training. By charting the course of development from birth, I tried to find infants with an uneven and fluctuating pattern who —I thought—would be those most likely to become schizophrenic. I studied twelve offspring of schizophrenic mothers. Seven children had abnormal development in infancy; some were unusual even in their first twenty-four hours. Six of these seven are now seriously disturbed, at eighteen to twenty-five years of age, although most were reared by loving, adoptive parents or grandmothers. Three have been diagnosed schizophrenic by outside experts who had no knowledge of their hereditary background or of my original predictions."

Although Dr. Bender was supportive, it was Max, her husband, who encouraged Barbara Fish to write her first paper. "I'd been analyzing the data on the first children when they were three years old, and found a peculiar dip in the growth curve of one infant who already seemed to me to be schizophrenic. I ran to Lauretta and said, 'He does just what you said he'd do!' She said, 'Of course.' So I didn't think I'd discovered anything. But when I told Max, he explained that it is important when someone finally offers proof of a scientist's theory. 'Write it up!' he said, and so I did," she remembered. Her first paper was published in 1957.

"When I applied to do a larger study the following year, my preliminary report met with disbelief, and I was unable to get financial support for the work. But Max encouraged me to continue and to accept the offer, in 1960, of Bender's job at Bellevue and New York University Medical School. So I found myself a full-time, academic, associate professor and then professor of child psychiatry at NYU, and director of child psychiatry."

At NYU she was told that her longitudinal study wouldn't bring any grant money. Dr. Bender had encountered the same obstacles. "Being a woman didn't help matters," Barbara recalled, "but that wasn't the main problem. At that point I was working under a department head who was very jealous of the achievements of his subordinates. True, he was a chauvinist—the men became professors five years earlier; I had to wait ten years, until he died! But he had had some very famous people working under him, men as well as women, who never got promoted to full professor. They were kept in the lower clinical rank."

Much of her time was spent on clinical, teaching and administrative responsibilities. On the side, she pursued the longitudinal research, continuing this even when she had her own part-time practice, and later, when she was the director of child psychiatry at NYU. Since the research began without any outside financial support, she had to limit herself to the number of infants she could examine without any help. Upon hearing that a schizophrenic mother was about to give birth, she would rush to the hospital to be on hand to observe the child.

But besides collecting data, she had a concern for the treatment and welfare of these children that went far beyond the limits of research. Often the babies were put out for adoption, and when this was the case she worked closely with social agencies. "We didn't know who was vulnerable or not, but it was important to see that they were placed in warm, nurturing environments," she explained. Sometimes, too, she intervened when the children were placed in foster homes where she felt they weren't given sufficient attention. "It was especially important that the apathetic babies not be ignored," she said. "We had to find parents who would wake them up."

The parents who reared these children knew that their natural mothers were mentally ill, but no one knew which child might become schizophrenic. "We couldn't tell them because we didn't know; no one had tested such a theory before. When mothers noticed that there were problems, we explained what might be wrong in specific developmental or behavioral terms, and tried to help. For example, in one child we detected a reading problem early. Instead of waiting until this little boy went to school and began to think he was stupid, we got help in time and he became a great reader in school," she related.

Year after year, a total of twenty-four children were seen regularly by Dr. Fish and then by her collaborators, who were unaware of the children's early backgrounds. The children would be tested and then have a long, searching interview. "I couldn't have stopped if I wanted to," she said. "As one of them said to me, 'I wouldn't see a regular psychiatrist, but I can talk to you.' "

The children grew, of course. She worked closely with their parents during their adolescent years, through the teens and on into young adulthood. Several had drug problems as teenagers. One mother had been concerned that her son, who was very bright, had not continued his education after high school. He went to Dr. Fish for his next examination, and "At the end of our talk I asked him about his plans. He wanted to go to college, so I asked what was standing in the way and whether he thought he'd go through with it. He said he thought he'd go when he was ready to, and I said, 'Fine.' Later his mother told me that he'd enrolled soon afterward. Then, recalling the help she had received over the years, this mother said, 'You saved our lives.' "

All the while, she published highly technical papers on her observations. A recent one explains her evidence that a certain biological predisposition for schizophrenia can be inherited, a major contribution toward understanding the disease. "People misunderstand heredity," she said. "It's not immutable. Environment can make an enormous difference in the lives these individuals will lead. This is why it's so important to recognize the indications early." Diagnosis of schizophrenic symptoms in children may prevent the disease from reaching its devastating adult proportions.

There seem to be two kinds of gratification in the work she has done. One, of course, is what any scientist feels when a long and difficult experiment yields some exciting new information. But as we talked that day I kept feeling there was much more here as well. The telephone on the patio table would ring occasionally. "I'm expecting one of my kids to call," she mentioned. Finally the call came. Although I shut off my tape machine, I couldn't help hearing a discussion about the arrival time of a plane from another city. I assumed that by "one of my kids" she meant one of the two children from her husband's first marriage, whom she had raised from the ages of nine and thirteen. They were now grown and she was proud of them, I knew. But when the telephone conversation ended, she began to tell me more about the person soon to arrive in Los Angeles. The "kid" coming for a visit, I realized then, was one of her experimental subjects, not one of her stepchildren. And she was proud of him, too. "Yes, I think of them as my kids," she said. "I've known them since they were very little babies."

Another thought struck me. Before I myself decided not to become a psychologist, I'd worked on the wards of a mental hospital and I'd found myself spending every waking moment thinking of "my patients," their problems and even their hallucinations. How does one find the delicate balance between involvement and detached objectivity which is necessary in order to work with disturbed individuals? I'd never found it. So I asked her, "How do you keep from getting too involved?"

She was thoughtful for a moment, then said, "I remember the first night I was out of medical school. I was in the emergency room. There was a diabetic in a coma and I was singlehandedly supposed to save this person's life. Well, that's a very different thing from testing urine as a medical student. I was up all night, drawing blood, giving insulin and running back and forth to test the urine.

The patient recovered, and I felt I had had my baptism by fire; I was really a doctor.

"But," she went on, "the first time you're responsible for someone who might have lived but did not, it's a dreadful thing. And it has to happen sometime in the course of your experience. Before penicillin, for example, you might have an alcoholic go out with pneumonia. Once you've been through that, you have to come to grips with the fact that it's not your fault. You've done everything you could do, you've used everything that was available to you. Of course, you have to be satisfied that you've done everything possible—maybe you had to run to the library or waken your supervisor in the middle of the night. You become aware of the limitations of medicine, and I think you lose that illusion of omnipotence you have as a young doctor. You care. Of course you care, but you know that you're not God. You have to accept the fact that you can't work miracles and that no operation, no treatment is a hundred-percent cure. . . .

"So," she concluded "I think the medical experience really helps."

Looking back over the years, she didn't find much that she'd have done differently. She had few regrets over not having had children of her own, she said, because she didn't think she could have managed it along with her many professional duties and raising her stepchildren as well. Thinking of the work she did without benefit of grants or funding, she said, "With some encouragement and better advice, I probably could have gotten money for the longitudinal study sooner. It's important to learn how to write a proposal if research is what you want to do."

For many years, too, she was burdened with extensive administrative work in addition to her teaching and research. "So often there's too much that you *have* to do in order to do the thing that you *want* to do," she said. "What I wanted to do was to teach and do research." Before accepting her present position at UCLA in 1972, she made sure that there would be ample opportunity to continue her research.

Her leaving the East for the West Coast was, however, contingent upon still another factor, one which many dual-career couples understand well. Her husband, Max Saltzman, was the manager of color technology with a large chemical concern in New York. The two of them talked the matter over seriously. "I wouldn't have come here without Max," she said. "He said, 'If the job is really good for you, then we'll go!' So finally he decided to take an early retirement, but it has worked out very well." Besides doing consultant work for industry, he has been able to turn a longtime hobby into a new career. Not so long ago he analyzed the chemical components in automotive paints. At UCLA he applies this knowledge to identifying and classifying primitive artifacts from their coloration, working with museum and university experts in the United States and abroad.

Yes, it has worked out very well. In my original letter to Dr. Barbara Fish, I'd written that I wanted to learn how she'd managed to keep going alone all those years. "When I read your letter, I laughed," she said. "I turned to Max and said, 'What does she mean *alone?* I had you, didn't I?'"

Undeniably, she's a lucky woman. The ingredients that seem to make for women's success are all there—a father who encouraged her intellectual interests, scholarships through school, a mentor and a highly supportive husband. Also, the timing was fortuituous; she'd already had nine years of training before she married. What strikes me as the most vital factor in this impressive career, however, is far less tangible, yet something she shares with women in fields very different from hers. It is the way she has consistently cared about her work, persistently going ahead no matter what, and doing far more than others might have done.

INROADS INTO PROFESSIONAL CAREERS

In the late 1930s, when Barbara Fish was a student at Barnard, *Madame Curie,* Eve Curie's book about her mother, had just been published. Many other young women read it, too, among them Dr. Rosalyn Yalow. "We were all going to be like Madame Curie," Dr. Yalow once told an interviewer. Thinking it unlikely that she would even be admitted to medical school, she made a choice hardly more orthodox at the time—to study physics. A woman among men and a physicist among medical doctors, she worked with her late collaborator, Dr. Solomon A. Berson, to develop a technique for measuring infinitesimal amounts of hormones and other substances in the blood. Hers was a revolutionary contribution to medical diagnosis and it won her the Nobel Prize.

The attraction that medicine, science, law and other professions have had for women, then as now, often has had to do with altruistic ideals. Much as the specific professions vary, these are careers which provide opportunities for saving lives and for making lives better. But only in recent years could women, like men, look to professional careers as a way of bettering their own lives.

Even more than other career women, professionals have been expected to accept sacrifice as part of the bargain. The long period of training took up the very years when other women were marrying and having children, and women's responsibilities to a home and a family were considered a decided drawback to a professional life. Rewards and recognition for original contributions might not be forthcoming either, but the work was supposedly its own reward. Early generations of women professionals forfeited much and worked selflessly, feeling lucky to be able to pursue the careers they had chosen.

After World War II the image of Madame Curie faded, and an all-out propaganda campaign heralded the return of women to home and family. Becoming a professional was far less acceptable as a young female fantasy.

A number of the women I interviewed who'd been college students in the late forties, the fifties and even the sixties remembered that they had shown promise for pursuing scientific or legal careers. Sooner or later, however, most were dissuaded from following these ambitions, convinced of their unsuitability. Today they are in managerial positions in small to medium-sized businesses, and they are doing very well.

For a long time science, medicine, law and other professions suffered, although, ironically, not even Russia's utilization of women in medicine and other such fields made this apparent. And women suffered, too, in struggling to find a niche for themselves in the professions.

Edna Alvarez, who entered law school in the sixties after having worked as a librarian in a legal library, remembered being the only woman in huge lecture halls where the men in their dark suits would file past her. "I didn't enjoy the breakthrough or pioneer aspect," she said. "Instead I felt very much alone and very uncomfortable."

Also during the sixties Virginia Tanzmann, having decided at fifteen that she wanted to be an architect, traveled to Cornell University to visit the architectural school there before applying. "I was told that because of my excellent record I would not be denied admission, but I was discouraged from applying. I was very politely told that the school did not want women," she recalled. At Syracuse University, however, she was warmly welcomed, and at the age of seventeen she enrolled in the six-year architecture program there.

Doris Sassower entered New York University Law School in 1952, and, like other women who'd squeezed past strict quotas to be admitted into training, she heard insinuations that she was taking up a place that rightfully belonged to a man. What she wanted to do, she decided, was to teach law, and during her final year she voiced this hope to the dean of the school. After congratulating her on the academic honors she'd won, he expressed surprise that she should hold a goal so unrealistic for a woman. Everyone knew that law schools didn't hire women.

When in fact she did not find a position on the faculty of a law school, she went into private practice with her husband. In 1957, however, as a member of the Equal Opportunities for Women Committee of the New York Women's Bar Association, she undertook a study of the attitudes of law schools toward hiring women as professors. But when her work was completed, the association didn't want her findings published. For over a decade she was unable to find women lawyers who were willing to join force and fight discrimination.

In 1970 she founded the Legal Task Force of the Professional Women's Caucus. The next year she filed a complaint against law schools receiving aid from the federal government, charging discrimination in faculty hiring and promotions, student admissions and financial aid. In 1972, in response to her arguments, the American Bar Association endorsed a resolution which called upon law schools to recruit women students, and to recruit, hire and promote women faculty members.[1]

Not surprisingly, women's representation on the faculties of other professional schools has also been scant. Professorships are prestige positions, and although more women are now achieving professional status, few so far have reached the highest levels within their respective fields. It would be difficult to say which male professionals put up the strongest attitudinal barriers against female colleagues. This depends upon particular specialties within each profession, upon what part of the country, too, and, ultimately, upon the individuals. Rank insults are rarer than they once were, but even the female professional with the best of credentials still experiences subtle condescension from male peers, as well as attitudes that constitute real roadblocks to her advancement.

The greatest progress that women have made so far within the professions in general has been at the bottom of the ladder. For decades women were effectively excluded from professional training, usually by means of rigid quotas. But, in response to pressure, women began gaining admittance in greater numbers by the early seventies, and their numbers have risen steadily.

In 1959 just 6 percent of all first-year medical students were women. By the fall of 1977, 4,149 women comprising 25.7 percent of the total were enrolled in first-year medical-school classes.[2] As recently as 1971 there were only about 9,000 women lawyers in the entire country. In 1977 the names of 15,817 women were listed in the *Directory of Women Law Graduates and Attorneys in the U.S.A.* and another 5,000 were presumed missing from the list. Also in 1977 there were 32,538 women enrolled in law schools approved by the American Bar Association—27.4 percent of the total.[3] In 1975, although there were almost one million scientists and engineers, women accounted for less than 6 percent of the total and only about one half of one percent of practicing engineers. That same year, though, women made up 8.9 percent of first-year engineering students.[4] Accurate statistics on architecture are difficult to come by; according to unconfirmed estimates, however, only about 2 percent of practicing architects but approximately 24 percent of the entering classes are now women.

Completing the requisite training and passing the necessary examinations still doesn't guarantee employment for women professionals or at least not the particular type of employment they would prefer. Competition in some specialties is rigorous for both men and women. In addition, many lawyers, architects and doctors as well as other professionals work in small firms which add very few if any newcomers to their ranks each year. In larger organizations, where evidence of discrimination is easier to trace, women are being hired.

Faced with difficulty in finding the jobs they would ideally want, many women lawyers, architects, accountants and others have chosen to open private practices of their own where they may be able to build a reputation more rapidly and where they can still find time for political causes, or for participation in either new networks or older professional organizations. The private practice, too, has obvious advantages for women attempting to juggle career with family responsibilities.

Of all the professions, law is the fastest-growing, although the number of jobs hasn't increased proportionately with the numbers of qualified lawyers. It's not hard to understand the attraction law holds for any woman who discovers that she has a certain combination of verbal and reasoning skills, and who notices, too, that legal training can open doors otherwise closed to her. And while most other professions demand an early career decision, it's possible to enter law after having majored in any of a number of subjects and even after having made a wrong start in a far different career.

There's power in law, after all. Women lawyers have an edge in being able to apply the tools of their trade directly in defending themselves or other women against treatment that is illegal as well as unfair. In the last few years, too, women lawyers have been forming networks and coalitions of various kinds. By working together, they can do much to enhance their own status and that of women generally. For the woman who knows her goals, her values and her objectives, a law career has much to offer.

And yet I've spoken with women law students who, amazingly, hadn't made any specific career plans beyond obtaining the law degree and, as they hoped, passing the bar examination. It might be exaggerating to suggest that women attorneys may soon find themselves in a situation parallel to that of women academics. There certainly will be job opportunities, particularly in government and in business, for persons with legal training. But some women now studying law without having clarified their objectives in doing so may be sorely disappointed. There is a need for more women lawyers, but at the same time, as Eleanor Holmes Norton pointed out, there is an inherent danger in seeing any one occupation as "the key to power in society."

Young women need to become aware of actual and anticipated opportunities early in the educational process. Colleges and even high schools have a responsibility to see that young women students are exposed to a variety of female role models. Women's networks can be helpful here, too. And social-science courses, even in high schools, should be providing greater insights into the distribution of power within the society.

There's power in other professions as well. The decisions of the medical-psychiatric establishment affect the birth and survival of our children, the care and treatment of our bodies and minds as well as the final breaths we draw. Women should have a voice in such matters, but as lay persons and activists women can make only limited impact upon the *status quo*. As doctors, psychiatrists and medical administrators women can challenge existing assumptions, undertake new types of research and advocate alternative ideas and methods.

And there is also great power in the scientific-technological community, which, besides giving us work-saving devices, is also responsible for the neutron bomb, for recombinant DNA, and for carbon dioxide replacing oxygen in the atmosphere while the search for alternate energy sources proceeds at a halting pace. There is surely no question that women should be fairly represented where such world-changing decisions are being made, and when they are chemists, physicists and engineers, women's opinions carry more weight. There remains, however, the question of whether *women* can bring humanistic values and a concern for future generations to science when some *men* have tried to do so but failed. Perhaps women will try harder than men have.

As things stand now, women professionals must still try harder simply to be able to work in their fields. And it will take time before women progress far enough up the ladder to put forth new ideas of their own.

XIV

A Woman of Independent Ways and Means—Lisa Clewer

WHAT constitutes success for the woman entrepreneur? Starting a corporation that eventually goes public? Making money while also having time for other things that are important? Organizing a company along democratic rather than hierarchical lines? Progressing faster and earning more than one's peers in the corporations or elsewhere?

Any of these goals and others, too, may be possible for the woman who decides to become her own boss. Women in business for themselves differ vastly as to specialties and scope and goals. What they have in common, however, is a state of mind that accompanies the need to go it alone rather than allying oneself with an existing organization and employer.

"Success to me is having options," Lisa Clewer told me. "Success is being offered five things, then selecting the two I want or being able to say no to all of them."

We were seated on the white sofa in her office, which is on the second floor of the house she recently purchased. The room still has flowered wallpaper, indicating that it was once a little girl's bedroom. So far Lisa has been too busy to change it. This is a far cry from the space she'd occupied until a few months ago. Her equipment and employees gradually had taken over a floor and a half of the three-story hillside house she'd shared with her former husband. Now, though, the equipment is gone and so are the employees, except for her secretary, who is typing away in what was formerly a maid's room.

Lisa has just relinquished the option to expand the multi-faceted graphics business she founded nine years earlier. Although she has retained a few favorite clients and projects, she now has more personal—and more elusive—goals of her own.

At thirty-five, she seems to have it all: accomplishments in business that utilize her writing and artistic skills, respect of peers and clients, even a fiancé with whom she can share much in the little free time there is. Also money and the things money can buy, such as the large English Tudor house with an aura of old Los Angeles, sedately situated on a quiet street that *is* old Los Angeles.

It hasn't been easy, however. Last December she was plagued with deadlines and work to get out just before the holidays. I'd met with her somewhat reluctantly the Sunday before Christmas to discuss work she'd hired me to do. "I hope I get a chance to celebrate Christmas this year," she sighed, and she truthfully didn't know if she'd be able to take even one day off.

Being in business for yourself has its penalties as well as its rewards. It's sometimes possible to take time off when no one else can, but it may be necessary to work all day and all night too, and on holidays when one's friends are free. Yet so many women dream of being entrepreneurs, playing their own game instead of someone else's. Why do some women do it? How do they do it? Is it worth the effort?

"Money has never been my primary motivation," Lisa assured me.

She didn't start out with much money or very many options either. She was born in Harlan County, Kentucky. Although her mother was known to be the prettiest young woman in town and her father the best-looking and richest, there ended the resemblance with the famous Southern lullaby. The two were separated before Lisa was born. She and her sister were almost teenagers before they lived together with their mother as a family. Until then her sister lived with a grandmother in Kentucky and Lisa lived with various relatives, shuffling back and forth between Harlan County and Detroit, where her mother had found work. "I only saw my father twice, but I remember him vividly," she said. "And I created a fantasy around him that helped soothe those troubled years. No matter how bad things got, there was always the dream that he'd come for me and take me to some exciting place to live with him."

Her mother eventually managed to make a home for the girls in Detroit. Lisa went to high school there, took business as well as academic courses, then started working her way through Wayne State University. "I majored in education because teaching seemed to be the only practical option for women. But since I knew I really didn't want to teach, school didn't make a lot of sense to me," she admitted. "I had good secretarial skills, so I managed to get good jobs. One was in the dean's office, where I learned a lot about college politics." She confessed, too, that she sometimes hired other students to do her library research for certain classes. "I've always valued my time. If something bored me, I didn't want to spend time on it."

She became engaged to a football player, but postponed marriage in order to see her father first. Then a few weeks before she was to leave to visit him in Las Vegas, news came that he had died. "It was an enormous shock. Meeting him had been the main goal in my life, and now—what was there? I decided to go to Las Vegas anyway and find out all I could about him, what sort of man he was, what his life had been like. Things like this matter when half of your parentage is a mystery," she said.

At twenty-one she set out for Las Vegas in search of her roots and any legacy there might be.

"Like a gothic heroine?" I asked.

"Yes . . . no. A gothic heroine created by Mario Puzo, maybe," she laughed. "I was naïve and friendless. It was a sink-or-swim situation, and I couldn't afford to stay naïve very long."

Her father died without a will, leaving his affairs in shambles. There was, however, a good-sized piece of commercially zoned property which was in the initial stages of development. "My father had had plans drawn up for a shopping center. It didn't seem right to let his dream slip away. I needed financing for it, so I tucked my plans under my arm and went to Los Angeles, San Francisco and Phoenix, talking to land-developers. They thought I was a cute kid, but I wasn't getting the money. In fact, I was getting ensnarled in some pretty heady stuff. Nobody wanted me to develop that property, and after a while they made that perfectly clear. But I learned how far you can get on sheer nerve. I came out with nothing for the lack of a little. The right contacts would have helped. Some expert legal advice would have helped, too," she said.

"But there seemed to be an omen here," she went on. "Something good had to come out of this. I realized that I'd ruin my life if I married the football player. I had just enough money left to get to Los Angeles, twenty-four dollars and ten cents. So I went. I guess I'm an optimist, really. If I had ten bucks and nothing else left in the world, I'd spend nine on a cab to Beverly Hills and the other dollar on a cup of coffee. I wouldn't worry. I'd just know that something good would happen. It always does. . . ."

She found a job and before long married a dashing Englishman who ran several California companies and who was a kind of mentor throughout their eight-year marriage. During that time he started an automotive franchise operation, but because of his other involvements he couldn't give it his full attention. He asked her to help out. The excitement of developing a business captivated her and she became deeply involved in the company as it grew to include two factories, five sales offices and eighty retail stores. "Not many women were doing things in business yet," she recalled. "I was having a marvelous time. Workers knew I was far more than the boss's wife. And I'd talk about what I did at parties to anybody who'd listen. People thought we must be poor since I had to work, but I didn't mind. I was learning a lot.

"One of the most important lessons anybody can learn in business, I learned early. Don't chase your money. I saw many people doing that. There'd be some basic flaw in the very concept of a business venture, and the people would refuse to admit they'd made a mistake. Even when that flaw became obvious, they'd pour more money in, throwing good money away. Instead of just taking a five-thousand-dollar loss, they'd let it snowball into a twenty-five-thousand-dollar loss. I know of one case—it turned into an enormous fraud because the people were trying to hide an initial problem in the concept."

I had heard the generalization that women have a harder

time than men writing off past investments in time or money. I asked Lisa about this.

"On the contrary," she said, "it may be easier for women to admit they've made a mistake than it is for men. Men are supposed to be the experts. But I've chased my money. It's so easy to say to yourself, 'I'll just make back the seven G's I've lost, *then* I'll get out.' Well, there ain't no law that says you'll get it back. . . ."

When continuing in the business would have meant chasing their money, Lisa and her husband severed their connections with it. "I decided to retire, do volunteer work, be a good wife and have a baby," she remembered. "But very quickly I was bored. I'd go to a cocktail party and I'd find myself talking business. Women, I think, can be worse than men about talking business at parties. I didn't know it yet, but I felt a void."

She began filling the void by handling some small advertising accounts. "Then, it seems hard to believe, but one phone call changed my life," she explained. "I called IBM because I needed a new typewriter. During the conversation I asked about their Composer typesetting machine. I'd seen one at a printing plant and was just fascinated by it." IBM delivered the typesetter, telling Lisa that someone would come out the next day to demonstrate how it worked. "Well, no one came out to show me how to use the damned thing, so I figured it out myself, not realizing that it cost close to five thousand dollars!" she laughed. The next thing she knew, she had a large retail fashion account and was renting and purchasing graphic equipment to handle jobs as they came in. "I was using our personal credit, but I knew it would work out," she said.

"All this was happening at our hillside house, all this equipment moving into the basement," she went on. "I had freelance artists coming in, and my maid somehow wasn't a maid anymore, but had turned secretary. The house was going to hell but we were doing all this work! We'd deliver everything rather than let clients see our set-up. No one would have believed we could be in business seriously with the photostat camera in a closet and other expensive equipment on rickety tables. We had only one phone, which would get lost now and then, and everybody was on top of everybody else. But what we did was professional. We overserviced, did everything faster and better than expected, even if we had to stay up all night—but I loved it! For once I was bringing together all my talents and interests. Art and design, writing and printing—I could do all the things I loved and get paid, too. I'd found my niche," she said.

"All this time I was learning, asking questions right and left. I'd ask my suppliers the most basic questions about graphics and printing, and those who took the time to help are still my suppliers."

The business get under way in 1969, and her husband was supportive of her efforts. Several years later, though, they separated and in the mid-seventies underwent what Lisa calls "a very civilized divorce." "I kept all my business assets and liabilities, he kept all his, and we split everything else as evenly as we could. I didn't ask for an accounting of what his business was worth and he didn't ask about mine. So many couples are encouraged by their attorneys to make unrealistic demands, to try for ninety percent, and terrible hostilities flare up. We didn't have that sort of thing." As it turned out, Lisa and her business were also allowed to stay in the house she and her husband jointly owned until 1978 when it was sold.

She was turning out advertising of all kinds, as well as educational and training materials, slides, premiums, anything involving words and pictures or both. "For the first six months we didn't have a name. We couldn't think of a word or two to describe what we did because we were doing everything, concept to finish, and at that time full-service graphics shops were practically unheard of. One of my skeptical friends who'd been in advertising for years jokingly called it Bumblebee Press, because, as he said, 'Aerodynamically, it just couldn't fly.' Well, concept, copy-writing, design, artwork, photography, typesetting, et cetera, et cetera, et cetera, just wouldn't fit on the door. We called ourselves The Works," she explained.

"One thing I knew was motivation. I learned about motivating people when I was a kid in Kentucky and evangelist preachers would come to town. We used to lie on a hill above the church, listen to the preacher and begin to rock . . ." she recalled.

"This experience has served me well in designing sales-incentive campaigns for companies," she said. One such internal-motivation program for Volkswagen dealers was called "Get the Bugs Out." This campaign, like many others Lisa has designed, helped pinpoint sales problems and motivate salespeople to move more products.

Often her function is that of responding to a clear-cut need that already exists, then filling that need in a way that's creative and will save the company money or help it earn more. Sometimes, though, after analyzing a company's situation, she must make them aware of a need that previously hadn't concerned them, selling them something they hadn't thought of buying. She explained, "It's like when you're an employee in a company and you want them to create a whole new position for you. You're asking them to buy a whole new concept. It's one thing to get a company to take that thousand they're already spending and pass it from one supplier to another. But to get them to take that thousand or two they've never spent before, that's something else."

Recent projects have been more closely allied with her own personal interests. One was the book *How to Find Your Own Roots*, which grew out of her interest in genealogy. She conceived of the project as a small book which could be offered as a premium by businesses. She wrote, designed and marketed it. Another booklet in process has to do with collectibles, "things anyone is apt to have stashed away in attics and closets—Mrs. Butterworth jars, Avon bottles only a few years old. People are dying for a book like this. It's great fun working on it," she said. This, too, will be a premium.

Another pet project is a magazine she publishes for a major financial institution in the Western United States. Demographic studies show that many of the firm's customers are senior citizens. "I have a serious interest in what happens to people when they grow older—I plan to do it myself! I want to cover how they cope with retirement, how they go on living after the death of a spouse, things other magazines have ignored until recently," she said. "Since I'm the editor, I can get across my ideas," she said, "ideas I think are important."

Although some women know all along what they want to do and what market there is for it, others, like Lisa, make the sudden but happy discovery that there's potential profit in doing the things that matter most to them. Important as that profit is, however, it's only part of the whole picture, even for Lisa.

"Where I get my kicks," Lisa said, "is from the sense of personal satisfaction. Then there's the glory and the good feedback. And later, I get paid. The money has to be there, but it's not the major motivation—does that make any sense? I try as hard as I can to meet my personal standards, and, naturally, I'm sometimes disappointed even when the client is raving about how good it is. It's easier to meet their standards than to meet mine. And, as in anything that involves creativity, things rarely turn out the same as when they revealed themselves to you in the burning bush. . . ."

Isn't it dangerous, I wondered, this intense identification with their work that women are apt to have? I asked her about that.

She smiled. "Yes, of course," she said. "When you pull off a big job really well, you're terrific. When you do a lousy job, though, you think you're a terrible person. I'm no different. Sometimes I have to admit, 'In the hands of somebody else, this would have been better.' I have to remind myself that I did the best I could do in the allotted time. I have to keep remembering, human beings aren't perfect. I think perhaps women do have to take pains to *distance* themselves from what they do. Maybe it's because what we are rewarded for is always so personal—the atmosphere we create in our homes, the food we serve. We're *not* the food, the poem or the advertising brochures, and yet that involvement is what helps make us good at whatever we do." She became thoughtful for a moment. "I think we have to find the *right* distance—the right balance between involvement and detachment. That may be one of the real secrets."

Listening to her, I'd begun to think that the life of an entrepreneur would appeal to many women who are interested in business but who find the game-playing in corporations too formidable and the chances for making it there too slim. What did she think? Would other women be well advised to go into business for themselves?

"Not as a way of avoiding the games played in business, no," she answered. "This is really harder. When you work for one firm, you learn the game going on there. As an independent, you have to understand the game being played in every place you do business. You have to know the protocol and be a step ahead of them, because, no matter how much they like you or what you're doing, you're still an outsider and not a member of their team. So you spend more time psyching out the situation and planning your moves, all the while without having the information an insider would be privy to."

There's a chance to make more money owning your own business, however, considerably more than most women make in working for large companies. Lisa agreed, then pointed out, "But there's always a chance you may go flat-out broke. The risks are greater."

"How do you feel about risks?" I asked her finally.

She gave me a sly smile. "I don't understand it yet. Maybe I do get off on risks. I've reached a point where I could make good money just doing what I've been doing. But, to me, progress is being able to look at certain things I've been doing and say, 'I will not do this kind of work anymore. I've learned what there is to learn here. It's time to move on to the next challenge. I know it won't be as safe or as easy, but I'll be stretching myself and learning.'

"You know, risk-taking can pay off," she continued. "I recently resigned a large graphics account because I no longer felt challenged by it. I liked the conceptual and consulting part of the work, but the follow-through and production were old-hat. Although I didn't have another account lined up to replace that income, I took the risk just the same. It was only when I resigned that I found out how much they valued my conceptual abilities. They asked me to stay on as a consultant only. I spelled out to them what I would and wouldn't do. They were panting! I had the feeling that I could have said, 'Okay, I'll consult for you at top rate if I have a half-gallon of Baskin-Robbins on my desk every morning at ten a.m.,' they'd have come back and asked me, 'Butter Pecan or Rocky Road?' Can you imagine?"

She's now doing less work, enjoying it more and earning as much as ever with fewer projects to produce. She also has more time for other interests. She's been spending that time writing, and she now has both a novel and a screen-play under way. Why did she want to try something entirely new? I said to her finally, "I have a hard time seeing why anybody who has achieved what you have would want to pull back and write, starting at the bottom of the barrel all over again. You've reached a point where you can do all kinds of things. Why not leave well enough alone?"

"That's exactly the same question I've been asking myself," she answered thoughtfully. "Looking back at the plateaus in my career, I can see them as steppingstones. Each time I've moved up, but also, each time there's been a change, a new ballgame, a new challenge. Maybe what I get off on really is that feeling of 'God, can I do it or can't I?' Yes, I wonder, why can't I just revel in what I've got?"

She gazed out the window into the sky, the palm trees and the rooftops. "In the beginning I started out with a lot of people helping me produce. I see my career as a cone. All the time there are fewer and fewer people around me. Or it's a mountain. I keep trying to climb further but I want to go alone. Until it's just me, alone and naked at the top of the mountain. Just think of it, naked!" Her voice became almost a whisper. "And I don't understand why I want the risk of being alone, naked at the top of the mountain."

I remembered a story she'd told me earlier. When she was a little girl in Kentucky, there was a mountain she'd always wanted to climb. She'd look at it and imagine what it would be like on the other side. Finally she set out one day and started climbing. It took a long time. She was scratched by briars and she nearly stumbled several times. "I was exhausted when I got to the top, but there was a wonderful feeling of having done it. Then I started down. Only after I was nearly to the bottom again did I realize I hadn't taken time to look over to the other side. I'd been to the top of the mountain and I hadn't looked around," she told me.

Now, thinking of her future, she said, "I'm not certain that I have an ultimate goal. I used to be wrapped up in what I was going to *be* someday. But now I'm more involved in *doing* than *being*. There are certain ideas I want to get across and to share with other people. It's as simple as that. And as complex." She shook her head.

ENTREPRENEURS—THE RISK TAKERS

A business of one's own. It sounds like the ideal solution
to many of the problems of women wanting careers. Although women start businesses of their own for some of
the same reasons men do—more money, greater independence, more options—being an entrepreneur has special attractions for women, now more than ever before.

Many women can't get what they want working for
someone else. But as an entrepreneur, even more than in
other areas, a woman should *know* what she wants. No
boss, no personnel department is going to decide her
priorities for her.

All too often the female entrepreneur is in business for
herself because some hiring committee of authority somewhere has already decided *against* her. Perhaps she is one
of many women who now want careers but whose qualifications do not match those of existing openings. Or, regardless of qualifications, she may be a self-starter who
doesn't have the patience to work her way up through the
ranks. Or she may have left the corporate world in order
to sidestep the sexist practices in hiring and promotion
still found there.

One entrepreneur, Toni Carabillo, was an English major
who went into public relations and corporate communications but who found herself stalemated in that career by
the mid-sixties. She was then employed by a well-known
think tank, where she edited and published an award-
winning corporate magazine as well as supervising other
publications, brochures and presentations with a staff of
six writers and as many designers. When her supervisor
left, she and a male colleague became top contenders for
the newly created position as manager of corporate communications. The man had public-relations experience, too,
but he had never managed the extensive range of activities
she had, nor had he ever been charged with as large a
budget. "The two of us were kept dangling for eight
months or so while management was supposedly trying to
decide who was the best for the job," she explained.
"Finally the man was chosen. I became assistant manager, but continued to supervise two thirds of the work

while the man had the title, the salary and all the perks that go with an executive job."

Through her association with the women's movement Toni began to hear stories of others who'd been similarly blocked in their careers. Eventually she decided that she could best use her experience in writing, editing, graphics, publishing and business in an independent venture. She and artist Judith Meuli started their own small firm, Graphic Communications, which provides a wide variety of printed materials for business and private organizations.

For women who have writing and art skills, plus some graphics or publishing experience and managerial ability, opportunities do exist, especially in large cities. Many large companies contract independently for a lot of their training or promotional materials. It's fortunate that the need for the printed word coincides with the large numbers of women with liberal-arts backgrounds who have also acquired an eye for business.

A different sort of entrepreneur has specific professional training and credentials in law, architecture, medicine or psychotherapy. Even those women professionals whose skills are much in demand may find they can enhance their opportunities by starting independent businesses. Architect Virginia Tanzmann, whose work consists mainly of commercial buildings and shopping centers, held a series of jobs before opening her own office. It isn't unusual for men or women in the early years of an architectural career to move from company to company, learning as much as they can and gaining valuable experience, too. Looking back at her experience working in architectural offices, she said, "I never had the feeling that I could advance on up the ladder as men do."

Although entrepreneurs aren't dependent upon others to promote them, they must promote themselves to a degree that most women haven't been able to do until recently. The woman entrepreneur may have to pitch and push and even defend her product or services more than a man in a similar spot would have to. The protocol and the style differ from field to field, of course; a hard-sell approach isn't always necessary or appropriate, but at some level the entrepreneur must have greater confidence than many women can muster.

Sometimes that confidence is born of a mixture of

fantasy and hard-edged realism. The women entrepreneurs who were professionals had this in common with those whose backgrounds and skills were somewhat more unorthodox and who had a harder time fitting into the existing structure. All were likely to have been little girls or adolescents who wanted to "make something of their lives." Although one's own business can be ideal for women launching late careers, most of the entrepreneurs I talked to, whether they started early or late, were impelled by dreams, drives and self-images, too, that had begun long ago.

One who is a friend of mine grew up on what she calls "a coconut island" off the coast of Colombia where she learned a dialect of English rarely heard in the continental United States. "All we knew of how the rest of the world lived was through Sears, Roebuck catalogues," she told me. First she dreamed of being a doctor. Working her way through religious schools, then college and medical training, she eventually became an anesthesiologist in Colombia. Another dream, though, was coming to the United States, and when she visited California fifteen years ago, she decided to stay. Unable to practice anesthesiology here, she became the manager of a medical corporation, but was soon at work developing a profitable sideline. It occurred to her that some full-length feature films which already had been produced but not distributed to theaters could yield profits if interested individuals could be found to invest. Starting on a shoestring, she got the investments and the investors together for several film projects.

She said to me, "When I'm dealing with other people's money, I have to believe in what I'm doing all the way. I have to know that a project is totally ethical, then financially solid. I research every detail before I'm satisfied." What comes through as she talks isn't toughness, but an inner core of confidence likely to inspire confidence in others as well.

This is a kind of confidence that doesn't allow for a defeatist attitude. These women saw themselves as creating their own opportunities—they saw a need and decided to fill it. They studied on their own, asked questions men might have felt awkward asking and learned all they could. Often they also saw themselves as lucky. "Accounts fell our way" or "Work poured in," they say. But they'd already calculated their chances carefully, and they saw the odds as having been stacked in their favor. They took risks fully expecting to win and refused to contemplate failure.

Marge Kinney, who had been in business with her husband and gained valuable experience in advertising and marketing, never considered going to work for someone else once she was divorced and faced the prospect of raising four sons alone. A job to match her varied skills and needs didn't exist, yet she knew that the services she could provide were in demand. She confessed, "In the beginning I was nervous before meeting with the chairman of the board of a big company, but I've learned to stand up for my ideas. I'm not afraid to go to the firing line." On one occasion she found herself disagreeing with nine men in a particular company about a project that was pending. She explained, "They all thought we had a winner; I was sure we didn't. I stuck to my guns and told the boss what I thought and why." The boss, who was her client, ended up agreeing with her, and he respected her for her honesty. "But a lot of men are intimidated at seeing a woman stand up for what she thinks," she added.

The trade-off isn't hard to see. Instead of coping with the sexism of bosses, one copes with the same attitude in clients and customers. It isn't necessarily easier to get an account than it is to get hired. It may be far harder to get in the door, and the process of getting in must be repeated again and again. And losing a major account, of course, can be fully as serious as getting fired. The element of risk is always there.

If the risks are greater, so are the potential rewards. While the number of women who earn six-figure salaries from large corporations can probably still be counted on one's fingers, quite a few more earn that much from their own enterprises. If a count were made of women heading companies, it's almost certain to turn out that more of them reached this level by having been founders or co-founders than through upward mobility within these companies. Besides the women who run or help run larger companies, there are many more who live quite comfortably on annual earnings of $40,000, $50,000 or $60,000 from various smaller enterprises in areas ranging from fashion to real estate. Some of the women I interviewed who held important jobs working in large organizations also owned and operated small businesses on a parttime basis.

Those women who have the drive to reach the top in their fields and who want to be well compensated, too, are likely to decide that the surest way is to drop out of the corporate world and compete alone. Ad-agency owner Jane Trahey, who is a writer and a playwright, did this after learning the advertising business while working for other people. Not wanting to start small, she took on a silent partner who backed her, then bought him out as soon as she could. She tells about this, offering much advice that would-be entrepreneurs especially should find useful, in her book *Jane Trahey on Women and Power*.[1]

Women have no scarcity of ideas for businesses, but starting out can be a difficult hurdle. Banks can no longer discriminate against women borrowers, and in 1977 the Small Business Administration specifically earmarked $100,000,000 in guaranteed loans to women. But banks can and do turn down loan applications that don't look like healthy risks. Previous managerial or professional experience with an employer, collateral, a good sales pitch and impressive contacts can help. Personal credit and references in your field are assets, too. It's usually wise to get to know the manager at your bank before asking for money, or to find a banker who is interested in your progress. Sooner or later you will need a "credit line" so that you can borrow money from a bank without having to apply for a loan.

A partnership can make it possible to get more credit as well as providing more capital for getting off the ground by pooling resources. Often, as for Jane Trahey, a silent partner is preferable, but women who go into business with an active partner have done well, too. Needless to say, the choice of partner is crucial. Women I met who'd teamed up with other women were pleased at how well it had worked.

Partnerships—even between good friends and especially between lovers—should be set up by an attorney. For any business, accurate records should be kept from the start, preferably with the assistance of an accountant. According to the Small Business Administration, more ventures fail because of poor management than from lack of capital.

Besides money, it takes sound help and advice to get a business started. It's now possible to attend special seminars and evening classes on how to start and run a small business, and some conferences for women starting businesses have had so many hopefuls show up that they could not accommodate them all. Networks of women entrepreneurs have also been springing up at national and local levels.

Some women do not want large or even medium-sized businesses for the very reasons they originally left or avoided such organizations. They may simply want to produce something that couldn't be produced elsewhere or to exercise a skill for which there is only a small demand, or they may want to devote time to their families or to political or artistic endeavors that yield satisfaction rather than money. Like Lisa Clewer, they may want options, a somewhat more open-ended style of living than is usually possible in this society. Money itself can increase one's options, but some women want other options that money cannot buy.

"When you're in business for yourself, you make your own rules," said Toni Carabillo. "For this reason, more women ought to have their own companies." Toni and her partner, Judith Meuli, haven't pushed the volume of their business because they feel it's more important to have the time and facilities to devote to non-business interests they care about. One of these is publishing the national NOW newsletter.

A business of your own enables you to establish priorities, both inside and outside the business itself. Entrepreneurs can achieve power over their own lives to a greater extent than many others can. Very few, however, achieve power in a broader sense so that their decisions have much real effect on the lives of others. For this kind of power, women must rise in government and in large organizations, particularly large corporations such as public utilities, oil companies and automobile companies.

Discussing this with Toni Carabillo, I mentioned the need for women in decision-making spots within such firms as General Motors. "Yes," she agreed, "but we ought to start creating corporate enterprises that operate in a different way, yet still survive. People who are happy produce better. When people have a stake in an enterprise, they're more committed. It's time we started developing alternatives to General Motors."

XV

Writing Without Tears—
Carolyn See

WHEN are you in the arts and when aren't you?

There's the pervasive notion that truly creative things must not converge with the commercial, that being successful in a commerial sense detracts from truer artistic or aesthetic goals.

Novelist Carolyn See has had a fair measure of both kinds of achievement, and there's no doubt in her mind as to which she prefers.

Her reviews have appeared in the *Los Angeles Times* for as long as the paper has had a book section and even before. I hadn't forgotten her quick wit or her name when I saw her for the first time at a booth in the middle of the 1977 Los Angeles Book Fair. There she was, seated cross-legged on a table in front of a gigantic poster edged with—no, it couldn't be, but it looked like—thousand-dollar bills. She was pulling in passers-by right and left, all the while smiling, nodding, chatting as she autographed copies of her novel *Mothers, Daughters*. I lined up with the others and left with a somewhat better idea of who this writer is as well as one very authentic-looking piece of play money with her phone number scribbled on it.

In the next year I attended several lectures she gave, in order to convince myself that the woman I had seen that day wasn't an apparition. Here was a calm, relaxed, happy, smiling writer. "Must be some kind of idiot," my friends would say when I described her. But they hadn't read or heard or met her, and any one of these might have changed their minds.

249

I finally called her for a lunch interview. As we munched health food, I learned that the lighter side of Carolyn See is a rather recent development. Like so many women who've been mothers and homemakers, she sees herself as a late bloomer whose self-discovery came after divorce. And in some ways she is like a lot of women who emerge late from home and family. "I'd never had a checkbook while I was married. I didn't drive until I was twenty-nine. I had a Ph.D. and I couldn't even ride a bike," she said, laughing at herself and pointing out that in the meantime she has learned to ride a bike and a skateboard as well as to do disco dancing, and she has started roller-skating.

Still, it would be very hard to make a case for arrested maturity here. By the time she was thirty she'd been married, had a baby daughter, lived in Paris for a year, earned her doctorate and written a novel. "Amazing," I said. She shook her head. "I was driven by anger, by sheer fury at the world at that time," she said.

The fury began during a childhood that was bleaker than most. "When I was eleven my father left and my mother worked as a typist. She was very unhappy, and I knew I didn't want a life like hers. My father is a writer. The year he left, he'd published half a dozen pulp Westerns. He's now seventy-seven and doing porno novels, thirty or so since he turned seventy, and awhile back he wrote some marvelous newspaper columns. But when I was little, he was a newspaper reporter for the *Daily News* in Los Angeles. Never heard of it? It was a liberal paper that went out of business. His friends were newspaper people who played poker and told stories and talked about novels. My father gave me the idea, I guess, that being a writer was the best kind of life to have. And I loved the newspaper crowd, all of them men except one woman, Virginia Wright, a drama critic, and a very elegant lady. . . ."

A role model? I wondered.

"Oh, no. I couldn't possibly identify with someone so— so elegant. But now that you mention it, I suppose it made some kind of impression, this woman being there among the men, working for a newspaper. But it didn't occur to me that I could be *like* her."

She went on, "To this day I'm intimidated by newspaper offices. I turn in my copy to the *Times* without having to show up there. I send things to the London *Daily Observer*. I have a lot of respect for newspaper people Some journalists, now, seem air-brushed. . . ."

She lived with her mother until she was sixteen. "My stepfather decided I shouldn't be around after my younger sister was born. So, when she was about ten days old, I went to live with my father. I will say that my stepmother probably did everything in her power to be nice to me, but all I could think of was moving out and having a place of my own."

She lived in furnished rooms and went to college, supporting herself entirely, and majoring in English without having any vocational plans. Neither of her parents offered her financial help, and it didn't occur to her to ask for any. "I sold Orange Juliuses, I was a waitress at Van de Camps, and once I spent a whole summer typing the name 'Arthur K. Rowe' at the bottom of a form letter. There was never enough money. Once my stepmother came by with ten dollars and I was so pleased because I was desperate! There were times when I didn't know how I was going to eat. . . . I'd always been good at school; this was the one stable thing in my life. School seemed to be a way to avoid a poverty-stricken, broken-down life, but even as a graduate student I didn't have any plans for getting a real job in the real world. That was something I couldn't even imagine. I was very sulky and very, very shy.

"I remember thinking that successful people must be very boring. I went out with fraternity men, and it was like going out with, well, lobsters. I didn't know what to say to them and they didn't know what to say to me. I thought anybody in business administration or law must be dull. I hadn't grown up expecting to marry an orthodontist who'd support me and my children," she said.

At twenty she married a Eurasian student who was going to be an anthropologist. "He was very elegant and very exotic. His family was so different from what I'd come from that I thought it had to be better, and in fact it *was* better! I thought we'd be a very cultured couple, but I still didn't think I'd be a writer. I didn't think much of anything at twenty. But a couple of years later I decided that by the time I was thirty I would have a baby, write a novel and go to Europe. And I did all those things."

Before she'd finished her undergraduate work, she and her husband took their savings and went to Paris to live for a year. "I wasn't writing or studying and neither was he. We were just 'hanging out' in a sleazy red-velvet hotel which also housed a brothel. I was pregnant and I loved Paris. The baby was born there and I had marvelous care. When she was only six weeks old, we took off for a trip to Yugoslavia, never thinking that maybe this wasn't the smartest thing to do with a little baby."

Returning home, she finished her work for a bachelor's degree and started graduate school at UCLA. It took a couple of years before she was hired as a teaching assistant. "At first nobody thought I could do it because I was so shy and I had this tiny little voice that no one could hear." Her husband was a teaching assistant, too. "We each had a half-time job, which added up to one full salary. We could go to Mexico now and then. It didn't occur to me to want anything more," she said.

A novel she wrote in graduate school won second prize in the Samuel Goldwyn writing awards. Telegrams came from publishers, and she sent the novel to one of them, who kept it for a year before rejecting it. "I had no idea what to do with a novel at that time. It was never published, but winning the prize gave me a lot more confidence than I'd had before. Shortly after that, I took my Ph.D. qualifying exams—the first of two sets of exams—and did better than I'd expected. Also, I started thinking that I could be a writer. But I was still a grim, angry person."

Her first marriage ended, but she wasn't alone very long before she met her second husband, a graduate student specializing in contemporary American literature, as she was. "After I'd passed those first qualifying exams, I thought I'd do my dissertation on Nathanael West. Meanwhile the man in my life, who became my second husband, was doing his on Horace McCoy, another Hollywood writer. When I announced what I wanted to do, the professor said, 'Are you working on Nathanael West because *he* is working on Horace McCoy?'

"I was enraged! How could he think that? I went home and outlined a whole different dissertation in the next week. My topic became the Hollywood novel, and I changed advisors, too. The anger kept me going, too, so that I finished three years before my husband did.";

Despite her early drive and self-sufficiency, however, Carolyn See became, she said, "a very dependent wife" in her second marriage. Her second daughter was born ten years after the first. Her husband, who would have liked nothing better than to stay home and write, now had to work full-time. Meanwhile she stayed home, took care of the two girls and wrote, too. "I can write no matter what's going on around me," she said. "Most women writers have to. We can't ask the world to quiet down while we *create great art:* we just *go do it.* Sometimes I think of it like ironing, just something to be done."

At first she concentrated on short stories, some of which she sent to little magazines. The first non-fiction piece she tried sold to *West,* a now defunct Sunday supplement of the *Los Angeles Times.* "I was amazed," she said. She contacted editors elsewhere and soon was selling non-fiction regularly.

But the second marriage had problems, and resentment was building on both sides. "The real blow came when he took off with another lady and wanted a divorce. It was like what my mother had gone through, the very thing I'd always dreaded, and it was humiliating to think that he'd found a cute, younger woman. It was a very heavy rejection. But afterward, when he'd really gone and I knew he wasn't coming back, I had one of the most wonderful surprises of my life. The very worst had happened and I'd survived. I'd died, sort of—so many women stay dead after a divorce—yet I had a chance to get up again. I was astonished that it could be this way, that here I was, having come through this, and I could have a good time. Not just be brave, *have a good time!*"

Magazine assignments eased her adjustment to divorce and earned a modest living for her and the girls. "It's not hard to become optimistic when things start going well," she said. She continued living in a rustic canyon house much like the one in *Mothers, Daughters.* "It was a regular Topanga shack, tiny, no inside staircase, you had to go outside to get from one floor to the other. The bedrooms were downstairs and there was no heat. But it was beautiful and we had to beat away visitors with sticks."

She survived three years of freelancing before deciding that a steady income would be necessary. Hired at Loyola Marymount University, she took on a full load of writing classes. "I needed the job for other reasons, too. When you stay home and write all the time, you get a little strange. This gives me someplace to go three days a week and talk to the same people. I have a wonderful time with my students. I kept on teaching because I enjoy it."

She wrote a second novel, *The Rest is Done with Mirrors,* which sold, and she recalls feeling grateful to be published by a hardcover house with a good reputation. "But I didn't know anything about sales or distribution or promotion. A first novelist has to be a little more flamboyant than I was," she said.

Her next book was a satirical exposé of the pornography business, *Blue Money.* She had every intention of making money from it and so did the publisher, this time. "I had a good advance and went on a tour," she said. At last she was able to improve her style of living, too. *Blue Money* bought the used silver Porsche which she still drives.

Soon, too, she'd saved enough to move to a much more comfortable canyon house with the same sort of rustic setting as her old one but with three stories, big picture windows, central heating and a *Better Homes and Gardens* kitchen. "There's nothing wrong with living well," she laughed, "only I didn't know that for such a long time. People think it's noble to suffer. That's sheer nonsense. Suffering isn't good for your soul or the rest of you. Poverty isn't good for people either, certainly not for people who have kids."

A woman's adjusting to life after divorce is the theme of her most recent novel *Mothers, Daughters.* The heroine is dating while coping with kids around and an ex-husband's visits, trying to find a new identity and meeting men who are trying to do the same thing. She said, "I think of her as a woman who is underwater. She goes down to the depths and sees these weird fish. During that world of divorce when everything gets so strange, you see every kind of weird creature. But she's swimming to the top and she can just begin to see the air and some bubbles. I want the reader to see that if she can just hang on a little longer, she'll get closer and closer to the surface. She'll be all right because she's on her way back up."

She spent a little more than a couple of summers working on *Mothers, Daughters*. "I took a lot of time thinking about it and working just a little bit. But I don't have trouble starting or finishing things. There's a technique I share with my students. I have them repeat again and again, 'My ideas come faster than I can write, my ideas come faster than I can write,' and pretty soon the ideas come. . . ."

She doesn't deny the autobiographical elements of her work. I asked her about the problem of identifying too closely with work one has created, about feeling self-conscious and lacking confidence. "When your work pleases you, when it's as good as you can do, then you can take criticism," she said. "You've got to work on the feeling that the work is not *you*. It's something else, something you did, that's all. I spend a lot of time working with my students on how they feel when they present their stories in class. I tell them to use all that negative emotion as energy to get the next assignment done."

After *Mothers, Daughters* was published, she knew considerably more about the book business. "A book can so easily go down the drain," she said. "You hear all kinds of horror stories from writers: 'The publisher didn't do anything! The publisher didn't even answer my phone calls!' Publishers expect writers to be victims. Most writers come on fighting; they'll call up the publisher and slam down the phone. Fighting is stupid, especially if you're a woman. Women, when they fight with men, are too conditioned to losing!

"Well, I figured I wasn't going to have another of those sob stories full of injustices and bad feelings. Instead of fighting, I decided I'd confront the problem at a different level. It's very interesting to see how far you can get by deciding what you want and making that known, then not getting mad or upset when people don't give it to you. You just keep going after the thing you want. You refuse to *hear* the rest. Writing is what I do, and I want to get paid for it, too. I don't want to be a member of some small elite who believe that the masses will never understand. You know, so many writers feel that autographing books is beneath their dignity. Once I got over being shy,

I realized that if I spent all my time guarding my dignity, I'd never have any fun. And if something is worth writing in the first place, it's worth promoting and selling, and that can be fun, too."

She continued, "I had a friend, Barbara Rosenstein, who wanted to learn about public relations. My publisher was saying, 'No, we can't give you this, we can't give you that, writers make such fools of themselves.' But I got a list of shows and she started calling them. I was on nearly every local talk show and some in other cities as well. I had a lot of fun, and it worked. The book did a lot better than the publisher ever expected it to and the paperback will soon be out. Meanwhile Barbara has become a partner in her own public-relations firm. It all worked out beautifully."

Carolyn applied the same positive principles to getting a break in television writing. This time she worked with another friend, Jackie Josephs. "She wanted to learn television writing and so did I. It's a whole different set of ideas and people, and we're finding it very stimulating, very exciting. The first script, which we wrote on spec, was rejected. They hated it! The very day we got it back, we wrote a letter explaining that she was an actress and I was a writer, and that we wanted to write award-winning comedies for this particular show. We pretended we hadn't even heard anything negative; we just let all that go by us. We prepared for our first Hollywood meeting, which writers are supposed to be terrified of, by getting ourselves into a wonderful, relaxed sort of mood. We sat there in the car, talking, laughing about how terrific it felt to be going to a meeting, until it was time to go to it. We took seven ideas. Six were turned down, and we said, 'Fine, what about the seventh?' They were apprehensive because we had no television experience; they told us we didn't know how to do it, so we said, 'Okay, we're ready to start doing it now.' There we were, cheerful, smiling, funny."

The two of them have now collaborated on two plays for the series *Family* and are planning other projects. "It's terrific to work with someone when you're writing comedy," she said. "We get together and we're outrageous."

Also, she's begun another novel, which she will probably call *Rhinemaidens*. It is concerned with the further development of ideas she dealt with in *Mothers, Daugh-*

ters. She explained, "There are, you see, two kinds of mythical women along the Rhine. There is the Lorelei, the beautiful creature who drives the poor fishermen to their deaths on the rocks below; then there is the Valkyrie, who is older, stout, loud and triumphant. It's as though she's shouting, *'I made it!'* The female characters in the book aren't just one or the other. They're all both. And every woman has a little of both," she said.

THE SEX OF ART

Is there a sex to art? The question revolves around a paradox. "Writing is essentially neutral, and that's one of the nicest things about it," Carolyn See said. "And yet the male characters are less important in my novels. My main characters are female."

To be good, art must somehow transcend sex. "To be a man or woman pure and simple" is not enough, as Virginia Woolf wrote. But art that is born of experience—and what art isn't?—will to some extent reflect the sex of its creator. Until now quite a lot of art has been masculine. For centuries women were portrayed in paintings and plays and novels as seen through the eyes of men.

Women's experience is different, so very different that until recently only a few women have picked up their pens or brushes. Talent needs training and it needs time and space. The female contemporaries of Leonardo and Mozart lacked the training, also the physical and the psychic space. No wonder the great symphonies and great paintings by women are missing. And no wonder that much of the art by women has been and still is dismissed as being of limited scope. The scope is different because the experience and the frame of reference are different.

Women's art today is not narrow or limited; it is as vast, varied and profound as the experiences of present-day women themselves. Women emerging, women in transition between old worlds and new, women rediscovering their history—there is no scarcity of materials from which women's art can be fashioned. Surely the so-called women's novels and women's films are more significant than a trend or a wave which will soon subside.

Must what women produce be called women's art? Many

women artists have transcended their female vision, and many, too, would prefer to have their work disassociated from their sex. Much art by women is for all people. But there are women artists today who've drawn their strength and their vision from experiences shared with other women and who are proud to designate their work this way. Judy Chicago is one of many artists who now call their work feminist art.

After phases of minimalist metal and plastic sculpture, Judy Chicago experimented in various media. In the early seventies she learned china-painting and created abstract portraits of women of the past. "I began to look upon the domestic object as a kind of metaphor," she said. Then she saw an arrangement by another artist, Ellie Stearn, of twelve place settings for twelve people, and the idea of a dinner party was born. At first she intended to do something small—a series of plates to be hung on the wall. Originally, too, she'd hoped to complete it all herself. But the project expanded into something far more complex as well as very different from anything done before.

The Dinner Party grew to become a mammoth multi-media installation of thirty-nine places at a triangular banquet table. It represents a dinner to which thirty-nine of the most prominent females ever to exist have been invited, their places arranged to show women's history. Each woman is represented by the crafts and techniques of the time and place in which she lived; each plate and runner is different. The plates are painted or carved, and the runners include leather and beadwork for Sacajawea, a Gothic arch with gold embroidery for a twelfth-century abbess named Hildegard, and lace and ribbonwork for Emily Dickinson. On the floor are the names of 999 other women selected from history, the result of researching over 3,000 names.

There had to be help, of course. Grants and gifts as well as Judy Chicago's own earnings from other work and lectures supported the project. Men as well as women, artists and craftspersons, volunteers, students and others adding up to a total of 250 individuals, worked with her in her Southern California atelier. She emphasizes that her role has been that of designing and "facilitating" the project. Diane Gelon is the coordinator and administrator.

"Ten years ago it wouldn't have been possible," Judy

Chicago said. "There is still an incredible prejudice against feminist art—a resistance to accepting the fact that women's experience is important enough to be the subject and basis of art-making." Women students who've worked with her have suffered disapproval from their schools, she also said.

She sees *The Dinner Party* as a challenge to existing distinctions between fine art and craft, also as a challenge to the elitism that dominates the art world, controlling styles and subjects and restricting audiences. Feminist art, she believes, is breaking new ground by making art relevant and accessible to increasing numbers of people.

ART AND MONEY AND OTHER PROBLEMS

Popular books, films, paintings and musical compositions can pay enormously well. The fact that they can pay, however, is not the initial motivation for most writers or artists or musicians. Usually the urge to do whatever one does in the arts begins at a very early age. Nearly every writer or artist I've ever known was scribbling or sketching something as a small child and kept on doing it. Making pictures or poems or stories eventually became an essential part of their lives. They were hooked or addicted.

One hears outsiders saying "You have to have talent," but talent is something that outsiders worry about far more than artists themselves. The founder and conductor of the New York Women's Symphony, Antonia Brico, looks at it this way: "You don't say, 'Do I have talent?' You say 'I want to do it. I'm going to leave no stone unturned to better myself. I want to do it and I will do it.' "[1] Although beginners enjoy hearing others praise their talent—and it may be important to hear such praise, too—it is not nearly so important as having the passionate compulsion to do the work. Talent, after all, is merely potential, and there's much talent in the world that never comes to fruition because, without drive and discipline, the work never gets done.

A woman today whose goals include financial rewards and living well could legitimately be encouraged to study for one of the professions or to start a business of some kind. While she might possibly reach these same goals sooner by writing a best-selling novel, there are heavy odds that she won't reach them at all unless she wants passionately to write that novel and believes that it is a good novel as she writes it.

But we've heard a lot about money motivations as the enemy of creativity, so much that many women are still working as waitresses or typists or paste-up people rather than doing any original work that might be tainted with money or commercialism. And I'm more concerned right now with the women who are waiting tables or typing or pasting while their novels, musical scores or canvases lie hidden or unfinished than I am with the woman who is condescendingly writing a would-be best-seller and hating every moment of it. The second woman will eventually shred her manuscript and do something else that pays. She'll be all right. But the artistic waitress may someday be old and poor and hungry, with only her ideals to show for it.

Women in the arts may need a job rather than a career while they're learning their art or craft. In any of the arts there is a necessary period of development when one attends classes or experiments or labors alone. It's hard to say how long this will last or what specific circumstances are ideal. For some women it happens during their college years, for others while managing households and rearing children. Those who must earn a living may decide to work at something totally unrelated to what they really want to do. Writers and artists I've known who worked in fast-food chains and factories assured me that this work had the advantage of not cutting into their creative energies. Painters who take jobs in commercial art or writers who learn to turn out promotional or business copy earn more money, but they run the risk of finding that twenty years later they are still doing something that is not quite what they wanted to do. There's no easy answer, except that, whatever one does for a living, and whatever one's personal life, there must be time and space, psychic space left over.

Awkward as this developmental stage may be, women in the arts, and some men, too, tend to prolong it. Women especially persist in believing that they're not ready and not good enough. It's the familiar feminine programming: by remaining positive, and modest, and by maintaining one's dignity, a woman will hide and wait year after year while males of equal or even inferior talent build a following and a reputation.

It's not fear of success or even scorn of money and commercialism that keeps artists starving in garrets as much as it is the beating they take from their inner yardsticks. One's personal, inner standards are so important in the arts that without them other goals do not mean much. Internal standards, however, can be so unrealistic and unreachable that the work itself is sabotaged. Many creative efforts remain forever in the revision or polishing stage, never finished and never submitted. Erica Jong has confessed that for years she could not pronounce her work done, completed. And many great projects are, of course, never even started. I remember a wise and wonderful seventeenth-century specialist in a graduate English class warning would-be writers away from the Ph.D. program, telling them to get out and write while they still could because in a few years they would be convinced of the impossibility of doing anything original or worthwhile.

In college, and for a few years also during the fifties, I knew both men and women who planned to write, paint or compose, and I don't recall that the men were any more determined than the women. Some of the men had backup plans—that is, alternate ways of making a living if art didn't pay; they were going to teach or enter the family business. The women seemed to believe that they could continue with their creative endeavors indefinitely, with or without financial recompense. Then, too, husbands were supposed to take care of money matters; and marriage, rather than conflicting with an artistic woman's career, appeared to be a way of subsidizing it. The women appeared to be at an advantage. Yet it was the men and not the women whose names I later saw on book jackets and album covers. This may have been sheer coincidence, but I tend to think that the men, because they were men, were more aggressive about putting their work on the line.

And there must be a point when the training or amateur phase is finally over, when it is time to put one's work on the line or on the auction block. Art starts to pay, not necessarily after an inner burst of confidence, but more likely after a realization about one's own situation. Sometimes there's a sudden flash. Nancy Shiffrin knew on her

thirty-third birthday that it was time for her to stop working at low-paying jobs, find an agent and start writing for
a living, and she then took the necessary steps to make
this a reality. For others, it may be a much later birthday
or a serious illness that ushers in a new awareness that one
is indeed mortal and that there is only so much time left
to do the thing one really wants to do.

It's not unusual, either, to produce one's first important
work when the wolf is at the door. George Sand began
writing novels when she had left her husband to live in
Paris with her impoverished lover. Others first wrote in
earnest when their children were hungry or when they lost
their jobs or when the unemployment checks ran out. And
women aren't the only ones who write their way out of
trouble. When Mario Puzo sat down to write *The God-
father,* he had not only run out of money but had very
nearly exhausted his credit as well. Also, a whole host of
former political men have turned into writers in order to
pay off astronomical legal fees and court costs.

Although necessity isn't always the mother of great art,
it can provide a powerful impetus for getting the work
done. And the necessity that follows a crisis can spawn a
serious career.

Unfortunately, a serious career and great art are incom-
patible for all but a very few individuals. Ours is not a
society that can support very many poets, fine artists and
composers, and some work will never be done, or will never
be seen, because of this. I wish I had some positive advice
for the woman whose creative abilities cannot possibly fit
into any of the popular or paying categories. Her life is
very likely to be one of sacrifice, martyrdom and probably
a job that's meaningless—in short, precisely the kind of
life women are now being encouraged to abandon. I hope
that she understands the psychic and material costs of
such a life, the high odds against recognition and the
gamesmanship involved in procuring grants and subsidies.
She will face competition far fiercer than that in the business world or the professions, and she needs all the help
she can get from mentors, networks and friends. I wish
her well and hope that she finds others who can advise her
better than I.

George Sand maintained that she did not live to write
but that she wrote to live. And today it is indeed possible

for more than a few women to have a good life as the result of their creative efforts. Besides the novelists, screenwriters and songwriters who number among the highest-paid women in the country, there are many more who live very well, independent of husbands' earnings or simply independent of husbands.

The ones I know best are writers, and opportunities are undoubtedly more numerous for individuals who work with words than for those in music or art. Some of my writer friends are former actresses, dancers and artists who eventually concentrated on writing. Most confined themselves to poetry or short stories until a crisis ushered in the necessity of earning a living. But they found that their apprenticeship had been well spent and they were, when called upon to do so, able to channel their abilities into something different—usually magazine articles. They were on their way.

Since magazine writing does more for one's ego and one's visibility than it does for one's bank account, however, some found they still needed another source of income. Some took jobs as editors. Carolyn See resumed teaching and Helen Colton began a counseling career, but these women and others branched into various kinds of writing: novels, non-fiction books, television plays and screenplays. All made some mistakes: working for publishers who went out of business without paying, collaborating with lovers, trying to write potboilers in which they did not believe and which were doomed to fail. Yet eventually something clicked. Sooner or later they found something into which they could plunge wholeheartedly and which was also something that would pay. For a few this turned out to be the serious novel that they had always wanted to write.

Things clicked sooner, however, for those who got in touch with others who could help. Iris Bancroft was encouraged to write fiction by her mentor, mystery-writer John Ball. With his help, she gained confidence in techniques such as plotting and characterization, at the same time finding out that she could handle a long manuscript. Until then she had only sold articles and short pieces.

But writers seem to be especially vulnerable to the problems that can sometimes plague mentor relationships with males. One woman admitted that it was a former lover who originally told her, "You think you're not ready, but I know better!" And he encouraged her to take the necessary steps to get her work published. "Initially, he'd nurtured my confidence, but as the affair grew stormy and complex, I suffered setbacks in my career, too," she said. "His eventual rejection of me as a woman and as a writer as well was very painful."

The women I spoke with generally gleaned more help from women peers who held common interests. Some informal networks of women writers read and criticize each other's work, discuss future projects and console each other through bleak times. They may also help each other to find agents, editors, producers or attorneys as well as comparing notes on the business aspects of writing such as marketing and promoting, contracts and deals.

The career of the artist is actually similar to running a small business, with the same freedom and excitement and risks. And while this may seem remote from the image of the serious artist, it is very much in the image of today's career woman, doing something she really wants to do, keeping an eye on long-range targets and seeing that she gets paid fairly along the way. Very few, like Carolyn See, would say that the whole process is fun, though most agree that there is satisfaction in having their work seen or read and enjoyed by large numbers of people. And most of them can't think of anything else they'd rather be doing.

XVI

Women Who Help Women– What They Say About Where We've Been and Where We're Going

TRADITIONALLY, women have been helpers, people who cared. Only in the last couple of decades, though, have women seen the need for helping each other and working together to make the world better for women in general. Nearly all of the forty women I interviewed were in some way involved in the lives or careers of other women.

A few of those I spoke with have careers in business, government or social agencies directly involved with women's causes and advancement. A number of others have arranged their careers in the professions or in independent businesses so that they can devote time and effort to activities pertaining to women. Some are or have been leaders in women's organizations or professional networks. A majority had made a profound commitment to women's causes. It seemed that most successful women, including those who had little or no involvement with feminism, were concerned with the changes and advancements women are making. Possibly, though, the women who did not wish to be interviewed were less concerned.

As I interviewed women, I tried first of all to get them to talk about themselves and their own feelings about their lives and their careers. Some did this more openly than others, but when I asked what advice they'd like to pass on to other women, they almost always had something to contribute. Nearly every interview eventually veered toward more general questions, such as women's progress or the lack of it, the obstacles to women's equality and the battles remaining to be fought. And it was here that their answers differed most of all.

Earlier, as they talked about themselves, they almost invariably revealed a very positive outlook toward their careers, their lives and their futures. This attitude more than anything else seemed to be the secret behind their success; it galvanized their commitments and focused their energies. Listening to them, I became infected with a breed of optimism I've been chronically prone to. For a time I was convinced that women could get ahead, become what they wanted to be and have the lives they dreamed of if only they began to believe, one by one, that they could do it.

I still feel that an individual's optimism or positive self-image is a necessary ingredient of success, no matter how success is defined. I began to realize, however, that social change is a difficult and often frustrating process in which optimism plays very little part. No matter how optimistic, even exuberant these women were in discussing their own lives and futures, they were less so when considering the futures of women generally.

Women who care very deeply about women's problems are troubled and frankly disheartened by the evidence of discrimination they see all around them. They're happy to be where they are, they feel that the struggle in getting there was worthwhile, but they're annoyed that other women will still have to struggle harder than men and that more women are not yet being welcomed into the mainstream.

Dr. Judith Stiehm has investigated the status of women from the point of view of a political scientist and social historian. Involved in teaching, research and writing, also attending women's conferences and being a mentor to younger women who are university scholars, she is pleased with the breadth and scope of her own career. Turning to the question of what gains women have made so far, she declared, "I have a very positive attitude, but I'm not an optimist. I don't think we're closing the gap between men and women anywhere in our society. I'm very unhappy about the myth of the next generation. People are saying that twenty years down the road it will all be different. They're telling us to look at the new group of women coming into management and other areas. The system is promising us that it will change, and these young women believe it will. There's no certainty that it will and I'm disturbed about the waste of all these women within the system."

"Time" is a four-letter word that polarizes people's views, especially women's. Yes, social change takes time. But we've been told to wait, be patient and look to the next generation by the same people who'd hoped we'd give up and turn back. Both as individuals and as crusaders, women want to accelerate progress. How much longer, women wonder, must we wait before men and women can compete equally for positions in the mainstream?

Meanwhile, is it worth it for those who try as hard as they can simply to know that they are blazing a trail for others and clearing the way for some future generation, yet stopping short of what they wanted for themselves? Many women understandably do not want to be pioneers. Instead they want to live well in the time they have.

And women who are concerned for future generations may have more on their minds than social change alone. They're concerned about time running out before answers are found to international questions of political and environmental importance. We don't know yet if women in the mainstream will change the direction the world is going in or, on the other hand, if women themselves will eventually be changed by the direction of the world. Women's supposed humanism may be no more than a result of our suppression, after all. And if this humanism turns out to be a function of female neurohormones, we might find ourselves disqualified because of it.

Women who succeed, who get what they want, believe that, yes, for them it's been worthwhile. Although the achievements and rewards of the women I talked to vary considerably, every one of them felt that her career was worth the effort or the sacrifice it had taken. Most had encouraging words, too, for other women who wanted to follow in their footsteps, but some were skeptical of popular advice telling women to put top priority on a career goal or to plan their lives year by year.

Grace Fippinger, whose career with New York Telephone Company evolved step by step rather than proceeding according to a plan, had this to say: "Today women can aspire realistically to top-level positions, and it's a satisfying experience to be able to help women move into jobs with greater responsibility and to watch them develop." On the subject of goals and five-year plans, however, she said, "It doesn't hurt to have something to aim for, but it can be harmful if, for instance, becoming a doctor is the end-all and be-all of one's existence. Some women and some men won't make it. If you construe not reaching your goal as having failed, or if you don't get where you'd planned to be in five years, then you may never do as well in whatever you settle for. It's better if you can decide instead to be a very good nurse or a very good pharmacist or a very good something else."

Not everybody is going to make it. There's not room at the top for everyone who would like to be there, and there's still very little room at the top even for women who are qualified. Women who have made it and who work with women trying to make it are highly conscious of the many who fall by the wayside. And some are concerned that as women reach for the kind of success men have been striving for all along, women, too, will have to cope with the same sense of failure and disappointment and frustration that many men feel at *not* making it.

However, if women continue to regard success differently than men do, if they continue to see it as inner satisfaction and self-actualization rather than specific titles and positions, increasing numbers of women will find opportunities within the mainstream to achieve this.

For the women I talked to, being successful meant being happy, not only in their jobs but in their lives with others. They were not willing to relinquish personal relationships for the sake of their careers and had tried to work things out so as to have the best of both worlds. But they couldn't pretend that it had been easy. Besides trying harder and exceeding the efforts of their male competitors, women who make it have often added personal responsibilities.

The system has demanded that they be exceptional human beings. If women not yet in the mainstream are more awed by the women than by the men who are there, it's not hard to understand why. There's the familiar argument that women have the right, too, to mediocrity, and although no woman wants to be mediocre, real equality would mean that unexceptional women have the same chances unexceptional men do now.

There have been gains. I specifically asked women in "helping" positions what gains made by women so far they saw as most significant.

One was Gloria Allred, whom I had not interviewed earlier. Twice elected to the presidency of the Los Angeles chapter of NOW, she is currently organizing the Women's Equal Rights Legal Defense and Education Fund in order to help inform women about equal-opportunity laws and to offer assistance in the prosecution of rape and battery cases. An attorney who made a late decision to study law, she had previously been a teacher working with children in the black ghettos of Philadelphia and Los Angeles, and at the same time a divorced mother with a young daughter to take care of. Her second husband urged her to pursue a legal career. She now has her own practice, specializing in cases involving women's rights.

"The most significant gain women have made," she said in answer to my question, "is in their awareness of themselves. Women have more pride now than before. Their anger and frustration used to be turned inward against themselves, but with increased awareness of the inequalities that exist in society, their feelings can be focused in an outward, productive way. Women now realize that something can be done."

There were others, too, who believed that no gain was more significant than the change in women's own self-perceptions and self-images. Those who've worked closely with other women in the last decade or so have seen them throw off the constraints of earlier programming, cease to be passive and powerless and view themselves as persons having options. Women have become creatures far different from what anyone previously suspected, defying not only conventional notions of what women were but also descriptions from medical, psychological and sociological texts.

However, as many women eagerly pointed out, these changes could not have occurred until women began working together. There'd always been a few women who'd refused to accept powerlessness and who'd managed to slip past the gatekeepers to travel paths where women weren't supposed to go. But these few didn't make a difference for women in general. Larger numbers of women began to undergo metamorphosis only after women began to form groups, providing each other with mutual support and exerting pressure upon the system.

Judge Joan Dempsey Klein had this to say on the subject: "It is significant, I think, that women are now identifying more and more with other women. As they seek each other out, they begin to find out who they are and where they are, overcoming guilt and ambivalence and other attitudes that can hold them back. I strongly urge women to affiliate with groups wherever they are. The collective power of women, I think, will have the greatest impact of anything in this century."

I've already recorded the initial experiences of several women in groups with other women. They suddenly found they were not alone. They learned, too, that not all the things which had gone wrong were their own fault and that some were the result of a system which survived partially because of the exclusion of women. Gloria Allred said, "Women tend to believe that what happens to them is individual or personal. An event that is the deepest crisis in a woman's life very likely has parallels in the experiences of many other women. Once she understands this, she'll look for ways to stem the tide of sexism in society."

There's a delicious sense of relief in learning that one is not to blame after all, in being able to point an accusing finger at society. For a while, too, many women cast the blame at men. But while it is occasionally possible simply to separate the external obstacles from the internal ones, as we understand ourselves and society better, the interconnections reveal themselves as more subtle and complex. In addition to the early socialization process which taught us how to be feminine, there is, as sociologist Dr. Cynthia Fuchs Epstein points out, the ongoing social process that can still undermine our aspirations in subtle and unconscious ways. "Even in encounters with total strangers," she writes, "women learned an etiquette of submissiveness and were subject to microcontrols of the lifted eyebrow, the putdown."[1]

Attitudes—women's and men's—change ploddingly and with great difficulty. Why do women of intelligence and achievement prefer to pair themselves with men they see as more intelligent and of still greater achievement? And they continue to do so unquestioningly. It cannot be simply that men themselves insist upon being first; women put men first even without realizing they are doing it. The system that closes its doors on women is one which rests on a foundation of just such underlying assumptions about how life should be. The myths that people live by lag far behind legislation.

Yet attitudes do change. In addition to some very noticeable changes in women's own attitudes, a few women now see perceptible differences in the attitudes of men in high places. Among them is Felice Schwartz, who, as founder and president of Catalyst has, since 1962, been directly involved in helping women with their careers. Her position is one which provides a close-up view of some very important changes as they occur. One of Catalyst's functions is to maintain a list of the names of women who are qualified and willing to become members of corporate boards. Ms. Schwartz pointed out that in the past ten years there has been a 550-percent increase in the women on the boards of the top 1,300 companies.

"I feel that very substantial gains have been made," she went on. "This isn't optimism or pessimism, but rather an extrapolation from what has happened so far."

I then asked her what gains she felt were most significant. She replied, "The outstanding gain that I have seen is that women are now in the consciousness of virtually every major corporate leader. Ten years ago this was just not the case. Now there isn't a leader in the business community who is not aware of women or who does not recognize that women are here to stay at every level. It was absolutely essential to have this happen. The acceptance of women has to begin at the top level. And it has only happened now. Until very recently a great many of these men had never seen women perform at a high level and had no assurance that they could. They'd seen their own wives and they'd seen women at lower levels. By now, though, nearly all of them have seen one or two or a few women whose performance they genuinely respect and this is changing their attitude."

She went on, "You see I've lived through the period when men thought this was never going to happen and subsequently the time when they thought it was a passing thing. And then some thought it might be avoided. Now, though, women have begun to arrive."

She is well aware that other women leaders are not in accord with this outlook. "I know my view is not widely shared," she said. "The evidence is not yet apparent, though we're seeing an influx of women into traditionally male fields and career lines and into education preparing them for careers in those fields. I feel we're going to see much more evidence a few years from now. The things preparing for the increase are under way. The inexorable process has been set in motion and there's no turning back." Other women agree that acceptance at the top level of the corporate power structure is crucial. But many do not believe it has yet been achieved. If Ms. Schwartz is correct, however, can acceptance at the upper levels of government and the professions be far behind?

And what will it take for women to achieve equality? Some women stressed continued political and legal pressure, further governmental commitment, and some felt the passage of the Equal Rights Amendment would be a turning point.

Others addressed themselves to the problems of attitudinal change. "We still have a long way to go in changing our basic attitudes," Felice Schwartz said. "The most important entails fully absorbing and understanding the concept of two-career families and the many things this implies. The careers of husband and wife must be seen as equally important, regardless of differences in their earnings or talents. Men, as husbands and as employers, must recognize that women's careers are very important to them. And there will be a difference in the way men regard their wives' careers as they see that their burden for the financial well-being of the family has been eased."

The implications of the dual-career family are many and complex. Among other things, they call for an upheaval of old value systems that have long been taken for granted. Dr. Judith Stiehm provided this analysis:

"What will it take? It will take men re-entering the family, men assuming responsibility in the home, assuming half the child-care duties. Everyone, men and women in our society, thinks that when you grow up, you shouldn't have to listen to women. Nobody wants to be supervised by women. So it's going to take fathers giving as much attention to fathering as mothers do to mothering, it's going to take male teachers of young children, males in all the roles that females traditionally play. What we have now is women in men's roles but very few men in women's roles. It's a one-way cross-over. The few males who cross the barrier to women's roles are severely punished. The things women do are still not valued. So much of feminism as it is being advocated is still the one-way cross-over."

Women tend to think that men's efforts in homemaking and child care matter only in so far as this frees them to do other things. But the significance is much greater and the eventual outcome more far-reaching. Ultimately there must not be men's responsibilities on the one hand and women's responsibilities on the other, but simply human responsibilities in which men and women share. The world of men cannot become our world until far greater numbers of women are admitted to the mainstream of society. And, paradoxically, the possibility for many women to make it in the mainstream depends greatly upon a renewed respect for the very things women have been doing all along. It also depends upon drastic changes in the relationships between men and women. Social change is an arduous and wrenching process. Meanwhile more women, though not many, will be making it. The question remains whether or not they will continue to do so on their own terms. If they do, their making it will indeed make a difference.

Notes and Sources

I. WOMEN AND SUCCESS

1. Phyllis Chesler and Emily Jane Goodman, *Women, Money & Power* (New York: Morrow, 1976), Epilogue, pp. 252–9.
2. Maragret Hennig and Anne Jardim, *The Managerial Woman* (New York: Anchor/Doubleday, 1977), ch. II, pp. 13–14.
3. Thomas S. Szasz, *The Myth of Mental Illness: Foundations of a Theory of Personal Conduct* (New York: Hoeber-Harper, 1961).
4. Cynthia Fuchs Epstein, "Mind, Matter and Mentors," in *The Frontiers of Knowledge,* Judith Stiehm, ed. (Los Angeles: University of Southern California Press, 1976), p. 29.

II. MONEY, DIRTY MONEY

1. Ruth Halcomb, *Money & the Working Ms.* (Chatsworth, Calif.: Books for Better Living, 1974).
2. Jane Howard, "Katherine Graham: The Power That Didn't Corrupt," *Ms.,* October 1974.
3. Carol Tavris with Susan Sadd, "20,000 Women Reveal Their Fears, Splurges, and New Confidences—About Money!" *Ms.,* May 1978.
4. Wyndham Robertson, "The Top Women in Business," *Fortune,* July 17, 1977.

III. POWER—USES AND ABUSES

1. Interview with Eleanor Holmes Norton, *Newsday*, January 23, 1971.
2. Cynthia Fuchs Epstein, "Separate and Unequal," in *Women in the Professions,* Laurily Keir Epstein, ed. (Lexington, Mass.: Lexington Books, D. C. Heath and Co., 1975).
3. Hannah Arendt, *On Violence!*. (New York: Harcourt, Brace & World, 1970).
4. Robertson, *op. cit.*
5. Eleanor H. Cooper, "Comparison of Men and Women in Recall of Public Events and Political Attitudes," unpublished paper presented at the Annual Meeting of the Western Psychological Association, Los Angeles, 1976.
6. Betty Lehan Harrigan, *Games Mother Never Taught You* (New York: Rawson, 1978).
7. Michael Maccoby, *The Gamesman* (New York: Bantam, 1978), ch. I, p. 27.
8. Maccoby, *op. cit.,* ch. V.
9. Raymond W. Novaco, *Anger Control* (Lexington, Mass.: Lexington Books, 1975), pp. xi, 8–12.

IV. RITES OF PASSAGE

1. For circumstances relating to women's success, see Hennig and Jardim, *op. cit.,* ch. VI, p. 76; also *Profile of a Woman Officer,* pamphlet published by Heidrick and Struggles, Chicago, 1978. For circumstances relating to men's success, see Michael Korda, *Success!* (New York: Random House, 1977), ch. I, pp. 7, 9.
2. Adapted from Theodora Wells, "Psychology of Woman," in *Humanistic Perspectives: Current Trends in Psychology,* ed. Barry McWaters (Monterey, Calif.: Brooks-Cole, 1977).

V. CASHING IN ON THE OPTIONS

1. Hennig and Jardim, *op. cit.,* ch. I, p. 10.

VI. HELP FROM FRIENDS, MENTORS AND OTHERS

1. Hennig and Jardim, *op. cit.*, ch. II, p. 72.
2. Daniel J. Levinson, research cited in Gail Sheehy, *Passages* (New York: Bantam, 1977), ch. XII, p. 189.
3. Sheehy, *op. cit.*

VII. IN THE RACE: THE JOYS AND CONFLICTS OF COMPETING

1. Hennig and Jardim, *op. cit.*, ch. I, p. 25.
2. Matina Horner, "Sex Differences in Achievement Motivation and Performance in Competitive and Noncompetitive Situations" doctoral dissertation, University of Michigan, 1968.
3. Adeline Levine, and Janice Crumrine, "Women and the Fear of Success: A Problem in Replication," *American Journal of Sociology*, vol. 80, no. 4, pp. 964–74.
4. Letitia Anne Peplau, "Impact of Fear of Success and Sex-Role Attitudes on Women's Competitive Achievement," *Journal of Personality and Social Psychology*, vol. 34, no. 4, pp. 561–8. Also see A. H. Stein and M. M. Bailey, "The Socialization of Achievement Motivation in Females," *Psychological Bulletin*, vol. 80, pp. 345–66.
5. Matina Horner, "Femininity and Successful Achievement: A Basic Inconsistency," in *Feminine Personality and Conflict*, J. M. Bardwick, E. Douvan, M. S. Horner and D. Gutzmann, eds. (Belmont, Calif.: Brooks-Cole, 1970).
6. Research cited in Laura Shapiro, "Did 'Fear of Success' Fail?" *Ms.*, July 1977.
7. Judith Stiehm, "Invidious Intimacy," *Social Policy*, March-April 1976.

VIII. IMAGES OF SUCCESS

1. Harrigan, *op. cit.*, ch. XIII.
2. John T. Molloy, *The Woman's Dress for Success Book* (New York: Warner Books, 1977), ch. VII, pp. 171–4.
3. Epstein, "Mind, Matter and Mentors," *op. cit.*, p. 33.

IX. GETTING IT ALL TOGETHER—BALANCING CAREER AND FAMILY

1. Elizabeth M. Tidball, study reported in *The Executive Woman*, February 1975.
2. Hennig and Jardim, *op. cit.*, ch. X.
3. Meron-Landolt, Monique de, "How a Woman Scientist Deals Professionally with Men," in "Women in Science: A Man's World," special issue of *Impact of Science on Society*, UNESCO, April–June 1975.
4. Sheehy, *op. cit.*, ch. 16, p. 340.
5. Stiehm, "Invidious Intimacy," *op. cit.*, pp. 12–13.

X. A WOMAN IN PUBLIC LIFE— ELEANOR HOLMES NORTON

1. Reprinted by permission of Hawthorn Books, Inc., from *Women Today: Ten Profiles* by Greta Walker, copyright © 1975 by Greta Walker. All rights reserved.
2. Statistics from *Time*, November 6, 1978.
3. "Women in Government," *Senior Scholastic*, February 26, 1978.
4. *Time*, *op. cit.*
5. Riva Berger, "Where Women Succeed in Politics," *Working Woman*, March 1978, p. 52.
6. *Time*, *op. cit.*
7. Berger, *op. cit.*
8. Blythe Babyak, "All the President's Women," *The New York Times Magazine*, January 22, 1978, p. 11.

XI. CLIMBING THE CORPORATE LADDER AND LOVING IT—MARCIA CARSEY

1. "Who Gets the Most Pay," *Forbes*, May 15, 1976, pp. 225–51. Out of 822 chief executive officers, those having technical background ranked fourth (9%), after those with backgrounds in finance (23%), administration (21%) and law (11%).
2. *Profile of a Woman Officer*, Heidrick and Struggles, *op. cit.*
3. Wyndham Robertson, "Women M.B.A.'s, Harvard '73,

'How They're Doing,'" *Fortune*, August 28, 1978, pp. 50–60.

XII. A WOMAN IN HIGHER EDUCATION—
JUDITH H. STIEHM

1. Cynthia Fuchs Epstein, "A Personal Perspective on a Career in the Social Sciences," paper prepared for the Conference on Career and Educational Opportunities for Junior and Senior Women, The University of Arizona, Tucson, October 29, 1977.
2. Statistics for 1900–70 from *Digest of Educational Statistics.* Those for 1975–76 are from *Salaries, Tenure and Fringe Benefits,* National Center for Education Statistics.
3. National Center for Education Statistics.
4. *Ibid.*
5. *Ibid.*
6. American Council on Education Statistics.
7. Epstein, "A Personal Perspective on a Career in the Social Sciences," *op. cit.*
8. Epstein, "Mind, Matter and Mentors," *op. cit.,* p. 31.

XIII. THE PROFESSIONAL LIFE—
BARBARA FISH

1. Liz Cameron, "Outside In: How Eight Women Attorneys Have Faced the Reality of a Sexist Profession," *Barrister*, vol. 5, no. 2.
2. Statistics from *Journal of the American Medical Association*, vol. 240, no. 26.
3. Statistics from *American Bar Association Review of Legal Education in the U.S.*, 1977.
4. Statistics from Engineering Manpower Commission, Fall 1975 enrollment survey.

XIV. A WOMAN OF INDEPENDENT WAYS
AND MEANS—LISA CLEWER

1. Jane Trahey, *Jane Trahey on Women and Power* (New York: Rawson, 1977).

XV. WRITING WITHOUT TEARS— CAROLYN SEE

1. Antonia Brico, "One Undeflected Step at a Time," in *The Frontiers of Knowledge,* Judith Stiehm, ed. (Los Angeles: University of Southern California Press, 1976), p. 21.

XVI. WOMEN HELPING WOMEN— WHAT THEY SAY ABOUT WHERE WE'VE BEEN AND WHERE WE'RE GOING

1. Epstein, "Mind, Matter and Mentors," *op. cit.,* p. 28.

Index

RUTH HALCOMB

As a college student, Ruth Halcomb held jobs in a variety of fields including retailing, hospital and social work; since graduating from Antioch College she has always earned a living by writing or editing.

A free-lance writer since 1969, she has contributed articles on psychology, medicine, nutrition, personal finances and women's interests to *Bride's, Ms., Parents', New Woman* and other publications. She is the author of six previous books of which the first, *Money & the Working Ms.*, received favorable media attention as the first feminist-oriented book on money directed specifically to women.

Ms. Halcomb lives with her teen-age son in Studio City, California.

The national bestseller by
the author of THE WOMEN'S ROOM,
now in paperback.

MARILYN FRENCH

THE
BLEEDING
HEART

A
LOVE STORY
FOR AND ABOUT
ADULTS

28896/$3.50

An extraordinary novel
about the devastating power
of marriage—and the unexpected
possibility of love.

 BALLANTINE BOOKS

COPING, LOVING and SUCCEEDING

Ballantine has everything to help the modern woman in today's world.

AL-28

Women of all ages *can look and feel their best with these bestselling guides to wardrobe, weight loss, exercise and skin care.*